I0037534

Economics Terms

Financial Education Is Your Best Investment

Published February 10, 2020

Revision 2.2

© 2014-2020 Financial Terms Dictionary - Thomas Herold - All rights reserved

Financial Terms Dictionary

Copyright And Trademark Notices

This book is copyright 2014-2020 Thomas Herold (the "Author"). All Rights Reserved. Published in the United States of America. The legal notices, disclosures, and disclaimers at the front of this eBook are Copyright (c) 2020 Thomas Herold and licensed for use by the Author.

All rights reserved. All trademarks and service marks are the properties of their respective owners. All references to these properties are made solely for editorial purposes. Except for marks actually owned by the Author, the Author (as both author and as publisher) does not make any commercial claims to their use and is not affiliated with them in any way.

Unless otherwise expressly noted, none of the individuals or business entities mentioned herein have endorsed the contents of this book.

Limits of Liability and Disclaimer of Warranties

The materials in this book are provided "as is" and without warranties of any kind either express or implied. The Author disclaims all warranties, express or implied, including, but not limited to, implied warranties of merchantability and fitness for a particular purpose.

The Author does not warrant that defects will be corrected, or that that the site or the server that makes this eBook available are free of viruses or other harmful components. The Author does not warrant or make any representations regarding the use or the results of the use of the materials in this book in terms of their correctness, accuracy, reliability, or otherwise. Applicable law may not allow the exclusion of implied warranties, so the above exclusion may not apply to you.

Under no circumstances, including, but not limited to, negligence, shall the Author be liable for any special or consequential damages that result from the use of, or the inability to use this eBook, even if the Author or his authorized representative has been advised of the possibility of such damages.

Applicable law may not allow the limitation or exclusion of liability or incidental or consequential damages, so the above limitation or exclusion may not apply to you. In no event shall the Author's total liability to you for all damages, losses, and causes of action (whether in contract, tort, including but not limited to, negligence or otherwise) exceed the amount paid by you, if any, for this eBook.

Facts and information are believed to be accurate at the time they were placed in this book. All data provided in this book is to be used for information purposes only. The information contained within is not intended to provide specific legal, financial or tax advice, or any other advice whatsoever, for any individual or company and should not be relied upon in that regard. The services described are only offered in jurisdictions where they may be legally offered. Information provided is not all-inclusive and is limited to information that is made available and such information should not be relied upon as all-inclusive or accurate.

You are advised to do your own due diligence when it comes to making business decisions and should use caution and seek the advice of qualified professionals. You should check with your accountant, lawyer, or professional advisor, before acting on this or any information. You may not consider any examples, documents, or other content in this eBook or otherwise provided by the Author to be the equivalent of professional advice.

The Author assumes no responsibility for any losses or damages resulting from your use of any link, information, or opportunity contained in this book or within any other information disclosed by the author in any form whatsoever.

About the Author

Thomas Herold is a successful entrepreneur, mediator, author, and personal development coach. He published over 35 books with over 200,000 copies distributed worldwide and the founder of seven online businesses.

For over ten years Thomas Herold has studied the monetary system and has experienced some profound insights on how money and wealth are related. After three years of successful investing in silver, he released 'Building Wealth with Silver - How to Profit From The Biggest Wealth Transfer in History' in 2012. One of the first books that illustrate in a remarkable, simple way the monetary system and its consequences.

He is the founder and CEO of the 'Financial Terms Dictionary' book series and website, which explains in detail and comprehensive form over 1000 financial terms. In his financial book series, he informs in detail and with practical examples all aspects of the financial sector. His educational materials are designed to help people get started with financial education.

In his 2018 released book 'The Money Deception', Mr. Herold provides the most sophisticated insight and shocking details about the current monetary system. Never before has the massive manipulation of money caused so much economic inequality in the world. In spite of these frightening facts, 'The Money Deception' also provides remarkable and simple solutions to create abundance for all people, and it's a must-read if you want to survive the global monetary transformation that's underway right now.

In 2019 he released an entirely new financial book series explaining in detail and with practical examples over 1000 financial terms. The 'Herold Financial IQ Series' contains currently of 16 titles covering every category of the financial market.

His latest book "High Credit Score Secrets" offers the most effective strategies to boost the average credit score from as low as 450 points to over 810. It teaches the tactics to build excellent credit, repair credit, monitor credit and how to guard that good score for a lifetime. It reached bestseller status in 2020 in three categories.

For more information please visit the author's websites:

High Credit Score Secrets - The Smart Raise & Repair Guide to Excellent
Credit
https://highcreditscoresecrets.com

The Money Deception - What Banks & Government Don't Want You to
Know
https://www.moneydeception.com

The Herold Financial IQ Series - Financial Education Is Your Best
Investment
https://www.financial-dictionary.com

The Online Financial Dictionary - Over 1000 Terms Explained
https://www.financial-dictionary.info

Please Leave Your Review on Amazon

This book and the Financial IQ Series are self-published and the author does not have a contract with one of the five largest publishers, which are able to support the author's work with advertising. If you like this book, please consider leaving a solid 4 or 5-star review on Amazon.

Herold Financial IQ Series on Amazon

Table Of Contents

Adam Smith

Adam Smith wrote the economic and political world shaking book *The Wealth of Nations*. This book marked the original birth of free market economics. It also spelled the doom of mercantilism, the dominant economic system of the day.

March 9, 1776 marked the publication of *An Inquiry into the Nature and Causes of the Wealth of Nations* that became known by the shorter title *The Wealth of Nations* around the world. Smith opposed mercantilism that predominated in the world economy of his day. Mercantilism believed that the amount of global wealth was limited and fixed.

The only way for countries to increase in prosperity lay in stockpiling gold and protecting markets from competition using tariffs. At the time nations felt they should sell their goods to others but not purchase any of their trade partners' goods back. This caused international trade to be extremely limited because of the trade wars and tariffs that constantly erupted.

The central part of Adam Smith's premise lay in the "invisible hand." He argued that mankind acted in his own best interests naturally. This would result in prosperity because the invisible hand of free markets would ensure the optimal economic production levels. Smith wanted all individuals to be allowed to make and exchange the goods they wished in free trade.

He believed that all markets around the world would function better if allowed to freely compete. A national government would not need to intervene much except to support the invisible hand and its magic. He promoted the idea that countries could achieve universal prosperity if they had the three elements of enlightened self interest, free market economy with strong currency, and limited government.

Smith believed that individuals should labor in their self interest with hard work and thriftiness. He believed in an enlightened form of self interest as the natural trait for most people.

His famous example surrounded a butcher who supplied meat. He did not do it out of a good heart. The butcher sold the meat to profit. By selling low quality meat he would lose customers and not make any profits. The butcher's best interests lay in offering quality meat to his customers at a fair price. Both groups realized a benefit with each transaction. Smith said that long term thinking would stop the majority of businesses from cheating their clientele. The government would enforce laws and penalties for those that failed.

This self interest extended to trade. Individuals who saved would invest for better returns and give industry the investment capital it needed to increase numbers of machines and promote innovation in business. This would boost the returns on invested money and cause the general living standards to increase.

Free market economy needed a strong currency to work well. Smith wanted a national currency backed up by precious metals so that the country could not depreciate the nation's money through waste and wars. Starting with this limit on spending, Adam Smith continued with free market government recommendations. They were to maintain low taxes and repeal tariffs so that free trade could flourish over international borders. Smith demonstrated that these tariffs were only hurting the lives of ordinary citizens by raising prices and cutting off trade and industry's efforts overseas.

Limited government proved to be the third big idea that Smith promoted in The Wealth of Nations. Governments should be limited to providing universal education to its citizens, national defense, infrastructure works, and the enforcement of law and justice. Governments were to intervene whenever people pursued short term interests or committed crimes. Larger governments only took money from their ordinary citizens' pockets.

Annual Percentage Rate (APR)

The annual percentage rate, or APR, is the actual interest rate that a loan charges each year. This single percentage number is truthfully used to represent the literal annual expense of using money over the life span of a given loan. Annual percentage rate not only covers interest charged, but can also be comprised of extra costs or fees that are attached to a given loan transaction.

Credit cards and loans commonly offer differing explanations for transaction fees, the structure of their interest rates, and any late fees that are assessed. The annual percentage rate provides an easy to understand formula for expressing to borrowers the real and actual percentage number of fees and interest so that they can measure these up against the rates that other possible lenders will charge them.

Annual percentage rate can include many different elements besides interest. With a nominal APR, it simply involves the rate of a given payment period multiplied out to the exact numbers of payment periods existing in a year. The effective APR is often referred to as the mathematically true rate of interest for a given year. Effective APR's are commonly the fees charged plus the rate of compound interest.

On a home mortgage, effective annual percentage rates could factor in Private Mortgage Insurance, discount points, and even processing costs. Some hidden fees do not make their ways into an effective APR number. Because of this, you should always read the fine print surrounding an APR and the costs associated with a mortgage or loan. As an example of how an effective APR can be deceptive with mortgages, the one time fees that are charged in the front of a mortgage are commonly assumed to be divided over a loan's long repayment period. If you only utilize the loan for a short time frame, then the APR number will be thrown off by this. An effective APR on a mortgage might look lower than it actually is when the loan will be paid off significantly earlier than the term of the loan.

The government created the concept of annual percentage rate to stop loan companies and credit cards issuers from deceiving consumers with fancy expressions of interest charges and fees. The law requires that all loan issuers and credit card companies have to demonstrate this annual percentage rate to all customers. This is so the consumers will obtain a fair comprehension of the true rates that are associated with their particular transactions. While credit card companies are in fact permitted to promote their monthly basis of interest rates, they still have to clearly show the actual annual percentage rate to their customers in advance of a contract or agreement being signed by the consumer.

Annual percentage rate is sometimes confused with annual percentage yield. This can be vastly different from the APR. Annual percentage yield includes calculations of compounded interest in its numbers.

Austrian Economics

Austrian Economics arose as a challenge to the then-dominant British tradition of economics originally championed by Adam Smith in his influential across the centuries work _The Wealth of Nations_. It was Carl Menger and his _Principles of Economics_ published in 1871 that presented the first alternative to the Imperial British ideas on the workings of the free market system. Menger founded the Austrian School officially, though other had come before him with ideas upon which he built.

Menger was assisted by contemporaries Stanley Jevons and Leon Walras. The trio in their various separate works fleshed out the original ideas of the subjective nature of economic value. It was they who for the first time explained the theories on marginal utility. This was the idea that stated the more units of any good an individual has, the less value he will place on any single unit of them. Menger and company also demonstrated the ways that money begins its life cycle in a free market. The most desirable commodity is wanted not because it can be directly literally consumed, but because it is useful in procuring other goods.

Menger's next influential work was his highly regarded Investigations. This twelve year later published book took on directly the German Historical School that viewed economics as the accruing of data for the benefit of the state. While serving as economics professor at University of Vienna, Menger returned economics back to its roots as the human action based science using deductive logic. He laid the groundwork for the later Austrian Economics' proponents and had students such as Friederich von Wieser who later impacted the critically important Austrian School economist Friedrich von Hayek. Even today, Menger's key works are studied as a fantastic beginning to the economics theory and thinking. All Austrian economists since Menger have considered themselves to be disciples of the great economics school and theory founder Menger.

The next great mind in the Austrian school was follower and admirer of Menger, Eugen Böhm-Bawerk of the University of Innsbruck, Austria. He expanded upon Menger's vast work and repackaged it so that he might apply it to a whole different range of economic questions and challenging topics such as price, value, interest, and capital. His influential work _History_ *and Critique of Interest Theories* was published in 1884 and remains a well-regarded review of the fallacies in the history of philosophy and economics. He first argued that interest rates are an integral component of the market itself. In his later *Positive Theory of Capital*, Böhm-Bawerk proved that the interest rate is actually the normal rate of profit in business.

As a result of these and other works, the Austrian economist battled extensively with the Marxists regarding the ideas of exploitation of capital, refuting the socialist ideas on wages and capital far in advance of the communists arising in Russia. In the final years of Hapsburg Austria, he served three terms as finance minister. This is where he was able to put into place his wise economics theories on sound money and the gold standard, balanced budgets, free trade, and the reversal of monopolies and subsidies for exporters of key goods. His writings, research, and practical application of economics helped to champion the Austrian School all across the Anglo-American and Imperial British world.

A last key Austrian Economics' founding scholar proved to be Ludwig von Mises. He published his perennial *The Theory of Money and Credit*, once again breaking fresh ground for the Austrian School. Here he fleshed out the application of the theory of marginal utility to money. Mises also worked out a full-scale outline of the Austrian School on the business cycle. After the First World War ended, Mises attacked the rising forces of political and economic socialist in his expository series of essays he purloined into the book Socialism. Here he demonstrated effectively how the practical application of socialism to nation states and governments would lead to the complete break down of society and eventually the end of the civilized world. This debate raged on, mostly in favor of the socialists, all the way until the crash of political and economic socialism around the world in 1989. From beyond the grave, von Mises had the last laugh.

Mises was such an influential Austrian Economics thinker that his converts and disciples from the socialist side included legendary Hayek, Lionel Robbins, and Wilhelm Röpke. They went on to lay the ground work for the revival of Austrian Economics in the U.S. and Great Britain still ongoing in the present days. Among his last and most influential of students, Rothbard proved to be one of the most adept proponents of Mises' ideas. He wrote *Man, Economy, and State* in 1963. The revival this began in the then-struggling Austrian School still continues to this day.

Barristers

Barristers are one of two types of lawyers used in many systems for different functions in the case law and courts arenas. The other designation of lawyer is a solicitor. Barristers' roles prove to be one of simply representing clients as their personal advocate in the courts of the appropriate jurisdiction.

Barristers' duties include actually speaking in court. Here, they present a case to a jury or a judge. They do not engage in preparation tasks such as advising a client, handling or accepting client instructions, reviewing or writing up legal documents, handling the daily administration of a case, or getting evidence ready for the court. These tasks are commonly handled by a solicitor when the two roles of attorneys are separated out. In this way, barristers function as the in court lawyer on behalf of the solicitor trial preparation lawyer.

Barristers enjoy unrestricted access and audience to the higher law courts. This stands in contrast to various other legal personnel, who are only allowed limited access to the courts after demonstrating appropriate qualifications. As such, barristers' occupation has much in common with the duties of lawyers who argue trials before civil law courts.

Barristers have little or nothing at all to do with actual clients. The solicitor of a client acts as intermediary between the two parties, even engaging the barrister to argue a case. Any client correspondence would be addressed directly to a solicitor, and not a barrister. Solicitors generally handle the barristers' fees and provide barristers with their instructions for actually arguing the case on behalf of the client.

Generally, barristers work as individual sole proprietors, as they are restricted from forming corporations or partnerships. Barristers are able to form chambers where they share office expenses and the use of clerks. There are chambers that have evolved into sophisticated and big operations that feel like corporations.

Barristers are useful for their highly specialized understanding of precedent and case laws. Generally practicing solicitors will often seek out a barrister's professional opinion when they encounter a rare or atypical section of law. Some countries permit barristers to be engaged by corporations, banks, or solicitor firms as legal advisers.

The long held traditional division between the roles of barristers and solicitors is gradually breaking down in numerous countries. In the British Isles for example, barristers long enjoyed their unique right to make appearances in the higher courts. Nowadays, solicitors are allowed to argue directly on behalf of clients in trial.

Solicitor firms are more commonly keeping the more difficult litigation tasks within their own companies anymore. Barristers are also allowed to deal with members of the public directly now, yet many still do not. This results from their narrow training pertaining to arguing before the courts that does not qualify them to offer legal advice to everyday individuals.

Barristers still argue cases on behalf of solicitors and their clients. These days, they no longer play a significant role in getting a trial ready. Barristers are mostly given briefs from solicitors that they will argue either one or several days in advance of a hearing.

Barter

Barter is a concept that pre-dates the invention of money. It proves to be the practice of trading goods, products, or services for other such products, services, and goods. Barter is a simpler way of transacting business, commonly without using money.

Although money systems have been in existence and well established for several thousand years, bartering for things as a practice is still alive and well nowadays. Systems of barter are used much of the time between one nation and another. Countries and companies occasionally engage in the practice as well. Barter is frequent in between businesses, and is sometimes also seen between a person and a business, or two different people. Within the U.S., bartering involves billions of dollars of services and goods that are exchanged back and forth in a single year. Per the International Reciprocal Trade Association that monitors bartering, over 400,000 businesses around the world bartered for more than $11 billion in just 2009.

Barter is sometimes referred to as counter-trade, in particular when it is used between two different countries. Bartering can be supremely convenient for countries that have an abundance of one or more resources or commodities but little cash on hand. Countries that produce huge quantities of wheat might exchange it directly with other countries for produce, oil, or textiles.

Where businesses are concerned, barter usually involves trading out services or products in consideration for advertising. Radio stations, television stations, and newspapers are common participants in barter, who may accept promotional goods for ads or on the air time. Other companies will exchange goods and services for stock in a company, or advice in consideration for services and goods.

Companies and individuals sometimes engage in barter as well. One company might give a consumer free merchandise in exchange for helpful sales leads. Individuals barter between each other for almost any item imaginable. Auction sites represent outlets for trading and bartering things. Interpersonal bartering is also carried out using online and print versions of classified ads. Today there are even barter clubs that help individuals learn more about and practice bartering.

In some countries like Spain, barter markets have arisen and spread. These swap meets forbid the use of money in any transactions. Participants simply bring along unwanted items and trade them with one or more parties for other items that they desire.

In times of national crises, bartering becomes more popular and commonplace. When currencies become victims of hyperinflation or devaluation, barter is resurrected. In these times and situations, barter can even supersede money as the principal medium of exchange.

Benchmarking

Benchmarking is a practice favored across many different industries and individual corporations. It refers to the idea of making a comparison between one's own company, processes, and operations against competing businesses within the entire market or only the businesses' own sector of the market. Companies can carry out this activity utilizing processes, products, approaches, or functions. There are a range of comparison points in such initiatives. Some of the most common include measuring quality, time, customer satisfaction, and effectiveness versus cost.

The goal and idea behind this Benchmarking lies in comparing and contrasting a company's own internal operations as measured against the competitors' own. It aims to create suggestions for bettering approaches, processes, and technologies in order to lower business costs, build up customer satisfaction and brand loyalty, and boost revenues and profits. This Benchmarking proves to be a critical component of initiatives for constantly boosting quality, as with Six Sigma.

There are many reasons that drive companies to benchmark. They often start with the idea that one of their approaches to business or internal processes may be improved somehow. Other corporations will draw these comparisons with competitors in an effort to discover problems within their own internal product delivery or service quality so that they can obtain a competitive advantage. The ultimate motivation in doing this activity lies in measuring up a company against the market leader or best in class corporation in a given industry. Many times companies will benchmark against corporations that are outstanding examples in a different industry to attempt to copy their success at a particular product, process, or method.

It is always helpful to look at a tangible example of a real world case study to better understand the concept. Southwest Airlines today is an industry-leading airline that did not always boast such a stellar reputation. A number of years ago, they notoriously analyzed the approaches, processes, and speed of delivery from pit crews in car racing. They did this with the goal of obtaining actionable ideas on boosting the time of their turn around on the ground and at the gate. As a result of this famous experiment with benchmarking, Southwest Airlines was successful in revamping their gate cleaning, maintenance, and customer boarding operations which helped the company to save one millions of dollars' worth of expenses each year.

Corporations which wish to engage in a benchmarking exercise do not have to come up with all of the data on their own. In fact a number of consumer organizations and industries themselves publish their own comparative data studies which companies can utilize to do a benchmark initiative. As an example, in the industry of used and new cars, Consumer Reports publishes an incredibly detailed section on the test results of both used and new cars. The fact that companies can often purchase such data means that they can pursue such initiatives without having to spend inordinate amounts of time and effort coming up with the comparison data in the first place.

Companies which are keen to boost their own customer service efforts could choose to compare their personal internal processes and measurements versus the ones which the industry leading success story company boasts. When they determine what their shortcomings are in the metrics, they can then decide to strengthen their processes and overall performance. To do this, the benchmarking corporation will study, consider, and then measure the operations of their successful competitor. They might go so far as to dispatch some of their employees to act as customers of the rival in order to obtain real-world experience in what the other company is doing so exceptionally well.

This means that a fast food restaurant chain which needs fast and accurate drive thru service to be successful would consider the efforts and results of its critical competitors. This is not an arbitrary example as the industry companies are well known for continuously studying and benchmarking against the various other competing companies in the sector. The best example of this is Pal's Sudden Service. They have won such prestigious awards for their speed and service that they opened an educational institute that now trains the employers and management of other businesses. A number of fast food corporations consider them to be the world class benchmark for themselves and their own operations.

Bipartisan

In the two party system found in the United States and other countries around the world, Bi-partisan signifies any resolution, act, or bill, as well as any action taken by a political governing body, where the two major political parties agree on the item or action in question.

Compromises between two parties are referred to as bi-partisan when they bring together the wishes of the two parties in a final version of a proposal or piece of legislation. When bi-partisan support can not be attained in a two party governing system, the end result is commonly gridlock. At this point, political party members and their home constituencies get angry with one another.

Bi-partisan is similarly used to describe the efforts of two radically differing groups who hold opposing views that they reconcile for a time or on an issue. Conservatives and liberals are two examples of such groups. If they can come to agreement on a course of action on a matter of urgent national importance, this is an example of bi-partisan efforts, or bipartisanship.

In the United States, the word bi-partisan commonly is employed to detail a political action or government policy that involves working together or compromising on behalf of the Republicans and Democrats, the two important political parties. Many politicians and political candidates cling to the mantle of bi-partisan efforts and policies, in particular during an election. In reality, these bi-partisan ideals are seldom actually put into place once a politician is securely and firmly in power.

In the history of the United States, precious little evidence exists to showcase that the answers to large, complex, and critical problems are found using bi-partisan agendas. The weight of evidence actually suggests that bipartisanship has little to do with the resolution of such conflicts and disagreements. Historians call bi-partisanship an invented construct that seeks to array itself as a noble tradition in order to hide its lack of results. In fact, in times of crisis, bi-partisan solutions rarely effectively deal with the problem.

The opposite of bi-partisan is partisan. American history actually demonstrates partisan ideas to be the more successful ones. The United States' civil liberties, existence as an independent country, and idea of equality before the law, as well as many of the most beloved and successful programs of the government, all started out life as extremely partisan causes. The truth is that many aspects that are central to American life were partisan accomplishments that previously divided the nation, even to extremes.

Bretton Woods Agreement

The Bretton Woods agreement represents the outcomes of a three week conference that the United Nations held to set up a new monetary system at the end of World War II. The U.N. organized this meeting called the United Nations Monetary and Financial Conference for July 1 to July 22 of 1944. They held it at Bretton Woods in New Jersey, which gave its name to the deal that ultimately resulted from the conference. The agreement itself proved to be a famed framework that set up a new exchange rate system.

Three significant outcomes resulted from this conference. Two of them are still a major part of the world financial system today. First the group agreed on the Bretton Woods Agreement which set up a new foreign exchange system. Besides this, the United Nations authorized forming the International Monetary Fund and also the International Bank for Reconstruction and Development.

A new foreign exchange system had been called for in the wake of World War II. The international economic system had been destroyed by the already more than five years of fierce global fighting. Allied nations decided even before they successfully concluded the war they needed to come up with a new currency and a plan to rebuild the devastated nations and world economy.

The conference saw 730 delegates attend from all of the 44 Allied countries. They met at the Mount Washington Hotel and spent three weeks coming up with the new currency system and financial institutions. On the last day of the conference on July 22, they signed the Bretton Woods agreement.

The new system rested on several key proposals. One of these involved currency convertibility. All currencies had to be converted for trade purposes and to settle current account transactions. The U.S. sat in a position of commanding strength as it controlled fully two thirds of all the gold in the world.

This gave it the basis to call for a new system of pegging foreign exchange to both gold and the U.S. Dollar. The final agreement had the currencies pegged to gold, but more countries added the U.S. dollar as it became clearer over the subsequent years that it was the world's new reserve currency.

Naturally not everyone felt satisfied with these outcomes to the agreement. Soviet Union (Russia and surrounding republics) representatives came to the conference and participated. They accused the institutions that the conference had created of being mere branches of Wall Street.

As a result, they refused to ratify the final important agreements. Many nations including those of Western Europe, South America, Canada, Australia, the U.S., and eventually Japan after the war did sign on to the agreements and these new institutions began operating in 1945 after enough nations ratified them.

Meanwhile, countries began to exchange their currencies at rates based on the set quantity of gold they held. Whenever an imbalance of payments would occur as a result of the artificial currency pegging system, the International Monetary Fund had the powers to intervene and adjust as necessary. This encouraged foreign trade and global economic growth. It caused expansion in the majority of the developed world following the war.

Besides the International Monetary Fund, the conference also created the International Bank for Reconstruction and Development that eventually evolved into the World Bank. These two organizations still thrive today and promote financial stability and international trade. They encourage worldwide monetary cooperation and economic growth that is sustainable. They also help to reduce poverty and push for higher employment.

Europe and other damaged parts of the world engaged in a long era of rebuilding and development after the war ended with the aid of these institutions. The Bretton Woods system itself became abandoned in 1971 when the U.S. unilaterally left the gold standard. It was replaced by today's free floating currency exchange system.

Bretton Woods Committee

The Bretton Woods agreement failed in 1973 with President Richard Nixon unilaterally abandoning the gold standard. Other countries soon followed suit, first with Switzerland and other European nations and eventually the rest of the world.

The death of the Bretton Woods agreement did not end dreams of restoring a semblance of order and low volatility to the since-then troubled currency markets. One man who was already in government service as Chairman of the Fed in the wake of the agreement's collapse was Paul Volcker. It was he who first seriously called for a new Bretton Woods Agreement back in 2014.

The old defunct 1944 based agreement had set up the U.S. dollar to be the global currency by linking and tying up its value to gold. This had produced thirty years of unprecedented stability in global currency markets and exchange rates. Volcker remembered the consequences of abandoning the agreement personally.

He observed that in the years since the agreement had ended, continuously recurring currency crises had plagued the world economy. Among these were the Mexican, Latin American, and Asian currency crises. In 2008, the global financial crisis and Great Recession had also rocked the world. This amounted to four major currency crises in only 35 years.

Paul Volcker argued convincingly that a new Bretton Woods Agreement would lead to an internationally coordinated financial and monetary system. This would provide much needed stability for the continuously troubled global economy. Such a renewed system would create rules to guide and foster better world monetary policy. He even foresaw the potential for a new global reserve currency that would take over from the U.S. dollar. This system would lead to a balanced equilibrium in various nations' balance of payments. In this way, countries around the world would be able to maintain sufficient foreign exchange reserves.

Paul Volcker made all of these suggestions and observations as he chaired the Bretton Woods Committee meeting in 2014. As the Chair Emeritus, he leads the body of worldwide leaders who wish to rebuild cooperation among the various international financial institutions. Among these are the European-based International Monetary Fund, the U.S.-based World Bank, international major and important central banks, various national Treasuries, and influential private banks.

The Bretton Woods Committee arose in 1983 around the ten year anniversary of the failure of the Bretton Woods Agreement. Two former U.S. Treasury officials suggested that it be established, democrat Secretary Henry Fowler and republican Deputy Secretary Charls Walker. Both men recognized the urgent need for a concerted, overt effort to make sure that leading global citizens spoke up regarding the critical importance of the IFI International Financial Institutions. The yearly meetings have continued without fail since 1983, with the 2016 meeting representing the 33rd year of the annual meetings.

Bretton Woods Committee members are comprised of around 200 different leaders from the heads of finance, business, academics, and not for profit sectors of economies. This includes numerous former presidents, industry CEOs, lawmakers, and cabinet level officials. They all have one belief in common that it is essential to maintain international levels of economic cooperation which is most effectively achieved via strong and efficient IFIs. Through their work on the Bretton Woods Committee, they spearhead worldwide endeavors to encourage economic growth, to foster financial stability around the world, and to reduce poverty wherever they find it.

The Bretton Woods Committee today puts on regular conferences, educational opportunities, and seminars. A great number of these activities were developed in order to address a large segment of the public. Other events are more exclusive and provide the Bretton Woods Committee membership with the chance to give their support, insight, and constructive criticisms to the IFIs management teams.

The Bretton Woods Committee has a track record of successfully working with all U.S. administrations to remind the elected leaders of yesterday and today that the twin ideas of enduring national security and worldwide economic prosperity are inseparably linked and improved by continuous movement forward on multinational issues.

Brexit

Brexit refers to the Jun 23, 2016 referendum on the future of Britain in the European Union. The term comes from the Grexit reference to the potential for Greece to leave the Eurozone shared currency area in past years. In this historic referendum, British voters have to answer the question "Should the UK remain a member of the EU or leave the EU?" Britain's electoral commission came up with the phrasing of the question and parliament accepted it.

The question of having a referendum on the issue arose in the 2015 general election in the U.K. Prime Minister David Cameron promised voters that he would offer the British people a final say on the issue of remaining in the EU if he won reelection. His ruling conservative party has been split on the Euro-skeptic idea and EU membership for around 40 years. The individual on the ground Conservative members are largely for exiting from the European Union over a variety of issues of sovereignty and border and legal control.

Those in favor of Britain leaving the EU believe that the restrictive rules hamper creation of new jobs. They also want to be able to decide on which laws to pass and on their trading partners. Though parliament in London passes laws, these can and have been overturned by the European Parliament and courts in Brussels.

Part of the reason the government decided to hold the referendum in early summer was to have it over before the next summer migration crisis begins in earnest. This migration problem has recently stirred up anger and fear in British citizens that they are losing control of their migration policy to the European Union in Brussels. Proponents of the leave campaign want to make their own immigration policy and decide on who comes into the country.

Those in favor of staying in the EU have their own reasons for their position. They feel that remaining in the block of European countries increases the nation's economic, military, and global influence around the world. Remain campaigners argue that Britain is stronger and more secure at home and abroad by being a part of this largest economic block in the world.

The voting base for this historic referendum is different than for general elections. Any British citizen who is older than 18 is allowed to vote. Citizens of the Commonwealth of Nations who reside in Britain are also eligible to cast ballots. There are 53 member nations of the Commonwealth. This means that residents in Britain of such countries and entities as Canada, Australia, New Zealand, Ireland, Malta, Cyprus, and Gibraltar will be allowed to vote on the Brexit issue.

Brexit supports have argued that the European Union has many incentives to continue trading with the United Kingdom. It remains a large importer of services and goods and carries out much of its trade with the block. They feel that they will be able to forge new and better trade agreements with the rest of the world. This would save them more than 8 billion pounds in contributions made to the European Union budget every year. They believe that the country will be able to join Norway, Iceland, and Liechtenstein as a European Economic Area member nation.

Those who favor remaining in the EU argue that leaving the block will create too much uncertainty in British markets. They argue that foreign companies will not be so likely to invest in Britain and others may move their EU regional or international headquarters to other countries should Britain cease to have unfettered access to the common market.

The Treasury has predicted that a recession created by leaving the EU block would cost households 4,300 Pounds per year in lost jobs, trade, and higher taxes by the year 2030. They argue that the pound will weaken substantially and push up the costs for weekly shopping, travel, and imported goods. Others are worried about what will happen to outside Europeans living in Britain and British expatriates who live around Europe after an exit from the European Union.

British World Economic Order

The British World Economic Order has also been called the Pax Britannica, or "world peace of Britain." What is often overlooked amidst the grandeur, splendor, and sheer military power of the Empire was that it was essentially an approximately 150 year lasting economic order that held sway over most of the planet in one form or another from 1763 at the end of the Seven Years War to the outbreak of World War I in 1914.

The empire itself originally began as an amalgamation of commercial projects which relied heavily on private-party risk and -provided capital to succeed. This was true with the colonizing of the original American 13 colonies, the Hudson Bay Company in Canada, and the East India Company and its ruling of the largest territory in the world (the Indian subcontinent) while still operating as a publically traded stock company on the historic London Stock Exchange. In essence, for the first hundred years or so of the East India Company, an investor could purchase shares in the whole country, land, resources, and population of India.

This changed because of the American colonial revolt in 1775 and the Sepoy Rebellion in India that had to be brutally put down by a previously disinterested and laissez faire styled government which reluctantly took over the reigns from the economic pioneers and their succeeding commercial enterprises. Despite this radical shift in the British World Economic Order, private ventures like the founding of Singapore by British businessman Sit Stamford Raffles in 1819 and the build up of unimportant fishing island backwater Kowloon into Hong Kong in China still occurred with enormous success throughout much of the 1800s. This "Britannic Century" following the final defeat of Napoleon in 1814 saw the zenith of the British World Economic Order which expanded, prospered, and flourished all the way until the outbreak of the financial ruinous and devastating First World War in 1914.

In practice there were four different versions of the British Empire from the end of the Napoleonic Wars to the end of World War I. The first were self governing dominions of the empire in far flung places such as Australia, Canada, the Caribbean islands, and New Zealand. The second was the crown jewel of the empire--- the Indian subcontinent. This strategically-centered, massive, and unquestionably wealthy territory allowed the British to project vast power and influence both militarily and economically from lands and islands extending from the Persian Gulf all the way to the South China Sea.

Third was the ragtag collection of smaller territories which were nonetheless important as way stations along the sea route to India or the new world. Among these were the great trade depots and eventually financial centers of the world like Singapore, Hong Kong, Bermuda, and the Cayman Islands as well as smaller enterprise beachheads including West and East African ports that had little impact on the vast interiors of the continent (at least for several generations until malaria could be conquered as a territorially-limiting disease).

The last type of empire was the purely commercial and diplomatic one, an unofficial realm that extended through such lands as Egypt, China, Hawaii, and Argentina/Uruguay. Investment, commerce, and shrewd diplomacy assured the British power and influence was almost as potent and lasting in these various quarters as it was in places like the Caribbean and Africa.

British commercial ventures enjoyed such historically unparalleled success throughout the world because of the uncanny British Imperial ability to substantially involve and include local elite rulers and minorities alike as willing and helpful partners in their endeavors. British law, rule, and investment may have built up Hong Kong and Singapore into the titans they have become in the world today, yet it was local Chinese hard work, enterprising nature, and all around partnership that ensured the necessary other critical ingredients were there for success. Great credit is deserved by the grand British Imperialists for their unquestionable genius in diplomacy with cultures, nations, and continents from one corner of the world to the other extreme.

Technology helped to assure the ascendency of this British World Economic Order and to bind together what they established with such hard-won efforts. This started with railways and faster steamships which could transport officials, armies, supplies, and armaments (when necessary) on both land and sea with unprecedented speed, effectiveness and importantly, cost efficiency.

Later they developed the telegraph and finally telephone which made it not only possible but relatively easy to police, govern, communicate with, and expand this one quarter of the world sprawling empire that stretched from the South Pacific islands through the Indian Ocean and Mediterranean all the way to the North and South Atlantic Ocean territories and islands. They accomplished this remarkable feat with the smallest army and administrative class of any massive empire in the history of the world. At one point, the British World Economic Order and Empire covered fully 90 percent of all islands on the earth and nearly one-quarter of the world's entire population

The British Empire and British Economic World Order they established in the 1800s had a noble purpose that was achieved in large measure all around the globe. Slavery was abolished by the might and power of the British navy, commercial influence, and diplomatic pressure where necessary working together to pursue a noble and enlightened agenda of the earliest human rights. Besides this, the Imperialists effectively spread scientific and technological advances and progress, free trade, the values and morals of Christianity, and the rule of law, order, and good governance. Without any doubts, these agendas were in the ultimate best interests of all tribes and peoples of mankind everywhere.

Budget Deficit

Budget deficits are accounting positions in which revenues are not sufficient to cover expenditures. As such they involve spending more than the entity takes in from receipts. This term is most often utilized to address government accounting and spending instead of individual or business spending.

This concept can also be applied to a number of government deficits that have been built up over time. In this case, the phrase national debt is employed. A budget surplus is the opposite of the budget deficit. Budgets are balanced when money coming in equals money being spent. Budget surpluses are rare and have occurred for only 6 times since World War II in the United States.

When economic conditions improve and become prosperous budget deficits may decrease as a share of GDP. This happens because tax revenues rise while the economy is growing and unemployment becomes reduced. It also lowers the government expenditures on programs like unemployment. If economic conditions instead deteriorate then budget deficits can grow as a percentage of the country's GDP. This is because government spending rises to help stimulate the economy and cover higher unemployment while tax revenues typically decline at these times.

Nations are able to fight budget deficits with some efforts. They can do this by encouraging economic growth. They might also choose to raise taxes or lower government spending. One easy way to promote better economic conditions is by decreasing the burdensome regulations and complicated tax rules for businesses. This boosts business confidence and results which inevitably increase tax inflows to the national treasury. Lowering the amount of government expenditures such as defense and social programs and improving the efficiency of entitlement programs like state pensions can also help countries to borrow less money.

The United States has been struggling with deficits since its founding in the 1780s. Alexander Hamilton served as Secretary of the new Treasury in the 1790s. He suggested that the states pay back their Revolutionary War debts via the Federal government using bond issues to assume them and pay them off.

The interest payments on these bonds caused deficits which were not finally eradicated until they paid off the debts in the 1860s. This set a precedent for the U.S. Every war the country fought after the Revolutionary War the nation paid for using debt. This led to increasingly larger deficits.

In the early years of the twentieth century, there were not many industrial countries that struggled with larger budget deficits and debt. This financial position changed dramatically during the First and Second World Wars. In these years, governments were forced to borrow extensively to pay for the expensive conflicts as they ran down their financial reserves.

The United States ran up enormous deficits of 17% of national GDP in World War I and 24% in World War II. The industrial nations were able to reduce their deficits into the 1960s and 1970s thanks to many years of consistent economic growth.

High budget deficits consistently will lead to high national debt. As a percentage of GDP, President Franklin D. Roosevelt earned the record for the largest national budget deficit. By 1949, he had amassed a national deficit of $568 billion that equated to nearly 130% of GDP.

While his deficits remained high because of the New Deal and war costs, they did decline to $88 billion under President Harry Truman. President Barack Obama holds the distinction of having the first $1 trillion deficit in all of history. He ran these up with stimulus programs to battle the Great Recession. In the full first four year term of his time in office, these deficits remained at over $1 trillion per year.

Bull Market

A bull market is one in which an entire financial market or a select grouping of securities sees rising prices over an extended period of time. It is also used to describe a scenario in which prices are expected to rise. While the phrase bull market is most frequently utilized to address the stock markets, it can similarly reference any items that trade, such as sustained rising prices in commodities, currencies, or bonds. The opposite of a bull market is a bear market.

The simplest definition of a bull market is one that is rising. Bull markets are those that witness an increase in prices of market shares that is sustained for a period of time. In bull markets, investors show great confidence that this rising trend will only continue to exist over a longer term. When bull markets are in effect, a nation's economy remains strong and employment levels prove to be higher.

Bull markets show the characteristics of high investor confidence, general enthusiasm about the future, and anticipation that strong and successful results will continue to occur. Forecasting with any certainty when such bull market trends will wane is challenging. Much of the problem lies in attempting to decipher speculation's role and the psychological impacts of investors that can often have a major influence on the markets in general.

Bull markets in stocks commonly develop as an economic slow down is waning. They begin in advance of an economy demonstrating a convincing recovery. As investors' confidence levels grow, they show this by their buying and investing in a belief that stock prices will gain in the future. Bull markets generally turn out to be positive and winning scenarios for most investors.

The phrase bull market is derived from the animal world, as is its opposite concept of bear markets. Bulls attack their prey by using their horns in an upward thrust, as when markets are moving up. Bears on the other hand swipe their victims down with their paws, as when markets are falling down. When the trend is rising, the market is a bull market. When it is falling instead, it is called a bear market.

Examples of bull markets abound in both the United States and developing countries. Throughout most of the 1980's and 1990's, the U.S. stock markets rose in a long running bull market. Prices rose by nearly ten fold in that time period. The Dot Com bubble put an end to this bull market at the turn of the century.

Around the world, there have also been numerous bull markets in foreign stock exchanges. In India, the Bombay Stock Exchange, known as SENSEX, experienced a dramatic bull market for five years from mid 2003 to the first of 2008. In this time frame, the index ran from 2,900 points on up to 21,000 points.

Bureau of Economic Analysis (BEA)

The Bureau of Economic Analysis is also known by its acronym the BEA. It is a bureau within the United States Department of Commerce. This BEA develops and publishes statistics for economic accounts that help a variety of groups to make decisions and to understand the economic performance of the U.S. Among the parties that follow their publications and statistics are business and government leaders, researchers, and members of the American public.

The publications which the Bureau of Economic Analysis produces prove to be among the most critical statistics of economics in the country. This includes such national benchmark economic indicators as the GDP Gross Domestic Product along with the balance of payments. The PCE Personal Consumption Expenditures Index is also compiled and released as part of their national economic data.

These and other statistics which the Bureau of Economic Analysis publishes have significant impact on important decisions in the U.S. Public policymakers, consumer households, individual people, and business heads use these numbers. They impact such important business, personal, and economic fundamentals as exchange rates, interest rates, budget and tax forecasts, investment plans for businesses, and the distribution of federal funds. These federal government grant monies total in excess of $390 billion. Numerous agencies distribute them to local and state organizations and communities.

Besides the two national bell weather statistics of GDP and balance of payments, the Bureau of Economic Analysis also puts together and publishes a variety of regional, national, international, and industry specific economic accounts. These deliver crucial information on a range of issues. Among these are relationships between various industries, economic development on a regional basis, and the position of the United States in the global economy as a whole.

Chief among the important statistics the Bureau of Economic Analysis keeps and uses are the NIPAs National Income and Product Accounts. They serve as a cornerstone for all of the agencies' other national and regional statistics. They include the country's gross domestic product numbers and other relevant measurements.

Many individuals are not aware of the depth of the international statistics which the Bureau of Economic Analysis keeps and provides on its website. Their international trade and investment country facts cover all of the nations in the world. These statistics are essentially complete reports on each nation's trade and direct foreign investment with the United States.

They provide information on the exports from and imports to the U.S. from each country. They also showcase the dollar amount of direct foreign investment to and from America for each nation selected. Included in this information is a detailed breakdown of the different types of imports, exports, and trade goods exchanged between each country selected and the United States.

Regional reports which the BEA provides cover GDP on a state by state and metropolitan area basis. They also deliver information on each state's and local area personal income throughout the country. The PCE Personal Consumption Expenditures is provided on a state wide level under this category of information as well.

For industry reports, the BEA offers a GDP by industry report and statistics. They also offer an annual industry accounts section which includes a 50 year survey of current business input-output and GDP figures.

Business Cycle

Business Cycle refers to changes in economic activity which economies around the globe undergo in a certain time-frame. Such cycles are generally framed under the concepts of recession or expansion. When an economy is expanding, it is growing in true terms, which means faster than inflation. This is demonstrated with economic indicators such as industrial production, personal income levels, employment levels, and consumer goods sales.

Conversely in times of economic recession, the economy is shrinking. Economists measure this with the same economic indicators as with expansion. In expansions, analysts measure the period from the bottom called the trough of the prior business cycle to the height (or peak) of the present cycle. With recessions, they instead measure them from the peak up to the trough.

There are organizations which decide what the official technical dates for any such business cycles actually are. Within the U.S., the group that makes these calls is the NBER National Bureau of Economic Research. The American NBER has decided for official purposes that fully 11 business cycles have occurred between the years of 1945 and 2009. They have also broken down the average times of such cycles.

The average business cycle length has run approximately 69 months. This means that they typically last for slightly under six years. Meanwhile, the average expansion in that time frame has run for 58.4 months long. In the same time period, the average length of contraction has amounted to a mere 11.1 months. This is good news as recessions or contractions are often painful and sometimes deep, bringing unemployment and financial hardship on millions of individuals.

The business cycle is also useful for investment positioning. Personal investors can effectively utilize it to allocate and position their various investments and funds. Looking at an example helps to clarify this idea. When an expansion is underway in the early months and years, the best cyclical stocks in different industries like technology and commodities usually outperform the other sectors. Within the recessionary periods, it is more effective to position in defensive sectors. These include consumer staples, health care, and utilities. Such segments commonly outperform their peers as they possess high and dependable dividend yields and reliable cash flows.

The NBER declared (per January of 2014) that the prior expansion began at the end of the Global Financial Crisis and Great Recession which ended officially in June of 2009. This represents the point when the Great Recession that held from years 2007 to 2009 attained its trough.

Economists consider that expansion is the normal mode of the American and Western based economies. Recessions are commonly far shorter and less frequent as well. Many people have wondered why recessions must happen. There is no general consensus among economists. Usually though, a definitive and destructive pattern of speculation that becomes carried away reveals itself in the end stages of the prior expansion. This is the case with many different business cycles.

As an example, the recession from 2001 had a mania which former Federal Reserve Chairman Alan Greenspan referred to as "Irrational Exuberance" that came before it. In this time, the various technology and especially "dot-com" stocks went from boom to bust in a short matter of months. Similarly the recession of 2007 to 2009 came after a time when real estate activity, primarily in housing, had experienced its greatest speculation in American history.

Since the 1990s began, the average time span for expansions has grown substantially. With the last three business cycles that ran from July of 1990 through June of 2009, the average expansion ran for 95 months, nearly eight years. At the same time, the typical recession lasted around 11 months. Some overly optimistic economists believed that this somehow meant the business cycles were finished.

This euphemistic hope became dashed when the world financial markets, banks, and economies melted down in spectacular free fall from 2007 to 2009. During this terrible time in the global economy, the majority of stock markets throughout the world suffered eye-watering declines exceeding even 50 percent in only 18 months. This amounted to the most severe contraction worldwide since the Great Depression of the 1930s.

Commonwealth of Nations

The Commonwealth of Nations is a voluntary membership organization that counts 52 different equal and independent sovereign countries on its roster. Within these nations live 2.2 billion citizens. More than 60% of these residents are less than 30 years old.

Included in the Commonwealth are countries which are among the smallest and largest as well as poorest and richest in the world. The member nations hail from five different regions including Europe, North America, South America, Africa, and Asia/Oceania. Fully thirty one of the members of this organization are smaller countries, a number of them being island states.

The Commonwealth of Nations' history stretches back to the days of the British Empire. This makes it among the oldest political groups of countries in the entire world. The vast majority of nations in the club were once ruled indirectly or directly by Great Britain. Many of these states chose to become independent and self governing even when they kept the monarch of Britain as their Head of State.

They created the Commonwealth in 1949 as a successor organization to the empire. In the years since then, other nations from the Americas, Africa, Europe, Asia, and the Pacific have also become members. The two most recent nations to join were Mozambique and Rwanda. Neither one had a historical connection to the British Empire.

Leaders of Commonwealth of Nations countries meet together every other year in order to discuss pressing issues of shared concern. Queen Elizabeth has attended all but one of the meetings since the organization began in 1949. The last meeting held in 2016 took place in Malta in the Mediterranean Sea. The next meeting is scheduled to occur in the United Kingdom in 2018.

Today membership in the Commonwealth of Nations is a matter of equal and free cooperation which is voluntary. The nations making up the Commonwealth count on the support of over 80 intergovernmental, professional, cultural, and civil society organizations. They ascribe to a body of guiding principles which are found in the Commonwealth Charter.

The group participates in a variety of projects to improve aspects of infrastructure, education, health, and all around society in its member states.

One of the important leadership institutions within the Commonwealth of Nations is the Commonwealth Secretariat. This office leads and guides the group with technical assistance, policy making, and advisory help to member states of the Commonwealth. It works to support governments in their quest to build development that is equitable, inclusive, and sustainable. Its work strives to encourage rule of law, democracy, good government, human rights, and economic and social development. It gives a platform for small countries and helps to empower the youth. The most important work of the organization is laid out at the biannual Commonwealth Head of Government Meetings (CHOGM).

The vision of the Commonwealth of Nations is to work to form and sustain an organization that strives towards mutual peace, prosperity, resilience, and respect while cherishing diversity, equality, and shared values. The Commonwealth's mission is to empower member state governments while it works with the overall Commonwealth nations and other countries in order to better the lives of every Commonwealth citizen and to help move forward their mutual interests around the world.

Consumer Data Industry Association

Consumer reporting has become a huge business in the United States. It makes sense that they would have a large and important trade association. The Consumer Data Industry Association is this organization that functions as the industry trade association for credit reporting companies in the United States.

While they have over 140 different corporate members, they represent approximately 200 companies in the consumer data business. These companies provide a wide range of services. Among these are risk management, fraud prevention, and mortgage and credit reports in the data reporting business.

Other companies offer additional services that are newer in nature. These cover employment and residential screening services, collection services for companies and individuals, and even check verification and check fraud services. Naturally the major consumer reporting agencies are important pillar members of the CDIA. These include Experian, Equifax, TransUnion, and Innovis.

This Consumer Data Industry Association works to provide education to all parties involved in the learning process of consumer data and information. This includes regulators, legislators, the media, and consumers. Their goal is to teach about the proper utilization of such information.

The members of this association also deliver analytical tools and data to help companies provide safe, fair transactions for their customers. Their products and services encourage competition and make better opportunities for the economy as a whole and their customers.

The products and services produced by the members of the Consumer Data Industry Association are enormously utilized. They are a part of over nine billion transactions that are processed every year. The goal of these companies is to offer better access to consumers. They also strive to create products and services which are centered on the needs of the consumers. Finally, they try to offer innovation in an industry that is constantly changing to keep up with rapidly expanding technology and the times.

The history of the Consumer Data Industry Association goes back to 1906. Its founders established it in Rochester, New York as the National Association of Retail Credit Agencies. The organization arose because American consumers were requiring more credit. At the same time, Americans were moving around like never before. Creditors needed a standardized and consistent form of credit information on these consumers. This way they would be able to assess their history of credit payment.

The CDIA underwent numerous name changes over the decades before settling on their present one as the services provided by their membership gradually evolved. In 1907 they became the National Association of Mercantile Agencies. After World War I this organization changed to the Associated Credit Bureaus of America. Under this identity they created the very first standardized system for credit data reporting following World War II.

In the 1960s they began computerizing the industry to keep better track of credit records. Nearly all credit became accessed through such automation by the end of the 1960s. The agency again changed its name at this time to Associated Credit Bureaus as it had expanded to become international. The government took notice of all this activity and passed the first of the consumer reporting industry regulatory laws the Fair Credit Reporting Act in 1971.

In 1991 they moved the office to Washington, D.C. to be near the regulatory and legislative bodies of the U.S. A final name change came about in 2001 as the group evolved to its present Consumer Data Industry Association. Today the organization is the representative body for all companies that deal with analyzing and managing credit data for consumers. Since the 1990s this has grown beyond credit reports to include background screening and employment reporting.

Consumer Debt

Consumer debt refers to debts which individuals owe because of goods they have purchased. These goods must be consumable forms which do not appreciate in value to qualify for the designation. Having huge amounts of consumer debts is generally considered to be negative for individuals since it raises the burden on their resources to keep up with the debt servicing. It also makes it harder to remit the installment payments which are often laden with interest. When these types of debts are not well managed, they can cause a consumer to be forced into bankruptcy.

There are cases where some analysts and economists feel that a little consumer debt can benefit the individual. These scenarios mostly center on instances where the debt is run up in purchasing an asset that will increase the earning power of the individual. Several examples of this are useful to consider. One of them surrounds buying a car with financing in order to reach a job which pays more. Another might be incurring student debt to obtain a higher degree that will make it possible to secure a promotion or better job.

There are differences between this consumer debt and those that governments or businesses owe. Consumer debt is also referred to as consumer credit. This type of debt can be obtained from credit unions, commercial banks, and sometimes the United States federal government. Among the two categories of consumer debt are revolving debt and non-revolving debt.

Revolving debt is represented by credit cards. These debts are called revolving as they were originally intended to be repaid every month when the bill comes due. In practice this does not often happen, as consumers carry balances forward much of the time. Non-revolving debts are fixed installment payment loans. They are not paid off fully in a typical given month. They are more commonly held against the underlying asset's useful life. Mortgages on homes are not considered to be consumer debt. Rather they are counted as personal forms of investment in real estate under the category of personal residential.

As of January 2017, the total debt of American consumers increased to

$3.77 trillion. This represented a 2.8 percent increase over the prior month. Around $2.78 trillion of this consumer debt was comprised of non-revolving loans. It had grown by 5.5 percent. Debts on credit cards represented $995 billion at this point. This had dropped by 4.6 percent in January versus December of 2016.

There are three reasons why Americans find themselves so deeply in debt today. These are school loans, car loans, and credit cards. School loans commonly last for ten years. They can also be pushed to an over 25 year repayment schedule by extension. The federal government guarantees most of these loans since there are no assets with which to back a college degree. The rates are low to encourage higher education. During the Great Recession, these loan defaults skyrocketed as the loans increased massively with many people who were unemployed "going back to school" to improve their prospects. The Affordable Care Act gave the Federal government authority to take over this national student loan program from Sallie Mae, the private company which previously administered it.

Car loans typically run from three to five years, which is considered to be the safe collateral life of the new vehicle. After this point, the value of these cars depreciates so highly that they are no longer considered to be valuable collateral. Banks simply repossess the vehicle if the borrowers default on the payment schedule. There are more of these loans now thanks to the low interest rates which encourage borrowing to buy vehicles.

Finally, credit card debt soared because of the Bankruptcy Protection Act of 2005. People could no longer easily declare bankruptcy, so they were forced to run up their credit cards in an effort to pay bills, especially healthcare. In July of 2008, the credit card debt peaked at its historic high of $1.028 trillion. This amounted to a per household average of $8,640.

Consumer Price Index (CPI)

The Consumer Price Index, also known by its acronym of CPI, actually measures changes that take place over time in the level of the pricing of various consumer goods and services that American households buy. The Bureau of Labor Statistics in the U.S. says that the Consumer Price Index is a measurement of the over time change in the prices that urban consumers actually pay for a certain grouping of consumer goods and services.

This consumer price index is not literal in the sense of what inflation really turns out to be. Instead, it is a statistical estimate that is built utilizing the costs of a basket of sample items that are supposed to be representative for the entire economy. These goods and services' prices are ascertained from time to time. In actual practice, both sub indices such as clothing, and even sub-sub indices, such as men's dress shirts, are calculated for varying sub-categories of services and goods. These are then taken and added together to create the total index. The different goods are assigned varying weights as shares of the total amount of the expenditures of consumers that the index covers.

Two essential pieces of information are necessary to build the consumer price index. These are the weighting data and the pricing data. Weighting data comes from estimates of differing kinds of expenditure shares as a percentage of the entire expenditure that the index covers. Sample household expenditure surveys are sourced to figure what the weightings should be. Otherwise, the National Income and Product Accounts estimates of expenditures on consumption are utilized. Pricing data is gathered from a sampling of goods and services taken from a sample range of sales outlets in varying locations and at a sampling of times.

The consumer price index is figured up monthly in the United States. Some other countries determine their CPI's on a quarterly basis. The different components of the consumer price index include food, clothing, and housing, all of which are weighted averages of the sub-sub indices. The CPI index literally compares the prices of one month with the prices in the reference month.

Consumer Price Index is only one of a few different pricing indices that the majority of national statistical agencies calculate. Inflation is figured up using the yearly percentage changes in the underlying consume price index. Uses of this CPI can include adjusting real values of pensions, salaries, and wages for inflation's effects, as well as for monitoring costs, and showing alterations in actual values through deflating the monetary magnitudes. The CPI and US National Income and Product Accounts prove to be among the most carefully followed of economic indicators.

Cost of living index is another measurement that is generated based on the consumer price index. It demonstrates how much consumer expenditures need to adjust to compensate for changes in prices. This details how much consumers need to keep up a constant standard of living.

Contango

Contango refers to an unusual situation in which a given commodity's future price rises to a higher amount than the anticipated future spot price. As such, it also means that the commodity in question has a future date spot price that is lower than the present price. It relates that investors will pay a greater price for a commodity in the future than the price for the commodity which economists and analysts expect the commodity to fetch. There could be a variety of reasons for this. It could be that individuals would prefer to offer a higher premium over the spot in order to hold the future date of the commodity instead of having to pay for storage costs and/or any carrying costs for purchasing the commodity physically now.

There are other ways of looking at such markets that exist in contango. It is at once a scenario where the price for delivery of the futures contract under discussion must adjust to the downside in order to level off with the futures price. Similarly markets that are in this state show a futures curve (or forward curve) that is sloping upward. The prices must converge closer to each other quickly. If they do not in fact do this, then savvy investors will rapidly recognize that they can begin to set up trades to profit from the unnatural situation by utilizing arbitrage trading. These scenarios are actually not only unnatural, but they are expensive for investors who maintain positions which are net long. This is because the prices for the futures are declining while they are long the positions.

It is helpful to look at a clear example to demystify the concept. Consider than an investor might take a long position using a futures contract at the price of $100. In one year, the contract becomes due. Should the anticipated spot price in the future sit at $70, then the market is in contango. This means that the futures price has to come down (or the spot price for the future must rise). They will have to converge together in some way or another at one point in the near future.

Contango should never be confused with Backwardation. In fact this is the opposite of backwardation. Such a backwardation state is viewed as the typical and natural position of the commodities markets. These markets are in this state as futures prices sit lower than the anticipated spot price in the future in a given commodity. Such a view point means that the futures curve or forward curve slopes downward. This is most optimal for those investors who carry long positions because they hope for the price of the futures contract to increase.

Consider this particular example. The Brent Crude oil trades for $45 per barrel while the contract futures price in a year from now is $55. This means that the commodity is in a state of backwardation since the futures price must increase to converge along with the spot price that is anticipated in the future.

Those investors who have long net positions in commodities which suffer from this state of contango naturally lose when it is time for futures settlement or expiration to occur. The only way that such investors will find it tolerable to remain long in such commodities will be to purchase the contracts at greater prices. This would lead to a negative roll yield though.

As an example, consider Frank the investor who is holding a long futures gasoline contract. It will expire in 9 months. Assume that gasoline is in this state with a $19 price level while the commodity itself trades for only $13. Nine months later, the futures contract has fallen to $16 while the spot has risen to $15. In order for Frank to remain long, he will need to roll his futures contract. He might do this by buying one futures contract at a higher price of $22 that will expire three months from then. The downside would be that he will continue to suffer losses as he rolls such futures contracts over into the future month for a higher price.

Contingency

Contingency in business relates to insurance products that generally are not included within the most commonly accepted types of insurance products such as property, casualty, marine, and financial services handled by the majority of insurance companies. The London Market began the industry of contingency insurance products.

These forms of insurance cover cancellation, non appearance, prize indemnity, transmission failure, weather, political risk, reduction in yield, and various other forms of unusual and esoteric coverage. These types of insurance products protect business clients from losses every bit as much as do typical insurance coverage.

Cancellation coverage pays a business or individual client back all of the costs and income associated with conventions, concerts, and other special events that are forced to be canceled or postponed for reasons beyond a promoter's control. Reduced attendance, ticket refunds, and obligations of contract may also be covered by this category of contingency insurance.

Non appearance contingency insurance protects a business' income should their scheduled famous performer not appear at the event as promised. Included with this type of contingency coverage are dangers such as sickness, extortion, accident, family catastrophe, and even incarceration of the performer. The total dollar amount that is covered includes not only the fee paid to the performer but also the revenue generated indirectly from the event appearance, including parking, ticket sales, merchandising, and concessions.

Prize indemnity contingency proves to be the widest type of contingency insurance business. Such products permit clients to be capable of insuring give away products and cash prizes to customers via promotions. To qualify for this coverage, a prize winning has to result from a lucky event.

Transmission Failure contingency safeguards a business' advertising money spent, or other revenues that would be generated, if a television signal somehow became preempted or interrupted. This contingency insurance is set up to provide coverage for a specific time frame or television event. Interruption has to be something that the insured is unable to control, such as catastrophic or segmented coverage.

Contingency insurance for the weather is commonly utilized alongside event cancellation coverage. These policies pay an insured entity if poor weather happens at a certain time on a particular day. Included in these types of weather are snow, rain, wind, lightning, or tornado watches and warnings. It might also be utilized in a promotion where weather turned out to be a factor in a prize being won.

Political risk contingency coverage pertains to an individual event that might lead to an event being canceled. Such coverage could pertain to delay, abandonment, or repatriation having to do with a covered event. Such coverage is available for limited time frames only.

Reduction in yield contingency is useful for casinos, amusement parks, and resorts. This policy actually pays if anticipated revenue from visitors or ticket sales does not reach the expected level because of a covered peril. If attendance is less than expected, the policy will pay to its limit.

Core CPI

Core CPI refers to the Consumer Price Index. This term revolves around the idea of core inflation. It reveals the longer term price trend in a given item or economy. Core CPI is a means of measuring inflation which leaves out some specific items, particularly those that experience volatility in their pricing. There is a reason for excluding these items. To learn what long term inflation actually is, volatility in prices over the short term and temporary price changes have to be eliminated.

Core inflation is most typically figured up by using the core CPI. This takes out some products like food and energy items, especially oil and gas. Both of these categories may experience short term price changes. Such short term shocks often differ from the bigger picture trend in inflation and provide a false reading of it.

There is another way of calculating core CPI. This is called the outlier method. This way of figuring core inflation takes away products that show the biggest price movements. Many of these items' prices fluctuate rapidly in commodity markets when speculators trade them for profit. Since their prices do not reflect actual alterations of supply and demand, it can make sense to exclude them.

The government is very concerned about which method of measuring inflation it uses. The Federal Reserve decided to switch from CPI to the PCE Index back in January of 2012. They prefer PCE because it offers trends in inflation which are less dramatically impacted by changes in short term prices. Different agencies find other ways to get to what they believe are more accurate means of measuring inflation.

The BEA Bureau of Economic Administration is concerned with eliminating those short term price changes that speculators and traders cause. To get around this, the BEA works with the gross domestic product numbers that already exist and calculates price changes from it. It then takes the monthly release of Retail Survey numbers and measures them against the CPI data-provided consumer prices. The BEA eliminates irregular fluctuations in the inflation data this way and gains more accurate long term trend information.

Determining core CPI inflation is important. It reveals the correlations between goods and services with their prices and the purchasing value of the general income of consumers. Should the costs of goods and services go up in a given time frame while the consumers' parallel income levels do not rise, the buying power of consumers is weakening. This is because their money's actual value is declining when measured against the costs of critical goods and services.

The process could be virtuous as well. Sometimes inflation occurs only on the income of consumers while the costs of goods and services remain constant. In this case, consumers gain greater purchasing power. This means that they will be able to buy an additional amount of the identical services and goods. Asset inflation can also benefit consumers. If the price of their house or the value of their investment portfolio goes up, the consumer has additional buying power also.

Core Inflation

Core Inflation refers to the change in the cost of goods and services without calculating the important categories of food and energy. The U.S. federal government believes this to be the most accurate means of figuring up true inflationary trends. They claim that both energy products and food components are priced too volatilely to be a part of the core inflation calculation and figure. This is because they constantly change so rapidly that they interfere with inflation readings.

The reason for this is that they are subject to the whims of the traders on the various commodity market exchanges. The majority of core food products like beef, pork, wheat, orange juice, and more and energy products such as oil, natural gas, and gasoline trade each and every week day all throughout the day.

As an example, traders of commodities will likely bid up the prices of oil and its derivative products when they believe its supplies will diminish or if they feel that demand will outpace supplies. It could be that a strike will interrupt production and oil supplies from Nigeria, Venezuela, or Angola. Because of this fear, traders will purchase oil at the prices today and hope to sell it for a higher amount at the anticipated greater prices tomorrow or next week.

That is all that it really takes to radically increase the price of oil. Should the strike wrap up quickly, then the oil prices will plunge when traders suddenly all sell out of their positions. This is why both energy and food prices depend on rapidly changing human emotions rather than real changes to underlying forces of supply and demand. Between this and the inelastic demand of food and energy which people simply have to possess in order to live, these commodities rise and fall crazily sometimes.

Consider how gasoline prices will change when their primary input oil does. Yet as people require gas to travel to school and work, they cannot delay their purchases and wait for prices to decline. Food prices also vary according to gasoline and oil prices as they are shipped by truck throughout the United States. In truth, most foods on your dinner plate have more frequent flyer miles than you ever dreamed of acquiring.

The Fed has a few tools to deal with higher than desired core inflation. The problem comes with their tools needing time to take effect on the broader economy. This might mean as much as from six to 18 months before changes to the Fed Funds rate will show a meaningful impact on the inflation rate in the U.S. As the Fed Funds rate goes higher, so will the bank loans and mortgage rates. Credit will tighten and slow economic growth. Corporations find themselves lowering their core prices in order to keep selling merchandise. This lowers inflation as it finally all feeds through to the economy.

The Federal Reserve targets inflation with their policies. They promise to not take action when the core inflation rate remains at two percent or lower. Consider a real world example. Inflation has a tendency to creep higher throughout the summer as people go on vacations. The Fed does not wish to raise rates each summer though, which would force them to proportionally lower them again in the fall.

Rather, they wait and see if such summer increases boost the prices of the goods and services ex food and energy permanently. Yet ultimately higher food and gas prices force up the prices of all other goods and services if they remain elevated for long. This is why the Federal Reserve will also consider the headline inflation rate, which is the opposite of the core inflation rate. This broader measure of inflation considers food and energy prices alongside all other goods and services.

The core inflation rate can be measured via the Core Price Index, or core CPI, as well as the core Personal Consumption Expenditures price index, or core PCE price index.

Cost of Living

Cost of living refers to the sum of money individuals require in order to maintain a given standard of living. The two concepts of standard of living and cost of living are therefore closely related. Expenses included in such a concept include all necessary costs for sustaining life, such as food, housing, health care, and taxes. This living cost frequently finds use in comparing the expenses to live between one city and another one. It is similarly closely connected with salaries and wages. This is because the levels for salaries are commonly measured up against the costs which individuals must pay in order to sustain their typical living standard in a given geographical area. Such living costs can and often do vary substantially from one part of the United States to the next.

The real Cost of living proves to be an important element in how successful an individual is in accumulating money and wealth. Even lower salaries will stretch longer in cities that are inexpensive places to live. At the same time, earning a big salary will hardly be enough to live decently in a costly city like New York City or London.

Mercer publishes its annual Cost of Living Survey that proves to be most illuminating on the differences in living costs from one major city to the next around the world. For their 2015 survey, they found the cities with the most expensive living costs to be Tokyo, Osaka (Japan), Moscow, Geneva, Hong Kong, Zurich, Copenhagen, and New York City. Among the American cities that boasted expensive living costs in 2015 were Honolulu, New York City, Los Angeles, Washington D.C., and San Francisco.

This leads to the Cost of living Index. Such an important index allows for comparisons between one significant city and another comparable one. To come up with a meaningful metric, the index takes into consideration elements that make up the basic living needs of people. It then compiles these into a total measurement that allows workers to reference and utilize when negotiating salaries in various towns and cities. This is particularly important for recent college graduates. They need to consider carefully their entry level jobs into their career and where they will work. For those already employed who are contemplating relocation for work, this index delivers a useful one-stop snapshot of food, rental, and transportation expenses in a prospective place of employment.

For the year 2016, the Cost of Living Index relied on New York City as its United States' and North American cities benchmark. With this as the base for that year, San Francisco boasted the most expensive living costs in all of the Americas. This meant that at least in that particular year, the rent costs for San Francisco proved to be around three percent greater than those of New York City. Food prices were an eye watering 22 percent higher than compatible levels of New York. On the other side of the spectrum, Reno in Nevada offered its residents a living cost which equated to roughly 43 percent less than the one in New York City.

This Cost of living figure also can be extrapolated to standard sized families. In the year 2015, the average living costs for the typical American family of four (two adults and two children) stood at $65,000. Keep in mind that this amount did not include any optional discretionary categories of spending for those goods and services deemed to be nonessential. This would include dinners out, entertainment, leisure activities, vacations, and also luxury goods.

The living costs figure presents policymakers with a challenge and ongoing debate in the highest levels of government. It centers on the national federal minimum wage. There is a significant shortfall between the government's minimally allowed wage and the income which families need to sustain a basic cost of living. This has grown progressively worse since the late 1960's and early 1970's to the point where no family can live decently on either one or even two minimum wage incomes any longer.

Cost of Living Index

The Cost of Living Index refers to a price index that was created so that businesses and individuals are able to compare and contrast the cost of living relative to other cities, regions, countries, and times. This theoretical index takes the measure of variations in the costs of different key goods and services. It also permits substitutions with other similar goods when prices fluctuate.

One thing that is interesting regarding this Cost of Living Index is that there is not only a single methodology and index that reveals the national (or international) cost of living. One of the most widely used systems for these indices is known as the Konüs Index. These formats utilize an expenditure function like those employed in considering anticipated compensating variation.

In the United States, the most widely recognized and cited version of the Cost of Living Index was developed and is continuously maintained by the C2ER Council for Community and Economic Research. It first appeared in 1968. This version has proven to be the most consistent index for sourcing city to city cost-based comparisons in the United States. Their COLI data is widely recognized by such American governmental organizations as the U.S. Bureau of Labor Statistics and the U.S. Census Bureau. Similarly the President's Council of Economic Advisors utilizes it routinely. Private national media outlets including CNN Money, U.S. News and World Report, Forbes, Kiplinger's, ABC News, and countless others reference this index for the cost of living purposes. This makes it the closest possible thing to a nationally recognized and utilized COLI.

The reason for the C2ER COLI success centers on their entirely transparent methodology for creating and their locally sourcing of data. Users of the index know precisely how they compile it. They have an Advisory Board made up of government officials and academic researchers which reviews their methodology and data continuously. This helps to explain why this COLI finds reference use within the Census Bureau Statistical Abstract of the United States. As the C2ER publishes it quarterly and collects data on local levels from more than 300 different independent researchers, this represents the only locally-based and –sourced Cost of

Living Index compiled on the United States.

The firm employs more than 60 goods and services within the index's underlying data. They precisely select these different representative goods and services in order to take into consideration the various consumer categories of spending. They assign weights for the various costs utilizing data from government surveys citing executive and professional households' spending habits. Each item becomes priced at a fixed point in time for every locality utilizing specifications which are standardized.

A number of characteristics set this particular renowned COLI apart from its various inferior competitors. The data is provided for both county and large city MSA metropolitan statistical areas. They organize it by six different categories. These include housing, food, utilities, health care, transportation, and miscellaneous services and goods. Naturally C2ER offer the composite index as their primary one. The data comes out quarterly, no later than three months following its collection, so it is both fresh and relevant. Besides all of the government organizations which rely on their data and COLI in general, the Brookings Institution and Bankrate.com also cite their well-regarded methodology.

All of the various mainstream cost of living indexes rely on the theory which the Russian economist A. A. Konüs developed. The theory is only somewhat hampered by the assumption that the consumers act as optimizers to receive the maximum utility possible out of the money which they possess and can spend. The weakness is that this standard baseline assertion does not always work out to be the case in practice.

Cost Push Inflation

Cost-push inflation is a scenario where all around price levels go up, creating inflation. This happens because of rising prices in the important inputs of raw materials as well as higher wages for labor. This type of inflation appears because of rising production factors costs. This leads to a lower amount of total supply and production in the economy. With a smaller quantity of good being produced as the supply weakens while demand for such goods remains constant, the final cost for the finished products goes higher. This creates the inflation.

Cost-push inflation most typically begins when the costs of production rise. This is many times an unexpected cost increase. It could come as a result of higher prices in input raw materials, an unforeseen shutdown of or damage to a key production facility (like with natural disasters or fire), or forced higher wages for the employees in production. The higher wages could result from an increase in the minimum wage that automatically boosts the salaries of the workers who were making less than the new legally accepted minimum standard.

In order for such cost-push inflation to occur, the associated demand of the product in question has to stay constant while the changes in costs of production are actually happening. Producers then feel they have no choice but to compensate for the rising production expenses. They raise their end prices for their consumers so that they can hold their profit margins as they attempt to keep up production with anticipated demand for the products.

There can be several unanticipated causes of this cost-push inflation. Natural disasters are a common example. There might be earthquakes, floods, tornadoes, hurricanes, or other kinds of large "acts of God" events that interfere with some component in the production chain. These create higher costs of production. Natural disasters that do not lead to higher costs of production do not qualify as an example of this type of inflation.

There are other actions that can eventually cause rising costs of production as well. It might be a strike of the plant workers that happens because of failed negotiations in contracts. It could also result from a rapid change in government as often happens in developing countries. This might create an inability for the country to keep up its prior levels of production output.

There are similarly cost-push inflation causes that may be anticipated but are still unavoidable. Present regulations and laws can change. These changes may be foreseen. Despite this, there could still be no practical means of offsetting the resulting higher costs that come along with the changes.

Cost-push inflation is one of the two main types of inflation. The other kind is demand-pull inflation. This is the opposite form. In demand-pull, higher production costs force up the price of an individual service or good. With demand-pull inflation, the increase in demand happens even when production may not be boosted to cover the rising needs. In such cases, the costs of the product will go up because of the resulting imbalance that is created in the natural demand and supply model.

Council of Economic Advisers (CEA)

The President's Council of Economic Advisors proves to be an agency of the President's Executive Office. They give the President unbiased and non partisan economic advice for coming up with both international and national economic policies. This council is made up of three people of whom one is the chair. They use analysis of empirical evidence based on economic research to come up with their regular recommendations to the President. They gather the most esteemed information they can to help the President in putting together the critical national economic policy and annual report.

In 2016 the Chairman of this CEA was Jason Furman. The two members of the group were Jay Shambaugh and Sandra Black. Distinguished one time chairs of the group include former Chairmen of the Federal Reserve Alan Greenspan and Ben Bernanke and 2016 Federal Reserve Chairperson Janet Yellen. This council receives significant support from a number of staff members. Among their support personnel are staff economists and senior economists, research assistants, and a statistical back office.

Congress established this Council of Economic Advisors for the President with its 1946 Employment Act. In this act, the legislation called for three members whom the President would appoint. The Senate was to advise on selection and give consent on the final selection of these members. Members chosen for the CEA are to be recognized for their experience, training, and accomplishments in the field of economics.

Their purpose in greater detail is to consider and explain the economic developments to the President and to review the activities and programs the government establishes for economic appropriateness. They are also expected to create and recommend policies to encourage production, better employment, and higher purchasing power in a freely competitive economy. One of the three members the President is to appoint as Chairman for the council.

The council specifically has five different duties in the performance of their role. They have to help with and give advice for the Economic Report that the President's office prepares annually. They are instructed to collect information that is timely and accepted on the economic trends and developments in the U.S. They can then analyze and understand if the trends are interfering with attaining the stated Presidential policy. The group has to put all of this information together and turn it in to the President.

A third role is to consider the activities and programs of the government. The CEA is supposed to ascertain which of these activities and programs are helping to advance the policy and which are hurting it so they can let the President know.

They must also create and recommend policies for the President that help to develop and encourage competitive free enterprise. These policies should help to reduce and stop economic fluctuations and to improve national production, employment, and purchasing power.

Finally, the Council of Economic Advisors was set up to create and provide a range of reports and studies that have bearing on national economic legislation and policies. These are to be drawn up as the President requests them.

Every month the CEA prepares a report for the Joint Economic Committee of Congress. This is known as the *Economic Indicators*. In this publication there is information on income, gross domestic product, business activity, production, employment, prices, credit, money, security markets, international statistics, and the finances of the Federal government.

They also produce reports and fact sheets on a nearly every month basis that address a wide variety of economic issues. These reports and the speeches and testimony of the members of the Council of Economic Advisors are all available to the public on their official website.

Credit Report

A credit report is an individual or business' credit history. This includes their record of borrowing and repaying money in the past. It similarly covers data pertaining to any late payments made or bankruptcies that have been declared. In some countries, credit reports are also referred to as credit reputations.

When an American like you completes a credit application for a bank, a credit card company, or a retail store, this information is directly sent on to one of the three main credit bureaus. These are Experian, Trans Union, and Equifax. These credit bureaus then match up your name, identification, address, and phone number on the application for such credit with the data that they keep in their bureau's files. Because of this match up process, it is essential that lenders, creditors, and other parties always provide exactly correct information to the credit bureaus.

Such information in these files at the three major credit bureaus is then utilized by lenders like credit card companies in order to decide if you are deserving of having credit issued to you by the creditor. Another way of putting this is that they decide how likely that you will be to pay back these debts. Such willingness to pay back a debt is usually indicated by the timeliness of prior payments to other lenders. Such lenders will prefer to see the debt obligations of individual consumers, such as yourself, paid on time every month.

The second element considered in a lender offering loans or credit to individuals like you is based on your actual income. Higher incomes generally lead to greater amounts of credit being accessible. Still, lenders look at both willingness, as shown in the credit report and prior payment history, along with ability, as shown by income, in deciding whether or not to extend you credit.

Credit reports have become even more significant in light of risk based pricing. Practically all lenders of the financial services industry rely on credit reports to determine what the annual percentage rate and grace period of repayment of a loan or offer of credit will be. Other obligations of the contract are similarly based on this credit report.

In the past, a great deal of discussion has gone on considering the information contained in the credit reports. Scientific studies done on the issue have determined that for the most part, this credit report information is extremely accurate. Such credit bureaus also have their own authorized studies of fifty-two million credit reports that show that the information contained therein is right a vast majority of the time.

Congress has heard testimony from the Consumer Data Industry Association that in fewer than two percent of credit report issue cases have there been data which had to be erased because it was wrong. In the few cases where these did exist, more than seventy percent of such disputes are handled in fourteen days or less. More than ninety-five percent of consumers with disputes report being satisfied with the resolution.

Currency Intervention

Currency intervention is also known as currency manipulation or forex intervention. These central bank-pursued interventions happen as they buy or sell their own national currency on the global foreign exchange markets. They do this to raise or lower the value of their currency.

Though these types of manipulations have occurred since the Great Depression, they are fairly new as a form of national monetary policy. Countries that have used this type of intervention heavily to limit the rise of their currencies in recent years are Japan, China, and Switzerland.

In general, central banks use currency intervention as a tool to contain the rising value of their own money as compared to those of other countries. When currency values appreciate, a nation's exports become more expensive and so are less competitive abroad. This happens because their goods cost more to buyers in their own foreign currencies. It explains why central banks prefer lower currency values which boost their nation's exports and improve economic growth rates.

The first significant use of currency intervention occurred on the side of the United States in the depths of the Great Depression. The American government counterbalanced imports of gold coming from Europe by selling off American dollars so that the gold standard would be upheld. Only when globalization had dramatically impacted economics did the large scale currency interventions of today become more commonplace.

China has been a major perpetrator of currency intervention in recent decades. They have been constantly concerned with keeping their Chinese Yuan value down against the dollar so that their all important exports did not become more expensive to their biggest customer. They aggressively sold Yuan and bought assets denominated in American dollars such as Treasuries in order to keep up a peg against the dollar.

The Swiss National Bank and Bank of Japan have also engaged in manipulation of the currency markets more recently to try to stem the over appreciation of their own national currencies. As the recipient of safe haven investment flows, these two countries find economic instability causes investors to seek their currencies the franc and yen for safety.

They have responded by selling their own currencies and buying those of main trading partners, such as the euro and dollar. Switzerland made headlines in January of 2015 when it suddenly abandoned its interventionist Euro ceiling as unsustainable. The Swiss franc gyrated as much as 30 percent higher in value in hours before settling between 10 percent and 20 percent more against the euro and dollar.

Currency interventions can be either sterilized or non sterilized. Sterilized interventions do not alter the money base of the country. Instead they offset foreign bond purchases or sales by performing the opposite transaction with its own currency bonds. Either means of intervening requires the central bank to sell or buy foreign currencies or bonds issued in such currencies. This allows them to decrease or increase their currency's value in global forex markets.

Central banks may also purchase and sell currency using transactions in forex spot or forward market instruments. They are literally buying or selling foreign currency with their own nation's currency in these cases. They pursue such actions in order to impact the near term valuations of their currency.

Economists question how effective such interventions really are. They generally agree that sterilized transactions cause little lasting effect. Spot and forward market purchases and sales tend to affect values short term but often do not last. Economists mostly concur that longer term currency interventions which are not sterilized can effectively impact exchange rates since they change the monetary base.

Cyclical Manipulation

Cyclical manipulation refers to government interference in the natural economic cycles. This can lead to extreme booms and busts over the long run as governments attempt to prop up booms and forestall busts. Cyclical manipulation is mostly accomplished through the altering of government set interest rates. This is accomplished on a regular basis by the Federal Reserve Board in the United States.

Economic cycles as a concept are occasionally referred to as Business Cycles. This idea is one that explores the alterations in economic activity that change over time. Elements contemplated in explaining economic cycles are comprised of GDP growth, employment rates, and household incomes.

Within economic cycles, two main types emerge. These are booms and busts. Booms are commonly seen when a strong economy is operating. Busts, or recessions, are tied to economic growth that proves to be below trend. In the U.S., the NBER, or National Bureau of Economic Research, turns out to be the ultimate trusted source that gives out dates of troughs and peaks which actually make up economic cycles.

The NBER is part of this cyclical manipulation in the United States. The first step of the manipulation is the way in which they refer to booms and busts. They euphemize them as expansion or contraction. When a few portions of the economic data are getting better, then this is expansion, and when these same indicators are declining, it is called contraction. Such definitions focus entirely on the data movement, versus the historical norms.

Cyclical manipulation is accomplished principally through the changing of interest rates by the Federal Reserve. When the cycle is one of boom, or expansion, they attempt to cool the economy down to prevent inflation. They do this by raising the interest rates to slow down lending and spending. Unfortunately, as economic activity then slows, this leads to an economy that can then fall into bust, or contraction.

At this point, the Federal Reserve begins cutting the interest rates, sometimes massively, in an effort to stimulate the economy once more. As the interest rates fall, businesses and consumers borrow and spend larger sums of money. This gets the economy going once again. The irony of this cyclical manipulation lies in the fact that the very effort of the government to keep the cycles from becoming extreme leads to changes in the cycles that the Fed wishes to prevent altogether.

Economic Cycles Theory believes that even though these highs and lows average together to create an average trend economic rate of growth, this trending growth rate remains stable over time. The government through the Fed attempts to manipulate these cycles to keep the growth rate along these trend lines consistently. There has been no effort made in the Economic Cycles Theory to explain the economic activity levels in long running time frames of decline, but only in growth. This policy of only focusing on growth is yet another demonstration of the cyclical manipulation.

Debasement

When economists speak of debasement, they are referring to lowering the value of the money in an economy which is utilized to purchase goods and services. There are a number of ways that this can be done and has been accomplished throughout history. These include reducing the amount of precious metals in coins, eliminating the commodity backing, deficit spending, fractional reserve lending, and re-denominating a currency.

The practice of debasement by reducing the amount of precious metals in coins dates back to Roman times. The Imperial Roman government reduced both the amount of silver and the size of their denarius coins over time. They maintained the same denomination in the process. The silver coins began as nearly pure 4.5 gram pieces that finally had only two percent silver content left in them when they were replaced altogether.

The U.S. engaged in this same practice after 1964. Half dollars, quarters, and dimes had all contained 90% silver through that year. They were altered to clad coins with copper cores and a nickel copper plating beginning in 1965. This means they ceased to be commodity money and became Fiat money with value only because of government decree.

More recently, governments began debasing their currency by eliminating the currency's commodity backing of silver and gold. The U.S. Congress abolished the silver certificate legislation in June of 1963 and stopped redeeming bills for silver as of June 24, 1968. The gold standard that had backed up U.S. paper bills died in 1971 when then President Richard Nixon abandoned the currency standard unilaterally. The U.S. and other developed nations have been using Fiat currencies completely since then.

Deficit spending is another means of debasement. As governments print excess bills or issue debt to pay for their spending, the engage in this. The dangers of this practice are that as the money supply increases, so too does inflation. The U.S. money supply has been tripled using this means in the years of the Great Recession from 2007 to 2012. The runaway government spending has increased U.S. federal debt four fold from the years 2000 to 2016 (from $5 billion to around $20 billion total).

Governments can also use banks in debasement. This practice is known as Fractional Reserve Lending. Banks are able to create money from thin air by loaning out significantly more money than they keep in reserves. Only a small percentage has to be kept on hand for the withdrawal of deposits. Money can be lent out versus kept on reserves to a factor of even ten to one. It leads to bank runs and bank panic if too many depositors attempt to withdraw all of their money at a time.

Currencies can be re-dominated by a government replacing an older unit of currency for a newer one. They do this by changing the currency's face value without allowing its foreign exchange rate to be altered. This re-dominating often causes hyperinflation. As bill values are changed by 10, 100, 1000, or even higher amounts, inflation can increase exponentially as well. When re-denominations became sufficiently high, the currency finally becomes worthless. This devastating result has transpired numerous times in history, most recently in Zimbabwe.

Debt Ceiling

The Debt Ceiling refers to an American budgetary and financial constraint which the nation self imposed beginning in 1917. Congress mandates this limit for the maximum amount of debt the Federal government may have at any point in time. Back on November 2nd of 2015, the U.S. Congress suspended the debt ceiling with the Bipartisan Budget Act of 2015. The ceiling remained suspended through March 15th of 2017, after the Presidential election. They did this deliberately to allow time for the new President (Trump) and his (Republican) Congress to establish themselves before they have to address the continuous debt crisis of the United States.

The prior debt ceiling was a whopping $18.113 trillion. Because the country was about to surpass this level on March 15th of 2015, then American Treasury Secretary Jacob Lew ordered a suspension to the debt issuance of the U.S. He began engaging in what analysts call "extraordinary measures" in order to stop the debt from breaking through the artificially created limit. To do this, he quit paying Federal government staff as well as the retirement fund contributions for U.S. Post Office employees. He began to sell the investments which these funds held as well.

The debt limit also covers a significant quantity of debt which the Federal government must repay itself. This includes the massive creditor the Social Security Trust Fund. Money owed to everyone outside of the U.S. government they call the American public debt. This amount represents approximately 70 percent of the aggregate Federal debt.

It was actually the Second Liberty Bond Act of 1917 which first saw Congress establish the initial debt ceiling. This law permitted the U.S. Treasury Department to sell Liberty bonds in order to pay for the then-vast costs of the U.S. military involvement in the First World War. By such an action, Congress gained the upper hand in overseeing total government spending for the first moment in U.S. history. Up to this point, the Congress had only held authority to approve particular debts, such as short term notes or for the Panama Canal.

By 1974, Congress found a way to gain absolute control over the budget process and effective spending in the United States. They called this new law the Budget Control Act of 1974. This new procedure for the budget envisioned Congress working closely in concert with the U.S. President to agree on what amount of money the country's government will actually spend. This all made the debt ceiling need irrelevant, since all it does is permit the Federal government to borrow necessary funds to pay for spending it previously approved anyway.

The reason this debt ceiling still matters is because Congress intentionally limits the amount of money which the U.S. Treasury may effectively borrow with it. If they do not continuously raise this artificially imposed limit, then the United States will default on its outstanding debt obligations. In general, the Congress has experienced no remorse for raising it. They raised it around ten times over the last decade, of which four of those times occurred in only 2008 and 2009.

This debt ceiling becomes a crisis in the event that both Congress and the American President are unable to come to an agreement on the country's fiscal policy. This has happened with alarmingly increasing frequency over the last few decades. It was an issue in 1985, 1995/1996, 2002, 2003, 2011, 2013, and 2015. The ceiling and associated government spending becomes an issue when the debt versus GDP ratio becomes excessively high.

The International Monetary Fund states that the maximum safe level for developed nations is 77 percent. After this point, holders of government debts then feel justifiable concerns that the nation will be unable to create sufficient revenues to repay the total debts.

Debt Consolidation

Debt consolidation is combining all of an individual's personal debts into a single larger debt. When people go though debt consolidation, they obtain one loan which they then use to pay down all smaller loans or outstanding debts. The idea is that this provides consumers with only a single payment that they make once per month. This is supposed to be simpler for consumers to pay and manage.

A main goal with debt consolidation is to obtain a lower interest rate. The monthly payment generally becomes lower through the process as well. Despite the fact that the payment is lower, the debt can be repaid faster. The lower interest rate makes this possible.

Debt consolidation is different from debt settlement. In debt settlement, higher outstanding bills are negotiated to lower more manageable amounts. In debt consolidation, individuals fully pay off all of their bills. There are no bad impacts on credit history and reports as a result of the consolidation process.

Consumers pursue debt consolidation through either an unsecured or a secured loan. An unsecured loan does not involve any collateral. This means that no personal assets back the loan. The lender extends the loan because the individual pledges to repay it. A credit card is a prime example of an unsecured loan. Many credit cards offer debt consolidation with a lower promotional interest rate to their customers. In general, the rates are higher on unsecured loans. This is because the risk is greater for the lender with an unsecured loan than with a secured loan.

With a secured loan, individuals receive the debt consolidation funds because they pledge an asset. These assets that secure the loan are usually a car or a home. Car loans and mortgages are both secured forms of loans. The downside to a secured loan is that a lender can seize the asset if consumers fall behind on the loan.

Debt consolidation with a secured loan happens through a variety of different types of loans. Among the more popular secured debt consolidation loans is a second mortgage home loan or a home equity line of credit. It is also possible to obtain a debt consolidation loan with a 401k. In this type of loan, retirement funds are the asset that underlies the loan. Insurance policies allow owners to take loans against the value in the policy as well.

Annuities are another vehicle that can sometimes be borrowed against. A number of special financing companies also issue loans against lottery winnings or lawsuit claims. In each of these cases, the element in common is that the asset secures the debt consolidation loan.

There are both pros and cons to consolidating bills with an unsecured loan. The biggest difficulty with these types of loans is obtaining them. Unsecured loans require fantastic credit in order to qualify. The interest rates are typically higher than those on secured loans as well. Still the rates are often lower than the ones charged by high interest credit cards. If these consolidation rates are not substantially lower than those of the bills on the debt consolidation loan, then it may not make a difference in the payments and payoff time-frame.

Debt consolidation loans that rely on credit card balance transfers can present problems. It is important to be aware of what happens after the promotional balance expires. The new interest rate may be so high that the loan does not provide any benefits over the terms of the old debts. There are commonly transfer fees with these credit card balance transfers. These can eat up a part of the savings that the debt consolidation should provide.

Debt Relief

Debt relief refers to the effective reorganizing of any form of debt so that the indebted party experiences at least some debt forgiveness. This could be complete or partial relief of debt from a large or even overwhelming burden. It is possible for it to take a wide range of scenarios. Relief might be offered in the form of lowering the aggregate principal in whole or in part. It might also be accomplished through lengthening the loan term or reducing the total interest rate and payments of loans which are due.

Debt relief also relates to debt forgiveness in order to stop the growth of the principal or at least to slow it down. This can be done for groups ranging from individual people to companies or multinational corporations to entire nations. From the days of the ancient world up to the 1800s, it primarily pertained to individual and household debt. This especially meant freeing of slaves from indebtedness or forgiving agriculture debts.

In the last years of the 1900s, the use of the phrase changed to cover mostly debt of the Third World. This began with the skyrocketing debt from the Latin American Debt Crisis that included such countries as Mexico and Argentina. By the early years of the 2000s, the phrase had greater application to individuals in wealthy countries that had been ravaged by housing and credit bubbles.

Debt relief in the 20th century came to apply to nations after the devastating effects of the First World War. Those debt payments from the allies of the United states were suspended in the dark depths of the Great Depression from 1931. Finland was the only country to repay these debts in full. Germany also received debt relief of its war reparation burdens from the United States, Britain, and France with the Agreement on German External Debts in 1953. This represented one of the first large scale applications of debt relief on an international scale.

By the 1990s, debt relief had become an urgent need for those under-developed nations which were heavily in debt. This became a mission in the 1990s for a number of Christian organizations, Non Governmental Organizations focused on development, and others partners who worked in an enormous coalition which called itself Jubilee 2000. As part of the campaign to push for debt forgiveness and relief, there were demonstrations at meetings like the G8 Summit in Birmingham, England in 1998. This helped the agenda for debt relief to reach the radar of international organizations like the World Bank and IMF International Monetary Fund as well as Western developed nations' governments.

It actually became public policy through an initiative called the HIPC Heavily Indebted Poor Countries program. This initiative started out in order to offer consistent help in the form of debt relief to those most impoverished nations of the world. It worked strenuously to make certain that the money donated went for reduction of poverty and did not get siphoned off to infrastructure or military buildup programs.

This World Bank-supervised project involved conditions which were much like those accompanying loans from the World Bank and IMF International Monetary Fund. They mandated strict structural reforms that often involved privatizing public utilities including electricity and water. The prospective nations had to institute Poverty Reduction Strategies and demonstrate substantial macroeconomic stability for minimally a year.

In order to cut inflation, there were nations goaded into reducing their expenditures on important sectors such as education and health. The World Bank may have deemed the HIPC protocols a triumph for the twin goals of poverty and debt reduction, but many scholars and analysts offered significant criticisms of the program.

Despite critiques though, the HIPC became extended through the MDRI Multilateral Debt Relief Initiative. After the Gleneagles G8 meeting of 2005 in July, the wealthy creditor nations signed on to the MDRI. This provided full, complete elimination of all HIPC countries' multilateral debts which they owed to the IMF, World Bank, and African Development Bank.

Debt Relief Order

A Debt Relief Order (also known by their acronym DRO) refers to a British legal system type of insolvency method which is relatively new. It was Chapter 4 from the Tribunals, Courts, and Enforcement Act 2007 that actually created these new orders. The advantage that such DROs offer is a less expensive, faster, and simpler means of receiving bankruptcy styled relief in Great Britain.

The DRO works well for those indebted individuals who possess no or very few assets (under 1,000 British pounds without owning a home), and who count tiny disposable income levels (which have to be under 50 pounds sterling each month). Individuals who meet these criteria and several others may pay only a 90 pounds one time fee and then make application for the Debt Relief Order without a court appearance. Participants can even pay this fairly reasonable fee in a period of installments before they file the application for the order. Such DROs took the full force of law for both England and Wales on April 6th of 2009.

There are a range of specific requirements that individuals must meet in order to qualify for such a Debt Relief Order. It must be clear the persons can not pay their debts. They must not owe more than 20,000 pounds in total unsecured bills. Homeowners do not qualify, nor do those who have over 1,000 pounds in total gross assets. They can only keep their car if its value is under 1,000 pounds. The debt holder has to live in Wales or England or at least have been resident or engaged in business in either place within the past three years. They also may not have been issued a DRO in the prior six years.

Besides this the indebted individuals may not be part of any other kind of insolvency proceedings. These include bankruptcies which are not yet discharged, voluntary individual arrangements, present debt relief restrictions, present bankruptcy restrictions, a bankruptcy petition, or an interim order. It is true that these Debt Relief Orders are still insolvency forms that will be publicly listed in the insolvency services website.

In order for Debt Relief Orders to be successfully implemented, there must be a government approved intermediary who handles the event with the relevant authorities. For intermediaries to be approved, they generally have to be debt advice organization personnel which have experience as debt advisors. Some of these approved organizations include the Consumer Credit Counseling Service, one of the Citizens Advice Bureaus, Baines and Ernst National Debtline, Think Money, Payplan, the Institute of Money Advisers, and members of the entity Advice UK. Any of these approved intermediaries are able to consider the information of the persons applying, discern if they are DRO eligible, and finally make an online application on their behalf. These intermediaries who are approved do not charge fees to submit such applications.

The Official Receivers are able to issue the Debt Relief Orders after they obtain both the fee and the application. No court involvement is necessary if the applicant is eligible. Otherwise they will reject the application out of hand. These Official Receivers also have the authority to rescind these DROs if more relevant information on the debtors' financial conditions appears after the order has been granted. There are also criminal charges and penalties allowed by the British law if the applicants knowingly perjure themselves or provide deliberately misleading information on their financial conditions, assets, debts, and other personal financial costs.

Back in November of 2014, the New Policy Institute released data (research funded by the Trust for London) on the quantities of debt relief orders throughout different parts of the United Kingdom. Unsurprisingly, the total numbers of these DROs for London in the years of 2009 to 2013 proved to be vastly less than the rest of England's average.

Deflation

Deflation is simply the prices of goods and services going down in a given time frame. Deflation is the opposite of inflation, which is the rising cost of goods and services over a period of time. This does not make deflation a good thing in the long run.

Another way of defining deflation is the increasing value of money versus various economic goods over a span of time. With inflation, money is becoming less valuable versus goods over time. Deflation happens as a result of the interaction of four factors. On the one hand, the supply of money in circulation might decline. At the same time, supplies of available goods might increase. The need for goods could drop as well. Finally, the demand for money could go up. If any of these four things happen either separately or in concert, deflation is commonly the result.

The easiest way for deflation to occur is as the supply of goods available on the market goes up at a more rapid pace than does the supply of money. The combination of these elements explains how some goods' costs go up while the costs of others go down at the same time. Despite this, deflation can pose certain problems.

The majority of economists today concur that deflation proves to be both a symptom of economic problems as well as a malaise in and of itself. Some buy into the concepts of good and bad deflation. Good deflation happens as companies are consistently capable of manufacturing goods for cheaper and lower prices because of gains in productivity and other ways of reducing costs. This type of deflation permits a strong and growing GDP growth, with lower unemployment, and rising profits.

Bad deflation is more challenging to grasp. Bad deflation rises as a result of the central bank, or the Federal Reserve, choosing to revalue the country's currency. Or, you could say that the supply of money declining results in this negative form of deflation.

The actual problem that deflation causes is that it creates uncertainty for businesses and their relationships. As a rule, business thrives on confidence and falters on the unknown. Borrowers have to make loan payments that turn out to be greater and greater amounts of purchasing power in deflationary time periods. All the while, the value of the asset that you purchased with the loan is declining. In these circumstances, many borrowers elect to default on the loan and its payments.

A declining spiral similarly exists in deflationary periods. Since businesses begin to enjoy fewer profits, they decide to reduce their employment roles. Individuals do not spend as much money as a result. Businesses then realize smaller profits and again cut back. This degenerates into a vicious cycle down before long, as it becomes self reinforcing. Consumers learn that larger ticket items such as houses and cars will actually cost less in the future and then delay their purchases.

Though deflation has been discussed as a potential problem for the U.S. economy with the economic downturn, the reality is far different. At the same time, from 2006 to 2009, the Federal Reserve massively increased the money supply by more than three hundred percent. This argues not for deflation in the United States' future, but for inflation instead.

Deflationary Bias

Deflationary Bias refers to a government approach to managing inflation versus deflation. Inflation means that prices are rising, whereas deflation signifies that the prices of goods and services are decreasing. It is helpful to consider a real example of these two opposing concepts in order to understand them and the problems deflation can quickly cause.

If individuals go to their local grocery store and discover that bread has increased to $2.50 instead of the previous price of $2.00, they will not be happy. This is inflation and represents inflationary bias. On the other hand if the individuals went down to the car lot and discovered that a car which sold for $25,000 before is now selling for $23,000, they would be ecstatic. This is deflation and represents a deflationary bias. In general, consumers will always prefer deflation to inflation, at least on the surface.

The picture becomes more complicated when debt is considered. On a consumer level, as home prices decline, the home owners suddenly find themselves holding a mortgage that may be higher than the house's actual value proves to be. As this becomes a severe problem, individuals who own the house and are paying down the mortgage little by little (over likely 30 years) will not be able to sell and move simply because the mortgage is so much greater than the value of the house. The debt laden homeowners become unwitting victims of deflation in these cases. As a result, they are unable to move to expand their job hunting possibilities and will likely cut back on spending as they realize that they are upside down in the home thanks to the ravages of deflation.

This logic similarly applies to business as well. Because contracts exist in fixed terms not real terms, as real prices rise or fall, losers and winners emerge every time. As inflation occurs, sellers in a contract prove to be the winners, along with debtors whose debt is priced less in real terms. When deflation happens, prices fall and the sellers and debtors become the all around losers as their debt now costs more to repay in real terms. The buyers and creditors are the winners in this deflationary scenario. Ultimately this means that regardless of accounting tricks and confusing statistics, both deflation and inflation create income transfers with zero sum game losers and winners.

Governments attempt to smooth out the precarious extremes of either deflation or inflation utilizing monetary policy. The problem occurs as some prices rise at the same time as others fall. Gas prices may be declining at the same time as new cars are becoming more expensive. This is where the various monetary policies of governments meet their match. As these policies are effectively massive but blunt instruments, it is impossible for them to flexibly address the two extreme scenarios simultaneously.

This leaves policy makers with one of two unappealing choices. They will have to show one bias or another in their approach to managing an economy. Will they pursue an inflationary bias or instead a deflationary bias? With the inflationary bias they will be favoring greater employment levels and higher growth over the shorter term time frame. With a deflationary bias they will be favoring lower employment and less growth over the short term. The problem is that these biases similarly impact both sellers and buyers of any assets as they cause the assets to be less or more valuable in real terms as the debt in which they hold them is constant.

The reason that central banks and policy makers hate deflation so much is because of the real world effects on holders of debt. They are in terror of deflation since it alters consumer and business psychology and spending. With the Western societies that are so heavily indebted, deflation is the greatest possible enemy. This is true for the consumers, businesses, and especially the debt-ridden sovereign governments alike.

It is why the policy makers around Europe and the U.S. are desperate to re-inflate their respective economies. Japan has been caught in a deflationary spiral for decades now. The terrifying result has been a long period of economic stagnation and malaise from which they have never escaped since the end of the 1980s.

Demand Pull Inflation

Demand-pull inflation is one of the two types of general inflation. It comes because of powerful consumer demand in an economy. When many different people choose to buy the identical product, this will result in a price increase. If this scenario transpires in an entire economy on all kinds of goods, then it becomes the demand-pull type of inflation.

Keynesian economists utilize demand-pull inflation to explain the events when prices begin to go up from an imbalance of the relevant demand and the total available supply. When all around demand within the economy greatly overtakes the full supply, prices rise. Economists have colorfully called this type of inflation the unavoidable and unfortunate result of too many dollars chasing after an insufficient quantity of goods.

This Keynesian theory describes what happens when there is an increase in employment. It subsequently results in a growth in total demand. Because demand is rising, companies engage additional employees to help them boost their total output. The more individuals businesses employ, the higher employment goes. Finally, business output is insufficient to keep up with their demand so the total cost of the good will increase to match demand.

Demand-pull inflation should not be confused with the other kind of inflation referred to as cost-push inflation. In the cost-push variety, wages and prices go up together and transfer from one economic sector to another. The two types of inflation move in basically the same way yet work because of different causes.

Demand-pull inflation demonstrates the way that rises in price begin. Cost-push explains how it is hard to stop inflation after it has started. The main concept behind demand-pull inflation centers on powerful consumer demand which exceeds total supply to substantially drive higher inflation. All markets are limited to a specific quantity of goods. When the demand for the finite goods becomes enormous, the costs of the goods must rise to be higher.

Ultimately, demand-pull inflation results from five different causes. When spending increases from consumers, then businesses become confident enough to put on additional staff to keep up with demand. A second is when exports suddenly rise and this causes the relevant currencies to become undervalued. A third happens when government spending rises.

Another is the expectation and prediction of inflation causes companies to raise their prices to keep pace with it. Finally, too rapid growth in the monetary supply can cause such demand-pull variety of inflation. When there is an overabundance of money within the economy then there will not be enough goods to go around without prices rising to compensate and reduce the demand.

Oil refineries provide a solid example of demand-pull inflation. If they operate at full capacity, these refineries create this type of inflation. Regulatory issues from environmental concerns make it difficult for refineries to operate at full capacity. This limits the available supply of oil products. It is not that there is an insufficient amount of oil or companies producing it. Instead the problem results from artificially imposed legislation that keeps the market from receiving the ideal supply of finished goods that are in high demand. This causes the oil industry to be among the largest contributors to supply-demand inflation.

Depreciation

Depreciation is the means of spreading out the price of a usable physical asset during the period of its practical life. Businesses engage in this process of depreciating assets for accounting and taxing purposes. Depreciation can also be the reduction of the value of an asset that poor market conditions create.

Where accounting and taxing purposes are concerned, the process of depreciation demonstrates the portion of the value of the asset in question that has been utilized. Where taxes are concerned, the rules are stricter. The IRS sets out the regulations for taking depreciation of tangible assets.

Businesses are permitted to deduct the expenses of the asset they buy as a business expense. They simply must abide by the IRS' rules as far as when and how much of the deduction they are permitted to log. This all comes down to which category the asset falls in and the amount of time for which it is expected to last.

In accounting, businesses attempt to correlate the cost of a particular asset with the amount of income that it practically earns the company. With regards to an item of equipment that costs them $1 million, it may have a practical life expectancy of 10 years. They would depreciate this asset over the course of ten years. The company would then expense out $100,000 of the asset value each accounting year. They would match up the income that the equipment generated the company every year as well.

Accountants can use depreciation tricks to impact the company's financial bottom line. This is because with enough depreciation, the income statement, cash flow statement, balance sheet, and statement of the owners' equity will all be impacted significantly. It is true that certain depreciation assumptions can have significant impacts on both the long term asset values and the results of short term earnings.

Other assets can see their value depreciated by unfortunate circumstances or poor conditions in the market. Two standout examples of this type include real estate and currencies. In the housing crisis of 2008, many home owners living in the most severely impacted markets like Las Vegas watched helplessly as their home values depreciated by even 50% of the value. The post Brexit vote results day saw the British pound plunge by over 10% in a single day.

Generally accepted accounting principles affect depreciation figures. This is because a company might pay for a long life asset in cash, as with a tractor trailer that delivers its goods to customers. According to GAAP principles though, this expense would not be shown as a cost against income then and there. Rather than this, the expense is listed as an asset on the company balance sheet. The value of the asset is consistently and continuously reduced out during the in-service life of the asset in question. As the expense is reduced, this is a form of depreciating the asset.

This is done because GAAP principles insist that all expenses must be recorded along with the accounting time-frame as are the revenues which they generate. In the example of the tractor trailer that costs $100,000 and lasts for approximately ten years, GAAP would look to see what the salvage value would be at the end of that time. Assuming it expected the trailer to be worth $10,000 at the end of the depreciating period, than the expense would be depreciated at a rate of $9,000 for each of the ten years (using the formula of cost − salvage value/number of years depreciating).

With long term assets, the depreciating typically involves two lines. There would commonly be one that displayed the price of the assets and another that demonstrated the amount of depreciating that had been charged off against the assets' value.

Depression

Depressions in economics are loosely defined as major declines in a country's GDP, or gross domestic product. The gross domestic product is made up of four major components. These include money that consumers spend, government spending for goods and labor, investment affected by government agencies and individual companies, and the net sum of the country's exported products.

All of these elements are combined to come up with the country's annual gross domestic product. Another simpler way of stating the GDP is in the counting of everything spent on services, goods, research, investments, and labor in the nation.

Depressions are then commonly said to happen as the country's GDP drops by minimally ten percent in only a year. There is not any consensus on the precise amount of decline in terms of percentage that must occur. Following the notorious stock market crash in 1929, the Great Depression that happened in the United States and throughout Europe demonstrated a sharp decline in GDP not only the first year but also over the following years.

In the months that came after this market crash, the U.S. GDP fell by in excess of thirty percent. After that it rose for a while, though not nearly to the pre-crash levels seen earlier in the U.S. This demonstrates the difficulty in simply defining depressions simply by looking at GDP declines and increases.

The Great Depression is mostly held to have continued until the very end of the 1930's decade. Real recovery nationally then did not begin until the outbreak of World War II in 1939. The reason that this is the case is that additional factors besides simply GDP declines have to be considered in evaluating what is and is not truly a depression.

The Great Depression had many negative characteristics besides simply falling GDP's. With plummeting industrial output, major numbers of jobs disappeared. As significantly smaller amounts of money came into workers hands, a great deal less could be spent on consumer goods or business investments. Without this money circulating back to businesses, firms were unable to hire workers back. The numbers of people dependent on help from the public assistance funds were greater. Job recovery did not materialize as hoped.

From time to time the Gross Domestic Product did rise in the 1930's. It never returned to the normalcy seen before the beginning of the Great Depression until the United States became fully involved in the Second World War. Demands for military equipment and weapons for the war did many things to help the American economy. Young men found employment in the army, industry suddenly had rising demand for military products, and job openings were more than the able bodied people available to fill them. At this point, women began entering jobs in industry in the place of men for the first time.

Nowadays, some respected economists worry that a depression like one not seen since the thirties could again be gripping the nation. This is because unemployment from the Great Recession remains stubbornly high, goods and services' prices are rising at a faster pace than payrolls in the majority of industries, and requirements for public assistance are higher than they have been since the end of the Second World War. The biggest fear today is that many of the jobs that are disappearing, such as technology and manufacturing, will never return, as they are migrating overseas to countries where workers are paid significantly less.

Devaluation

Devaluation involves an intentional adjustment to the downside for the currency value of a country. This is done in comparison to a currency standard, basket of currencies, or a single currency. This practice turns out to be a monetary policy tool for those nations that are either using semi fixed exchange or fixed exchange rates, like with China. Sometimes individuals confuse this tool with deprecation. The opposite of devaluation proves to be revaluation.

The government which issues the currency is the party that chooses to devalue it. Devaluations are always intentional, while depreciations instead result from activities beyond the scope of the government sector. A country has several motivations for devaluing its currency. The leaders might be attempting to fight against imbalances in their nation's balance of trade.

By devaluating, they make the national exports more affordable which helps them to compete more effectively in the global market place. It also makes their country's imports more costly for the citizens. This helps domestic consumers to choose to buy goods offered by their own domestic businesses. It strengthens the national economy.

It may seem like an appealing choice to devalue a currency. In reality, there are negative side effects to pursuing this option. When the leaders make the imports more costly, they protect their own native industry. These companies can then descend into inefficiency since they do not have much serious foreign competition any more. A greater number of exports as compared to imports also will increase the total demand. This often causes higher inflation at some point.

There are a number of different examples of official devaluations in the world. It may happen because of a variety of different reasons, yet government choices always lead to it. Egypt is a classic example. The country has long struggled with continuous strain from the black market demanding USD American dollars. This black market rose to prominence because of a shortage in foreign currencies that discouraged domestic and foreign investments in the Egyptian economy and also negatively impacted national businesses. The Egyptian government chose to put down the black market deals by devaluing their own Egyptian pound against the US Dollar by 14 percent back in March of 2016.

At first the Egyptian stock market delivered a favorable response after the currency devaluation. The black market reacted by depreciating the USD to Egyptian pound exchange rate. This caused the central bank to intervene. They were forced to announce a further devaluation of their currency again on July 12, 2016.

China also began to quietly devalue their currency throughout 2016. They did this in preparation for the U.S. presidential election results of November. Since both American candidates Donald Trump and Hillary Clinton were speaking out against the relationship with China, the country figured this would give them the opportunity to revalue their currency following the election in a move that would make it seem to be cooperating with the new administration. This makes the Chinese complicit in two rounds of currency devaluation, one to set up for the later intended opposite devaluing action.

Disposable Income

Disposable income proves to be the remaining income after an individual has met all of his or her income tax obligations. It is utilized as a means of ascertaining the health of an entire society, as well as a person's general economic condition. Disposable income also turns out to be among the main measurements for determining personal wealth.

Although they are sometimes used interchangeably, disposable income should not be confused with discretionary income. Discretionary income is simply any income that remains following paying the taxes and other customary living expenses. This means that the value for disposable income is a greater amount than discretionary income proves to be in practically every case. Still disposable income does not really deal with the day to day costs of living that people encounter in their normal lives.

For you as an American, disposable income typically proves to be anywhere from ten to fifteen percent of the personal income of an individual. All of the rest of the money goes into one of a number of different taxes. Naturally, this would be individually determined as a result of the amount of income that you have, the withholding allowances that you enjoy, and the state in which you reside. Similarly, for other countries, disposable income can be figured more or less by examining the typical tax rates.

Disposable income commonly decreases in difficult economic times, such as recessions and depressions. This does not happen because of an increase in taxes. Instead, it is more a factor of the likelihood of it falling in challenging economic times as companies cut back on employee payrolls. Because of this, lower disposable income will mean that people have more difficult times in fulfilling their present obligations. This will make them far less likely to take on new financial responsibilities.

When people do not make enough money to be taxed, then their disposable income may actually prove to be about the same as their total income is. This is similarly the case in nations that do not charge their citizens personal income taxes. In such cases, gross income and disposable income are identical.

Besides being used for spending on needs and expenses, it can also be saved and invested. Through wisely purchasing cash flow investments with disposable income, the resulting disposable income in the future can actually be consistently higher as regular investment income comes in to the person's account. Disposable income used for capital gains investments will commonly lead to one time gains on sales, which will only temporarily increase disposable income for one time.

Dollar Standard

The dollar standard came about as a result of the breakdown of the Bretton Woods agreement and international monetary system. In 1973 the U.S. (and then other developed countries) had abandoned the gold standard. The central bankers and finance ministers of the world could not reach agreement on a new standard for managing monetary relations and international trade. What emerged was a nameless new system that the nations did not officially consent to or sanction.

This de facto dollar standard received its name as the world moved away from gold as its main reserve currency and into U.S. dollars. Gold had underpinned the Bretton Woods system along with the monetary systems of the 19th century. The decision to move away from it as the ultimate backer for paper currencies had major implications for the world economy and trade.

The biggest result of the dollar standard was that it permitted the United States to finance unbelievably huge current account deficits and government spending simply by selling its trading partners and other countries its dollar denominated debt instruments. Under the previous Bretton Woods system and classical gold standards from past centuries, these additional imports that exceeded exports would have to be settled with gold.

The positive effects of this dollar standard are that it brought about globalization on a scale never before seen. This happened as the nations of the world were able to sell their goods and services to the U.S. on credit. It permitted economic growth to accelerate far more rapidly than would have been possible otherwise. This was especially the case for major swaths of the developing countries. It also served to keep interest rates and consumer prices extremely low in the U.S. Inexpensive manufactured goods could be produced with cheap overseas labor and then brought into the U.S. in dramatically growing quantities.

There are also three negative consequences of such a global dollar standard that may prove to be disastrous in the future. The first is that some international nations amassed enormous stockpiles of dollar reserves because of their financial account surpluses. This led to their economies overheating and their asset prices inflating enough to cause economic catastrophes. Asian Crisis nations and Japan are the most stunning examples of countries which suffered harm from these effects. These states escaped from the looming economic depressions thanks to their national governments taking on huge debt to bail out their banks which had gone bankrupt.

A second major problem is that the flaws of this dollar system have led to massive asset price inflation in the U.S. This resulted from America's creditors and trading partners choosing to reinvest their surplus dollars back into assets which were dollar denominated (especially stocks, company bonds, and real estate). This constant chasing of U.S. investible assets created bubbles in the American stock markets, pushed property prices throughout the U.S. to levels that were unnaturally high and not sustainable, and helped to misallocate corporate capital on an epic level.

Finally, the dollar standard's rapid creation of credit permitted nearly every industry to over invest. This has led to an overabundance of capacity and deflationary pressure which is reducing the profitability of companies throughout the globe.

Thanks in large part to the excess this new monetary system permitted, the U.S. economy is struggling under historically unprecedented debt burdens in government, corporate, and consumer segments. The world which finds itself overly dependent on exporting to the U.S. on credit struggles with difficult choices. They can continue the process even though they are fearful of overexposure to dollars and dollar denominated assets. They might also change dollar surpluses back into their national currencies which would raise the value of these currencies and hurt exports and overall growth. Some like China are pursuing a third way by acquiring as much gold as they can with their dollars, albeit slowly enough not to cause a rush for the dollar exits.

Dumping

Dumping in economics refers to a country attempting to enforce its own firms' predatory pricing on other nations in the context of international trade. It also happens if a company exports its goods to a rival nation for a price that is under the one it would charge in its own domestic market or at a lower cost than the expenses it incurs to produce the goods. The reason companies and nations do this is typically to build up their foreign national market share. Sometimes they engage in this despicable practice so they can drive away their competitors.

The technical definition of dumping boils down to charging other countries cheaper prices for similar goods in their foreign markets than they do charge in their domestic market for the identical good. Many economists call this undercutting the nominal value in the act of international trade. Dumping has been officially condemned by the WTO World Trade Organization and an agreement which the member states all signed. This is especially the case when it inflicts material harm on a national industry within the nation who is importing.

There can be no doubt that the term dumping comes with an extremely negative connotation. Free market capitalist proponents consider this to be a thinly veiled kind of protectionist policy. The advocates of labor maintain that businesses must be protected from these forms of predatory practice in order to reduce the more painful consequences of trade between unequally developed economies.

International dumping has not been so successful except for in a few examples. One such case is the Chinese steel dumping dilemma. For years, the Chinese have sold steel at prices which are well below those any other nations' steel producers can match. They sell it for less than their own cost. They are also sometimes selling their steel at lower prices than they do within China. The venerable steel industry in Great Britain has been all but destroyed because of this practice. Britain was once the world's largest steel producer. Other European and American steel makers have similarly suffered from the illegal Chinese steel dumping practice.

A more controversial case pertains to OPEC's Saudi Arabian led efforts to drop the price of oil over the past several years. Because competition from American shale oil industry had become so intense and America and U.S. companies had massively increased their oil and natural gas outputs, Saudi Arabia became concerned by the excessive supplies of oil washing over the world energy markets. They decided to eliminate the U.S. shale oil company business through a covert form that might be considered dumping.

Saudi Arabia had the ability to produce oil for a substantially lower cost per barrel than the more expensive fracking process that releases the shale oil in America (and Canada). They decided to force down the prices of oil within OPEC by making the other Persian Gulf (Iraq, Iran, Kuwait, Qatar, Bahrain, United Arab Emirates, Oman) and non Gulf (primarily Nigeria and Venezuela) countries sell their oil at a lower price. They manipulated these price levels for oil down to the point that oil traded in the low $40's per barrel. At this point, the price of oil had declined to below the cost of production for several of the oil producers in the OPEC cartel, but not for Saudi Arabia.

As the Saudi's hoped, the American shale oil producers began to lay off workers and shut down production. Many of the firms in the U.S. shale industry shuttered their doors at least temporarily and some permanently. Saudi Arabia successfully dumped the Gulf and OPEC oil on world markets at prices lower than their rivals could conceivably match, permanently harming the domestic industry in the U.S. (and to a lesser degree Canada with their oil sands projects). The Saudis claim it was not dumping as they at least can produce oil for $20-$30 per barrel. So far, no action has been enforced by the World Trade Organization against either the OPEC oil cartel or Saudi Arabia for this underhanded ploy. There is still controversy regarding whether or not this particular case is technically dumping.

Econometrics

Econometrics refers to the utilization of math and statistics in the discipline of economics. Economists include these branches of study in order to test their hypotheses and theories. They attempt to predict future trends by employing it. The idea is to consider economic models and test and re-test them by using statistical trials. They finally contrast and compare the ultimate results against known real-world examples. This is why economists often divide up the study into the two groups of applied and theoretical.

Economists work econometrics by merging math, economic theory, and statistical hunches. Through these combinations they are able to analyze various theories. They harness a variety of tools including probability, frequency distributions, regression analyses, statistical inference, times series methods, and simultaneous equations models.

It is always helpful to consider a real life example to understand a difficult concept like Econometrics. Economists might choose to work this discipline in order to consider the idea of income effect. Many economists will theorize that individuals who boost their income will also expand their spending levels. The way they can test out such an economic hypothesis so that it becomes proven and accepted is with the tools of this discipline. These include multiple regression analysis and frequency distributions.

The field of Econometrics became discovered and advanced by the three renowned economists Ragnar Frisch, Lawrence Klein, and Simon Kuznets. The lot of them received the Nobel Prize in economics for their achievements and work with this discipline of economics.

Utilizing Econometrics in practice is not as difficult as it might at first seem. Step one is to consider a data set so as to come up with a particular hypothesis. This must give reasons for the shape and nature of the data. In such a first step, the variable which the employing economists will consider they must specifically define. Relationships between independent and dependent variables must also be detailed. It is this stage of the discipline which depends enormously on the economic theories to be tested for their usefulness as the study progresses.

In the next step, the economists will have to select their particular statistical model or tool with which they will test out the economic hypothesis. For a model to be considered effective, it will have to outline particular relationships mathematically between the dependent variables and the variables which explain them in the given test. The most typical tool economists use is the multiple linear regression model. It is because they consider this to be the most practical tool in the discipline. The reason for this is that the relationships can be expressed in a linear fashion. It is appropriate to many situations since the most typical relationship between data sets proves to be linear. All that this means is that a change in one variable will lead to another positive correlation with the other variables.

A third step revolves around entering in all of the data set information to a software program specifically created for econometrics. Such a program will utilize the economist chosen statistical model in order to tabulate the preliminary results. It employs the entered economic data to come up with these results.

Finally they come to the most critical (and also coincidentally last) step for proving a hypothesis using Econometrics. The economists in question gather the program's outputted results and prepare a real-world type of test. It is this test that gives the economist the knowledge regarding the validity of the model that was proposed and tested. For the model to be useful, it must deliver reliable and accurate predictions which can be back tested and so proven. When the economists uncover the results they anticipated, then they know that their hypothesis is in fact a theory. Should the results not be what they anticipated, additional inferences or other hypotheses will be required.

Economic Collapse

Economic Collapse refers to the total breaking down of an economy in a territory, region, or nation. Such an end result is the most possibly serious rendition of an economic depression. When this type of collapse occurs, it often requires years or even decades for an economy to escape from distress. When a true and complete collapse of an economy happens, the events which transpire around it are ugly. Poverty levels massively increase, jobs disappear entirely, and civil unrest and widespread crime become more commonplace.

Many individuals who contemplate such a possibility in developed nations like the United States wonder how they can effectively prepare for such an Economic Collapse. The truth is that it is difficult to effectively avoid personally simply because the warnings of imminent collapse are not easy to see coming. Consider the real world example of the nearest event to an economic collapse the United States has suffered from since the end of the Second World War.

On the day of September 17th in 2008, the entire American economy nearly collapsed. This was the date when terrified investors pulled out an all-time record of $140 billion in deposits from money market accounts. Money Markets are the storage vehicle for the daily cash funding of countless companies and corporations. Had such enormous withdrawals lasted for only one week, the whole U.S. economy would have ground to a screeching halt. Businesses would have closed to never reopen, trucks would have ceased carrying their loads around the country, and most dangerously grocery store shelves would have been empty.

What staved off this particular episode of Economic Collapse was the quick thinking of both the Chairman of the Federal Reserve and the Secretary of the United States Treasury. The pair saw the signal of the enormous money market account withdrawals and instantly understood the meaning of it. This is because Chairman Ben Bernanke proved to be a scholar of the Great Depression while Secretary Hank Paulson had served as a long time veteran on Wall Street. They quickly crafted a bailout plan together which flooded the markets with sufficient cash to calm and arrest the panic.

The best known example and closest the United States has been to a complete Economic Collapse is the Great Depression of the 1930s and 1940s. This began with the infamous 1929 stock market crash that started on Black Thursday, the date of October 24th in 1929. Only a few days later by the following Tuesday, stock markets were down an incredible 25 percent. It took only a weekend for a huge number of American investors to watch their entire life savings disappear into the ash can. The recovery to the levels seen October 23rd of 1929 did not occur until 1954, nearly 25 years later. It is the nearest the American economy flirted with total economic catastrophe. It proves how susceptible to another such near disaster the U.S. economy still is today.

Such an actual American economy collapse would be devastating for the entire planet. It would lead to worldwide havoc and panic. Dollar and U.S. Treasuries' values (many of them held by foreigners) would crash and burn. Interest rates in the United States would skyrocket higher. Investors would trample each other in their efforts to cash out of dollars into euros, Swiss francs, and gold. Hyperinflation would infect any economy which was closely tied to the United States as it spread from the U.S. to its closest trading and investing partners.

Unfortunately, the history of the world is replete with examples of total or partial Economic Collapse. It tends to happen in cycles every so often. The classical world collapsed economically and took the mighty Roman Empire with it. The Byzantine Empire suffered economic collapse and this led to lasting economic decline for huge portions of the Greek world, the Balkans and parts of Eastern Europe. An economic collapse that came along with the Thirty Years War in continental Europe devastated everything from farms to commerce in the first half of the 1600s.

There have also been slow motion and partial economic collapses which have occurred in the last few centuries. The Spanish Empire experienced a slower collapse economically which led to economic stagnation for over a century in the Latin American, Caribbean, and Spanish-ruled world. Over the period of the two world wars, the British Empire suffered from a slightly milder form of collapse economically. This impacted much of the quarter of the world which was a part of the empire at the time. It led to the dissolution of the greatest empire the world has ever seen and the subsequent independence of more than 50 countries (including India, Canada,

Australia, New Zealand, half of Africa, and most of the Caribbean and Pacific islands) in a matter of two decades.

Economic Commission for Latin America and the Caribbean

The Economic Commission for Latin America and the Caribbean is a key United Nations body which is referred to by its various acronyms of UNECLAC, ECLAC, and the Spanish acronym CEPAL. This regional commission of the U.N. has a mandate to foster economic cooperation between the various member states.

There are 45 member nations in total. This includes 13 in the Caribbean, 20 in Latin America, and 12 which lie outside the region. There are also 13 members who are associated but not full members. This is because they are territories which are not independent (such as the United States Virgin Islands), commonwealth of the Caribbean (such as the Cayman Islands), and associated island countries. The ECLAC produces a number of valuable statistics which cover the nations in the area. It also makes cooperative forms of agreements pairing up these nations and nonprofit organizations of the world.

The Economic Commission for Latin America and the Caribbean arose in 1948 at the behest of the United Nations. It was originally called the UNECLA UN Economic Commission for Latin America. In the year 1984, they passed a resolution in the United Nations to bring in the nations of the Caribbean into the organization's name. This commission is under the ESOSOC UN Economic and Social Council and reports to them.

The current executive secretary of the Economic Commission for Latin America and the Caribbean as of 2017 is Alicia Barcena Ibarra of Mexico. She has served since July of 2008 in this head leadership role.

There are several important locations of the Economic Commission for Latin America and the Caribbean. Its headquarters lie in Santiago, Chile. There are two sub-regional headquarters as well. These are the Central American head office in Mexico City, Mexico and the Caribbean head office in Port of Spain, the capital of Trinidad and Tobago.

Other important country offices exist in four nations. These include Buenos Aires, Argentina; Montevideo, Uruguay; Brasilia, Brazil; and Bogota,

Colombia. The organization also maintains a liaison office in Washington D.C. in the United States.

The member states of the Economic Commission for Latin America and the Caribbean include Venezuela, Uruguay, the United States of America, the United Kingdom, Trinidad and Tobago, Suriname, Spain, South Korea, St. Vincent and the Grenadines, St. Lucia, St. Kitts and Nevis, Portugal, Peru, Paraguay, Panama, Norway, Nicaragua, the Netherlands, Mexico, Japan, Jamaica, Italy, Honduras, Haiti, Guyana, Guatemala, Grenada, Germany, France, El Salvador, Ecuador, the Dominican Republic, Dominica, Cuba, Costa Rica, Colombia, Chile, Canada, Brazil, Bolivia, Belize, Barbados, Bahamas, Argentina, and Antigua and Barbuda.

The associated members of the Economic Commission for Latin America and the Caribbean are the United States Virgin Islands, the Turks and Caicos Islands, Sint Maarten, Puerto Rico, Montserrat, Martinique, Guadeloupe, Curacao, the Cayman Islands, The British Virgin Islands, Bermuda, Aruba, and Anguilla.

It was the creation of this Economic Commission for Latin America and the Caribbean that became an instrumental part of the so-called "Big D development." Economists and regional historians blame the founding of this ECLA and the subsequent policies it recommended for the ensuing problems including dependency and structuralism. This is because though the group was established in the period following the Second World War, its roots in fact date back to the era of colonialism which saw the European powers such as Britain, France, and Spain and the United States as economic overlords of much of South America.

It was the League of Nations which came up with the idea for a need to economically restructure South and Central America and the Caribbean. Stanley Bruce drew up the document which he presented to the League of Nations in 1939. This had a major impact on the establishment of the United Nations Economic and Social Committee in the year 1944. At first the ECLA did not have effective policies for Latin America.

In subsequent decades though, it dramatically altered the balance of economic power in the region as member nations became prisoners of the interest and principal repayments on loans for development projects. These

were forced upon them by the World Bank, IMF, and the Economic
Commission for Latin America and the Caribbean.

Economic Embargo

An Economic Embargo is a type of government-mandated order. They limit the exchange of goods and commerce to a country which they specify. Sometimes they affect only particular goods which represent a threat to the importing nation's vital economic or security interests.

Such embargoes are typically established because two nations find themselves in a political spat or economic disagreement or because of a combination of the two. The idea behind such an economic punishment and restriction is to economically isolate a nation. The enforcer hopes to make life difficult for the people and ultimately government of the nation so that it will have no choice but to carry out the desired actions of the embargo issuer.

There are two different main forms of economic embargoes. A strategic embargo will stop the trade in any type of military hardware, equipment, or goods with the victim nation. Trade embargoes are far more restrictive. They stop any individual or company from exporting given goods (or sometimes all goods) to the nation which is targeted. In today's world, a large number of countries depend on global trade to function and prosper. This is why an economic embargo can prove to be such a potent weapon to influence the behavior of a nation without having to go to war.

A trade embargo may lead to severe negative consequences for the victim nation and its economy. The U.S. often relies on the mandates issued by the United Nations in deciding which countries to inflict economic and trade embargoes against. In many cases, allied nations will combine their collective economic and trade powers to issue joint economic embargoes. This restricts trade with the targeted countries in an effort to force them to make strategic changes for world peace or to engage in better humanitarian behaviors.

The United States has become famous for its imposition of a few long-lasting economic embargoes against other sovereign states. Among these are ones which have been in place on nations that include Iran, North Korea, and Cuba. Back in the decade of the 80's, a number of countries with the U.S. enforced a trade embargo against the once-prosperous nation of South Africa. They did this because of several issues the combined governments opposed, including apartheid (segregation and official discrimination against the native African black population by a ruling white minority) and a drive for nuclear technology and weapons capability within the country.

America- enforced embargoes leveled against some of these and other nations particularly leave out the trade of certain goods, such as necessary items. In these cases, they focus more exclusively on weapons, ammunition, and weapon systems or luxury item goods. Other forms of trade they leave in place. Comprehensive forms of economic embargoes are more devastating to the victim nations since they stop all types of trade between the victim nation and the inflictors.

After the terrorist attacks which began with September 11, 2001, American-led embargoes have increasingly tended to focus on threatening nations like the Sudan. This country and others such as Iran are well-known for their historic and present-day ties to terrorists and their funding around the globe. This makes them a direct threat to American national security interests and those of its allies and friends around the world.

The U.S. has occasionally also been the recipient of such economic embargoes. During the 1970s, the American economy suffered great harm because of the infamous Arab Oil Embargo. The Organization of the Petroleum Exporting Countries, or OPEC, enforced this oil embargo and created misery through skyrocketing gas prices, fuel rationing, and even gasoline shortages at the pump.

In the United States, it is the American President who has full authority to inflict embargoes in war times. This he can do under the existing Trading with the Enemy Act. Besides this, the President may also rely on the existing International Emergency Economic Powers Act to enforce national emergency based commercial restrictions. Such embargoes become administered by the Office of Foreign Assets Control within the U.S. This is a division of the Department of the Treasury that helps to find and freeze the ultimate sources of funds for both terrorist operations and drug businesses.

Economic Globalization

Economic globalization turns out to be an either hated or praised global phenomenon. It means that the economic picture and scenario for any given nation is dependent significantly upon the involvement of other often-time competing nations. A great number of countries who are friends supply resources to one another which the other countries simply lack.

Such resources can include imported technology, products, raw materials, services, and individual labor. Many critics have astutely observed that this process will eventually lead to closer integration and finally a one-world government, as has been gradually occurring within the European Union. This idea entails a centralized single government for all countries under one flag.

A popular engagement under the auspices of economic globalization is international trade. In this activity, countries exchange essential and luxury services and goods between one another. With countries that possess abundant natural resources, they rely on this system of trading to sell their unique resources so that they can improve their national economic situations.

International trade such as this has gone on for many centuries. The Silk Road which connects Asia and Europe in ancient trade demonstrates this. A modern day example of such international trade proves to be the toy industry. In this business, numerous toys sold in the United States and Europe carry the phrase "Made in China" upon their surface.

Economic globalization pertains to both economics and finances for countries, but it also impacts cultural identity and national politics as well. Tax treaties and trading policies are fashioned between various nations in order to protect either state from threats like terrorism or to control their trade. Multinationals can actually alter a nation's appetite for foods. Corporations such as McDonald's have managed to shift the eating preferences of consumers in Asian countries that believe rice should be the mainstay in their daily diets. European fashions from Paris, London, and Milan have managed to influence the styles and tastes of Asian and American consumers who import them to sell in their clothing shops.

It is easy to view economic globalization through either advantageous or disadvantageous lenses, depending on the perspective of the person judging it. The positive side effects are that it provides additional job opportunities and sometimes offers greater salaries. This often leads to faster and more economic growth and eventually an increasing standard of living. Such international cooperation has also fostered greater and longer periods of international peace between countries. It has further led to better cultural exchange through understanding and awareness of other cultures and countries. Technology has played an outsized role in this capacity.

Critics of economic globalization have much about which to vocalize their complaints as well. Many critics have successfully made the case that the disadvantages substantially outweigh the benefits. One negative issue is that it helps countries to burn through global natural resources on a larger and faster scale. This is a result of the higher demand for scarce raw materials which has grown with many developed and developing countries alike.

A second downside is that it enables human rights violations. Numerous nations are able to more easily exploit labor of other countries' populations when they are developing countries. Still other critics from the developing world point to how economic globalization is basically a disguised means of richer countries colonizing those which are poorer and less powerful. They do this by seizing control of the overall economic picture of the poorer countries. Regardless of how critics or fans view this economic globalization, neither camp is able to deny the amount of impact which it continuously has on the global development of today and for the foreseeable future.

Economic Growth

Economic growth represents a boost in an economy's ability to create and produce services and goods. This is compared from one period of time against another. There are two ways to measure this phenomenon. It may be quantified either in real or nominal terms. When real terms are used, economists have to adjust them for the effects of inflation.

Historically and routinely, total growth in an economy is determined and expressed in the form of either the old standard of GNP Gross National Product or the more recent standard of GDP Gross Domestic Product. There are also other infrequently utilized metrics for measuring growth in an economy.

The simplest way to express such economic growth is by utilizing total productivity. Gains in productivity often correspond to an increase in the average marginal productivity. In other words, the typical worker within a specific economy becomes more productive as the economy is growing. Economies may also obtain growth even without such an average marginal productivity increase. This happens when there are more births than deaths (higher birthrate) or as additional immigrants come into an economy and begin to work. It can also result from technological revolutions. Examples of this are the Industrial Revolution, the computer revolution, or the Internet revolution.

It is always true that economies experiencing economic growth will be able to produce a higher quantity of services and goods than they did before the growth transpired. Yet there are those services and goods which command a higher value than competing goods or services. Examples of this abound. Smart phones or laptops are considered to have a higher value economically than bottles of water or a shirt. This is why growth in an economy is effectively figured up by measuring the total value of goods and services which the economy produces instead of simply the quantity.

An additional dilemma comes as different consumers put varying values on identical services and goods. For example, for residents of Alaska an effective heater would command a higher value than it would for residents of southern California. Similarly, in Florida efficient air conditioners have greater value than they do in Canada. Other individuals prefer fish to steak, or steak to fish. Value is always subjective. This is what makes measuring the value of all goods and services challenging. It is ultimately why the current fair market value is what economists employ to determine value for the purposes of measuring economic growth.

Interestingly enough, only a few means exist to create growth economically. A relatively straightforward one is through the uncovering and exploitation of better or newly discovered physical economic resources. Before gasoline was discovered to have the ability to generate energy, petroleum had very little economic value. Gasoline and hence petroleum began to create economic growth once this discovery was made. This was true for those countries with an abundance of petroleum they could export as well as for countries that utilized the gasoline to more effectively move goods across their nations.

A second means of producing economic growth is by increasing the size of the labor force. When every other factor is equal, a greater number of workers will produce additional services and goods. Much of the impressive economic growth in the United States through the 1800s came from a constant inflow of productive and inexpensive immigrant labor.

The third means of creating such growth is by developing better capital goods or higher technology. Such capital growth and technological improvements are closely correlated to the level of business investment and savings. Both are needed for firms to pursue a significant amount of R&D, or research and development.

The final method for boosting economic growth lies in better specialization of labor pools. In other words, the workers have to increase their skills at their crafts. This boosts productivity because of extra practice or through experimenting with new or improved methods. Investment, savings, and specialization are the easiest to control and most reliable means of increasing the growth in an economy.

Economic Indicators

Economic indicators are bits of economic data generally pertaining to the macroeconomic larger picture economy. Investors utilize them to decide on the investing climate as they consider the all around state of the economy. There are many different economic indicators which the government usually releases. Five of the most important are gross domestic product, consumer price index, employment indicators, PMI manufacturing and services, and central bank minutes.

Gross Domestic Product is the dollar value of every good and service a country produces in a set amount of time. It can be delivered in real and nominal formats. Real GDP makes adjustments for changes in the value of money. This indicator is one of the most anticipated by financial markets for its importance. Increases in GDP indicate an economy that is growing. Declines in it demonstrate an economy that is slowing. National growth rates like this are often utilized to judge the affordability of a country's sovereign debt. They also determine if companies operating in the country are likely to be profitable.

Consumer Price Index is an inflationary figure. It looks at the household purchased goods and services and measures their changes over time. This statistical estimate is compiled by taking prices from a group of representative items. This CPI is often used to discern how much inflation is. Markets watch CPI figures to determine if inflation is getting too high. When there is higher inflation it causes interest rates to rise and lending to decline. Deflation causes more lending and better interest rates. Inflation reduces the relative value of a currency and is bad for savers.

Employment determines the citizens' wealth and economic success. This makes employment indicators like unemployment and payroll data, income trends (earning more or less), total labor force, and percentage employed telling. These numbers are particularly important in developed countries that see most of their national income created by consumer spending. Declines in consumer spending often lead to an increase in unemployment. This in turn feeds into lower GDP numbers.

PMI manufacturing and services is part of the Purchasing Manager's

Index. Markit Group developed this with the Institute for Supply Management. They survey businesses every month to learn about business purchasing manager's activities in acquiring input goods and services. The most crucial of these surveys are the PMI Services and PMI Manufacturing indices. These are considered to be important leading economic indicators. When demand for business products declines then companies will decrease their buying of raw materials instantly. This gives a picture of problems in an economy long before consumer spending or retail sales figures will.

Central banks play such an important role in any nation's economy that their releases are very important. Markets study every word that comes from central bankers to learn what is in store in the future. Central bank minutes prove to be the official information releases that give out useful commentary on the economy and signal what actions the central bank will take in the future.

The United States has the Federal Reserve. It provides its well known beige book. In this book are economic conditions related anecdotally by each of the branches of the Federal Reserve Bank. These types of notes are also released by a great number of other central banks. Among these are the Bank of England, European Central Bank, and Bank of Japan. They are released publically on a routine schedule. Central bank minutes releases also give a clue as to when the group will raise or lower the national interest rates which affects everything from consumer and business lending activity to savings deposit rates.

Economic Inequality

Economic Inequality concerns disparity financially between various groups of individuals. There are no societies in the world where all people fall into precisely the identical class economically. In other words, all individuals do not have the same amount of material or financial resources. Unfortunately, just the opposite is more common.

In many nations, some people have such vast income and wealth differences from others who live in dire poverty. On the other extreme, the wealthy live ultra luxuriously. This causes great and intense debate as the effects of economic inequality spill over into other parts of life that would normally not be determined by one's economic standing.

In most economies and countries, there are poor people, rich people, and then many medium classed ones which live in the middle. This is most clearly demonstrated in respect to the richest class. They earn and possess substantially greater resources than all of the other classes, particularly versus the bottom one. It is this whole scenario that economists call economic inequality.

Two different focuses surface as analysts consider such economic inequalities. Wealth is the first of these. This refers to the quantifiable amount of money and possessions that people have. Such wealth massively affects the lifestyle of individuals as it is almost exclusively the determining factor of what people can buy and what choices they have in their daily lives and when making longer-term plans. The wealthy naturally have higher standards of living than the rest of the classes.

The other critical financial indicator for measuring the level of economic inequality has to do with income. There are a number of individuals who possess no or little wealth as they have next to no meaningful income. In most cases, the people who command the greatest amount of wealth and so enjoy the highest standards of living are similarly the ones who enjoy the most significant levels of income.

It is interesting to realize that this kind of inequality economically is more severe in some nations and regions than it is in other ones. Nations that do not have sufficient social services find that the disparities are greatest and painfully obvious. In some of these countries, some individuals are extravagantly wealthy while others on the other extreme live in appalling conditions or suffer from starvation or at least severe malnutrition. Other countries have adequate social service networks and find that the gap between the richest and the poorest proves to be less severe. This still will not stop significant differences from appearing between the different groups and their actual lifestyles.

The debate rages on regarding economic inequality because of a variety of reasons. One strong argument against wealth and income disparities is that these dramatically impact the ability of citizens to obtain core services and basic items that ought to be easily available to all people. This includes such things as food, clean drinking water, legal representation, and adequate health care. Another complaint regarding inequality concerns the unfair access to impacting the political environment that the rich enjoy.

In recent years, the United States has been ranked among the most unequal of all developed nation rivals. In fact the OECD ranks the U.S. as second highest in inequality levels once it takes market incomes and adjusts them for the redistribution impacts of income transfer programs and tax policies (like unemployment compensation and Social Security payouts). According to their measurements, only Chile has a greater level of economic inequality from all 31 developed nations.

Similarly, the U.S. economic inequality has become the highest since 1928 in recent years. As of 2012, the highest earning one percent in the U.S obtained 22.5 percent of all pretax income. The bottom earning 90 percent enjoyed only 49.6 percent of the national income share.

Economic Occupancy

Economic Occupancy refers to the rate of paying tenants for an apartment building or some other rented out space like an office building. The managers and owners of apartment buildings and complexes commonly measure their success with both physical and economic occupancy rates. While these two concepts are related, they are not exactly the same. With physical occupancy, this pertains to the percentage of the total apartments (or commercial office suites) that the owners successfully rent. The rate of economic occupancy describes how many of these tenants are actually paying rent. The economic assessment speaks volumes more than the physical occupancy rate, since ultimately the economic one explains the apartment complex of office building's financial performance.

Another way to think of economic occupancy pertains to the percentage of rents which the owners and managers successfully collect from their tenants as measured against the total sum of money which could physically be collected. This ultimately describes how successfully or unsuccessfully management is optimizing potential revenues.

A number of reasons present themselves for why a building's unit might not be paying rent. The simplest explanation is that the units could be vacant. There are also gaps which exist from when one tenant leaves a unit until another finishes moving into the unit. Some buildings or complexes will find they need to offer discounts to lure in tenants. This might be half off the first rental month costs. Other tenants could depart while still owing the management company rents or fees. Many times, the manager of the apartments, maintenance head, or security guards will live rent-free on the property as part of their benefits as well. The downside is that while it is useful to have such key personnel living on site, it lowers the revenue stream on the property every month.

Figuring up the true economic occupancy is simple. This requires the property manager to divide the actually collected rent by the potential maximum collectable rent if every tenant paid the full price. It helps to consider a real world example of the concept. For any complex that possess 20 occupied apartments which rent for $1,000 per month, perhaps 16 actually pay the rent for one reason or another. This would amount to

$16,000 divided by $20,000 for an 80 percent rate. Yet the physical occupancy would amount to a full 100 percent in any case. The best case scenario is to have as close as possible an economic occupancy as physical occupancy rate.

The measure for economic occupancy has various helpful applications. It demonstrates any complexes or office buildings which are suffering from serious issues. If the rate is low, then problems exist with either rent collection, tenant turnover, or both. It may mean that the complex or office building management is inadequate or the base of tenants is unable or unwilling to pay their rent because of property problems. Low rates of occupancy eat into the ability to pay operating costs of the property. Ultimately they mean that profits will be lower or outright losses will be present instead.

Realtors often use the economic assessment over the physical occupancy rates when they are attempting to value an apartment complex or commercial office building. Those properties which are losing money display an inability to retain their tenants. It is also important to compare apples to apples with this measurement. Calculating the economic occupancy on a week by week basis will show a bias of high economic results the final week of the month and a low result the first week of the month. This is why realtors will prefer to have the occupancy calculated economically on a month by month basis, as it filters out the discrepancies of weekly fluctuations.

Economic Output

Economic output refers to the amount of goods and services which a nation, industry, or company creates over a set time period. These might be utilized in later stages of production, traded, or otherwise consumed. The idea surrounding national economic output is a critical one in the world of economics. This is because economists opine that it is not enormous quantities of money which truly make nations wealthy, but rather their national output amount.

Other phrases that analysts and economists often use interchangeably with economic output include output and gross output. This should not be confused with GDP Gross Domestic Product. Value which is added on a national scale is the definition of GDP ultimately. On a local level, this is often called gross regional product or even gross area product. While the two ideas of GDP and output bear some similarities, they are not identical. Both concepts do measure the productivity economically of a particular nation or region for a given time period.

Economic output itself quantifies the total value for all services and goods. The problem with this idea is that it involves a double counting of all intermediate purchases. Looking at an example of this dilemma helps to clarify the issue at hand. If a furniture maker purchases its wood directly off of a saw mill at $150, they might then increase the value of it to $450 by creating an article of furniture. The output involved would be measured as $600. This represents all value in every sale involved for this particular chain of economic activity. The problem is that this method includes the wood value two times. It becomes doubly counted when it is the intermediate stage good and again in the final price or value for the article of furniture.

GDP on the other hand concentrates on only the services' and goods' additionally added value. Another way of defining this lies in the economic output minus the intermediate inputs included. When economists take out the goods' value which already came through the market once before, it allows for a more accurate assessment regarding the output. The strict GDP formula is then GDP equals the gross output minus the intermediate inputs. In the example above with furniture, the GDP equaled up to merely

$450 because the formula takes out the $150 in wood inputs from the final sales price of $600.

In the real world, the overwhelming numbers of companies produce products which they make utilizing many materials that go through a few different suppliers hands in the production process. Each supplier will add its own value. Only in the end would this value be tallied into the cost of the ultimate product. The important take away from this is that there is a significant difference between GDP gross domestic product and economic output.

One of the great economic questions of all time that economists wrestle with pertains to why the national output for a given country will constantly fluctuate, sometimes dramatically. There is no one easy answer on which economists have consensus opinion unfortunately. Instead, economists generally concur that there are a variety of factors which cause output to rise and fall. With growth, the majority of economists can agree on there being three principal sources of economic growth.

These are labor increases, factors of production efficiency increases, and capital increases. This is a two-edged sword though. Growth to the factors of production inputs can also be negative. In fact when any factor leads to a decrease in the efficiency of production, capital, or labor, then the growth rate will subsequently decline. This finally translates to a drop in economic output as well as in GDP.

Economic Participation

Economic Participation refers to the labor rate of participation. This means that it measures the total active population participating in the labor force. Another way of saying this is that it pertains to the numbers of individuals which are actively seeking out work or who are already employed. The two categories are important to consider, as in economic recessions a number of active labor force workers will despair of finding a job and simply give up the search for employment. This means that the Economic Participation rate will decrease as this happens.

Such an Economic Participation rate is a key measurement to utilize when considering a body of unemployment statistics. This is because it reveals the numbers of those individuals who show interest in being a part of the active work force. Such people either have a job or are actively looking for one. They usually must be considered from 16 to 18 years of age or older to be eligible for inclusion in the category. Those individuals who are not physically capable of working or who lack the interest in working will not comprise the participation rate. This includes retirees, imprisoned people, students, and homemakers or stay at home moms.

This is an important metric to consider alongside the official unemployment rates. The reason is that many individuals who are called unemployed might not really be true participants in the active work force. If analysts only contemplate the unemployment rate by itself, they might arrive at the conclusion that a greater number of individuals are not bringing home income.

This does not meant that they are not actively contributing to the level of the economy. It might be that such individuals choose not to work for a variety of reasons. They could be spending retirement savings, building their skills as college or university students, or spending their spouse's earnings as stay at home moms. It explains why both unemployment statistics and the Economic Participation rate should be reviewed together to fully appreciate the true employment picture of an economy and country.

This Economic Participation rate becomes even more critical to understand when recessions bite. As an economy goes from reasonably good to particularly bad, many workers will simply give up looking for work after many months unemployed. At this point, they could simply abandon the workforce. The labor participation rate would then decline. The reason is that these individuals would no longer be classified as actively looking for employment. This explains why in recessions, sudden plunges in the labor participation rate would be carefully considered and evaluated.

A case in point is the effects of the Great Recession on the ongoing Economic Participation rate. The labor force impact from this worst economic collapse since the Great Depression of the 1930's proved to be absolutely devastating. The recession officially began in December of 2007. Per the NBER National Bureau of Economic Research, the unemployment rate stood at 5 percent that month. When the recession officially ended in June of 2009, this unemployment rate reached 9.5 percent and then climbed on to peak out at 10 percent by October of 2009.

In the eight years since then, the unemployment rate has nearly touched five percent again. Yet the labor participation rate has never recovered from the Great Recession. Many economists believe that this devastating recession and global financial collapse caused the acceleration of structural changes in the labor force participation rate. The rate has ranged from 67 percent back in 2006 to today's near 62 percent in 2017.

The decrease in the economic participation rate has been broad based and consistent since 2009 in fact. Many baby boomers decided to retire early as their job opportunities suddenly evaporated. Many individuals used government grants and loans to go back to university or college. Some women stopped working to be stay at home moms as the job opportunities were so scarce.

Economic Sanctions

Economic sanctions turn out to be both financial and commercial penalties which a nation or several nations level against a targeted nation, organization, or individual. Such sanctions can cover different types of punishments. Among these are tariffs, trade barriers, or financial transacting restrictions.

What is interesting about these is that they are not always applied thanks to an economic dispute. In fact they can be forced on other countries, organizations, or individuals because of several different types of military, political, or even social concerns. Such sanctions are often utilized to realize international and sometimes domestic policies or goals.

These economic sanctions may be deployed as an extension of international foreign policy. They are typically forced on smaller and weaker nations by one or more larger and richer ones because of two different reasons. It might be the weaker nation is actually a threat to the greater nation's security, as with Iran's aggressive nuclear weapons program versus the United Nations. It might also be that the more powerful country feels the weaker state is practicing human rights violations on its own people, as with Syria versus much of the rest of the world's countries.

This is why economic sanctions might be employed as a means of forcing the stronger countries' wills on the lesser one. Some of these policies pertain to achieving more open and fair free trade or for punishing and stopping violations of basic human freedoms and rights. In modern times, these forms of sanctions have often been utilized in lieu of waging actual military conflicts in order to reach desirable end results and outcomes without actual loss of human life.

The problem with these sanctions according to many analysts and economists is that they mostly harm the ordinary citizens of a nation rather than its government or military-industrial complex. Besides this, these kinds of sanctions are not always effective in achieving their hoped for results. Regime change is a classic example of this type of foreign policy. Though it is the most common basis for such sanctions, it is rarely successful.

Haufbauer et al. have studied these types of sanction policies and determined that in only 34 percent of the relevant instances did they work out successfully. An analysis of this study by Robert A. Pape ended with the conclusion that in only five out of the forty claimed successes did the results really stand out, which dropped the successful rate down to only four percent.

The reason for this is governments have a wide range of choices for trading partners and even financial conduits which they may go through. Consider the case of Iran and its frightening nuclear weapons program. For most of a decade the democratic nations of the world united to force a range of restrictive economic sanctions via the United Nations on the Islamic Republic. The sanctions were never one hundred percent effective, as countries including North Korea, Cuba, and Venezuela still continued to trade freely and openly with Iran. Some multinational companies and even a few countries secretly conducted trade with Iran as well.

The world's largest international bank (according to balance sheet) British multinational giant HSBC is the best known example of a company cheating on these specific economic sanctions. The United States' justice department found the banking giant with significant operations in 71 countries and territories guilty of helping the Iranian government to circumvent the international sanctions regime. While HSBC received several billion dollars in penalties, this did not reverse the damage to the sanctions' policy that they had already done.

These economic sanctions similarly impact the national economy of the country which imposes them to a lesser degree. When they erect restrictions on imports, the country imposing them will find its consumers suffer from less selection of goods. As export restrictions occur, the companies from the imposing nation(s) lose their access to and investment opportunities in the victim country. Other rival companies from foreign nations will take over these opportunities instead.

Economic Surplus

Economic surplus relates to supply and demand. They are also referred to as total welfare. There can be two different types of such economic surplus, consumer surplus and producer surplus.

A consumer surplus happens when a given product or service's price proves to be less than the greatest price level consumers would be willing to pay. This is something like an auction. Buyers go in to an auction with a maximum price amount that they are willing to pay.

Consumer surplus transpires when these buyers can obtain the product for a lesser price than their limit. This reflects a gain. Oil product prices are a real world example of potential consume surplus. When the costs for a gallon of gasoline decline to a lower amount that the consumers typically pay, the consumer realizes a profit in the form of an economic surplus.

Alternatively, a producer surplus happens as companies are able to sell their goods for more than the lowest price at which they were willing to sell. Using the same example of an auction, the auctioneer or house might have a minimum reserve on an item where they begin the bidding. The house will not accept lower than this price. They would realize a producer surplus if the auctioneer obtains a higher price than the reserve limit for the product.

This happens when the buyers keep bidding on the price of the item and thereby increase the price of the good until someone finally wins and buys it. The producer realizes more money than initially expected in this example of economic surplus. It is important to realize that producer and consumer surpluses are effectively zero sum gains. This means that the benefit of one is the loss to the other group.

There are side effects from either type of economic surplus. With a consumer surplus, this will lead to an eventual shortage in the producer's supply. This is because supply at that price simply can not stay abreast of the demand. People like to purchase additional quantities of any product available at an attractive price point. Alternatively, a producer surplus will result typically in an overabundance of supply. This is because prices are too high for consumers willingly to purchase much of the given product.

Economic surpluses happen because of an atypical disconnect between demand and supply on a certain product. It could also result if some consumers are ready and able to pay a higher price for a good or service than are others. If instead prices were fixed on the product while all consumers anticipated paying the same price, then shortages and surpluses would not exist.

In the real world this rarely occurs. This is because different businesses and consumers have various price points at which they are willing to sell and buy. In selling items, the competition is constant to produce the most and best product for the greatest value. With prices rising and falling because of demand and supply, surplus happens on the side of the producer or the consumer.

When demand becomes too great for a given product, the vendor providing the cheapest price will sell out. This leads to general market price increases, or producer surpluses. Similarly, prices will decline if supply is high and demand is insufficient, leading to a consumer surplus. Surpluses commonly arise if the product price is set too high at first at more than consumers will pay.

Egalitarianism

Egalitarianism refers to a philosophy that believes in some type of equality. The main idea behind it is that all individuals should be regarded and dealt with as equals, at least pertaining to political, religious, social, economic, or cultural equality. The tenets of egalitarianism hold that every human being has an equal moral value or basic worth.

It can be used as a political philosophy that claims that everyone ought to be treated as an equal, provided with the identical economic, political, civil, and social rights. It could alternatively be a social philosophy that pushes for the decentralizing of power and the breaking down of economic barriers between different people. Some individuals believe that this egalitarianism is the natural form of society.

Egalitarianism deals with the studies pertaining to social inequality. Unequal societies lead to many of the world's great social problems. Among these are infant mortality, homicide, teenage pregnancy, obesity, incarceration rates, and depression. A comprehensive type of study that was performed on the major economies of the world showed that a strong connection exists between all of these challenges in society and issues of social inequality.

Egalitarianism exists in numerous different forms. The most typical basis for it arises from political, religious, or philosophical backgrounds. Political precedents of egalitarianism date back to the Age of Enlightenment in the 1700's. At this time, modern government founders referenced egalitarian principals of morality that they lived by, such as the American concept of certain inalienable rights endowed to them by their Creator. These were laid into the modern framework of countries like the United States and France.

Religious egalitarianism is heavily rooted in Christianity. This Christian egalitarian world view states that the Bible is the basis for the common equality of men and women, as well as every economic, racial, ethnic, and age group. This comes from Jesus Christ's example and teachings, as well as other lessons taught throughout the Bible.

In philosophy, egalitarian ideas grew in substance and practice over the last two hundred years. Various sub-philosophies have arisen from this general philosophy, including communism, socialism, progressivism, and anarchism. Each of these concepts favored political, economic, and legal versions of egalitarianism.

Some of these egalitarian philosophies have gained significant and wide standing support with both the general population as well as the intellectuals in numerous countries. This does not mean that such ideas are actually put into universal effect though. On the other hand, democracy does involve many ideas of egalitarianism, at least in the political sphere. Representative democracy proves to be the ultimate realization of such political egalitarianism. Critics of this idea say that even though votes are given out on a one vote per one person basis, the actual power still rests with the ruling class and not the common people.

Elastic Demand

Elastic Demand refers to a factor of demand which is affected by the price. When the quantity of a good demanded responds substantially based on a change in the price or another factor inherent in demand, then the demand for the good in question is said to be elastic. When prices for a good or service decline even a little, consumers will often purchase a significantly greater quantity of the particular item. When prices instead go up a little, the consumers will typically cut back on their purchases while they wait on the prices of the good or service to return to the prior level.

When services and goods feature elastic demand, this describes items which the consumers are happy to comparison shop around for a more attractively priced substitute. The reason for this truth is that the buyers are not desperately in need of having the given item. This could be because they do not require it each day, or because there are many similar comparable choices which may be offered at more advantageous prices.

It is actually the laws of demand which lead the correlation between quantity purchased and price per item. This law claims that the price of an item is inversely related to the amount which consumers will purchase. As prices go higher, it is human nature for individuals to purchase fewer items. Elasticity of demand describes by how much the item quantity they purchase will drop as the price rises.

Where goods and services are concerned, there are actually two more kinds of elastic demand. Both of these quantify how the numbers purchased will specifically change as the price declines. These are inelastic demand and unit elastic demand. Inelastic demand simply means that the amount of the goods or services which consumers demand will change less radically than the associated price will. Conversely, unit elastic demand means that the amount of a given good or service which individuals demand will alter at the same percentage rate by which the price varies.

To figure out the elastic demand formula, one simply takes the quantity demanded percentage change and divides this figure by the price percentage change. Demand is said to be elastic as the percentage change of the quantity which consumers demand is greater than the associated price change percentage. This would mean the ratio is higher than one. As an example, if demanded quantity increased by 10 percent as the price declined by an associated fiver percent, then the ratio would be .10 divided by .05 for a total demand elasticity result of 2.00. It would mean that the demand was highly elastic.

Another scenario which may result is called perfectly elastic demand. This happens if and when the demanded quantity increases to infinity as the price declines by any percentage amount. Of course in the real world this is not possible. It does serve to illustrate the point that elastic demand possesses a ratio higher than one.

Conversely, inelastic demand is present as the demanded quantity increases by a smaller percentage than does the drop in price. Consider this example. When the quantity demanded increased by two percent as the associated price dropped by five percent, then the ratio proves to be .02 divided by .05. The result is .40 demand elasticity, which is under one. This means the demand is inelastic, and the item can not be easily substituted or replaced by the markets.

Unit elastic demand is present as the demanded quantity varies by exactly the same percentage amount as the price change does. This would mean the ratio proved to be exactly one. The example with this base case is easy to understand. If the demanded quantity rose by five percent as a result of an associated five percent decline in the price, then the .05 divided by .05 would yield a result of one.

Embargo

In its most straight forward form, an embargo represents a ban on trading. The word is derived from the Spanish word "embargo" which means obstruction or hindrance. Such trading bans are either entire or partial prohibitions on both trade and commerce on either one specific nation or several of them. These actions are intended to be intense diplomatic penalties which are deliberately imposed in order to garner a particular national interest result out of the nation which is the victim of the embargo. These acts are like economic sanctions in their effects and comprise legal barriers to free trade. They should never be confused with a physical blockade, which is an actual act of war.

With embargoes, nations are able to ban altogether or partially limit imports or exports, impose specific tolls or taxes, develop quotas for limitations of goods, seize or freeze freight, assets, and bank accounts, make illegal transport vehicles or freight, and restrict the transportation of a certain product or technology when it is considered to be a strategic or high technology.

An embargo proves to be a government order which limits commerce and the exchange of goods or services with a particular nation or for particular goods. It is typically because of a negative economic or political climate between two countries that it occurs. The idea behind such a restriction is to isolate the offending nation and therefore cause hardships for its governments so that it will address the issue which underlies the dispute.

Strategic embargoes stop a nation for dealing in or receiving any kinds of military goods or advanced technology with military applications. General trade embargoes keep any individual within a nation from exporting to the receiving country. The embargo has become a potent tool, still short of outright war, for impacting the policies and behaviors of a state. This is more and more the case since a great number of nations depend on international trade to prosper in the post modern age.

Such trade restrictions can cause massive negative results for the afflicted economy. When allied nations get together to sign joint embargo deals in order to restrict trade benefits for particular pariah nations, they often do this to cause positive humanitarian changes or to lessen perceived dangers to the peace of the globe.

The United States has utilized a few long lasting embargoes against other nations. These have included such rogue states as Iran, North Korea, and Cuba. South Africa also endured an extended embargo period from not only the U.S. but also Britain and much of the European Union because of these countries' collective opposition to the government-mandated policy of apartheid. These American led embargo restrictions leveled against particular pariah states allow basic humanitarian goods to trade but prohibit military and technological hardware and luxury goods from arriving.

When an embargo is comprehensive, it is more punishing still since it cuts off all trade for that receiving-end nation. Since the 9/11/2001 terrorist attacks on the twin towers, the American embargo tool has been more often focused against nations like Sudan that possess obvious connections with terrorists and their financing and those who pose a danger to national and international security policies.

The street is not always one sided even for the United States. The U.S. has also been targeted by vindictive embargoes over the years. The decade of the 1970s saw the American economy suffer grave harm because of the infamous oil embargo. The OPEC Organization of the Petroleum Exporting Countries' member states imposed this set of trade restrictions that led to rationing, fuel shortages, and roaring higher gas costs in the U.S.

It is actually the POTUS President of the United States who has full authority to level trade and strategic embargo weapons against other states in wartime, under the auspices of the Trading With the Enemy Act. The International Emergency Economic Powers Act also provides the President with the powers he needs to create and enforce restrictions relating to commerce in times of national emergencies. The Office of Foreign Assets Control actually handles the specific arrangements and details pertaining to an embargo within the U.S. This Department of the Treasury division engages in a mission critical role to find and freeze any funding sources for drug smuggling and terrorism as it relates to the internal borders and international interests of the United States.

Emerging Markets

Emerging markets prove to be those countries of the world that possess business and development activities that stand in the midst of fast paced industrialization and growth. Today, twenty-eight different emerging markets are considered to exist around the globe. By far and away the largest of these are China and India. The largest regional emerging market today is the ASEAN-China Free Trade Area that began operating on the first of January in 2010.

The concept of emerging markets dates back to the 1970's, when the term used to refer to these particular markets was LEDC's, or less economically developed countries. The comparison alluded to their levels of economic development as compared to the U.S., Western Europe, and Japan. Such emerging markets were supposed to offer higher risk levels for investors as well as the opportunity to make greater profits.

As this term had a slightly negative connotation, the phrase emerging markets replaced it. Some have claimed that this newer term is deceptive, since no one can be assured that a given country will actually migrate from less developed to a more substantially developed one. This has generally proven to be the case, but there are exceptions. Argentina has occasionally digressed from more to less developed.

Numerous examples of these types of emerging market economies exist, since twenty-eight different ones are labeled. These include countries that are grouped in more advanced emerging economies, such as Brazil, Mexico, Taiwan, South Africa, Poland, and Hungary. The secondary emerging economies are as follows: China, India, Chile, Colombia, Egypt, the Czech Republic, Indonesia, Morocco, Malaysia, Peru, Pakistan, Russia, the Philippines, Turkey, Thailand, and the United Arab Emirates. This list is compiled and occasionally updated by the FTSE group based in London, Great Britain.

In the last few years, several competing terms have arisen to challenge the emerging markets phrase. One of these is that of rapidly developing economies that refers to emerging markets like Chile, Malaysia, and the United Arab Emirates. All of these nations are experiencing torrid paces of growth.

The biggest of the emerging markets have earned their own acronyms in the past several years as well. Chief among these are BRIC, signifying Brazil, Russia, India, and China. BRICS includes the above four nations along with South Africa. BRICM is the original four BRIC nations and Mexico. BRICET signifies the first four BRIC members plus Turkey and Eastern Europe. BRICK includes the original four nations of the BRICK along with South Korea. Finally, CIVETS is comprised of Columbia, Indonesia, Vietnam, Egypt, Turkey, and also South Africa. Although none of these countries are particularly aligned by policy or ideology, they are currently gaining a more important role within the overall world economy, as well as in international politics.

For an investor who wishes to invest in these economies, there are several different investment vehicles available to them. Among these are both Exchange Traded Funds and Mutual Funds. One of these is the iShares sponsored MSCI Emerging Markets Index ETF with a symbol of EEM. Another is the iShares run MSCI EAFE Index ETF that has a symbol of EFA. Though these funds' prices can be up spectacularly in good years, they can also experience precipitous declines in periods of instability, such as during the worldwide financial crisis of 2007-2010.

European Union

The European Union proves to be both an economic and political cooperation and block. It is made up of 28 independent European countries. There are several common representative institutions that bind the nations together. The European Council is a body that represents the various national governments. The citizens are represented by the European Parliament.

The common interests of the Europeans are represented by an independent group called the European Commission. These three bodies democratically legislate particular issues of mutual interest to the countries that belong. Most of the countries in Europe participate in the European Union in some form. Three countries that have opted not to are still associated members of the European Economic Area. This includes Norway, Iceland, and Liechtenstein.

Several European countries established the EU following the Second World War and its devastation. They wanted to encourage better economic cooperation and ties. The philosophy behind this was that countries which traded more closely shared an economic interdependence. This would make them less likely to engage in future wars and conflicts.

The group they created out of this philosophy in 1958 became the EEC European Economic Community. France, Belgium, Luxembourg, the Netherlands, Germany, and Italy were founding members that pledged to work towards closer economic cooperation and ties. Over the years since then, more and more nations joined to form an enormous common market.

The original economic union has increased its powers and scope to become a political union as well. As a result of this, they changed the name from European Economic Community to European Union in 1993. These areas of political cooperation include security and external diplomatic relations, migration policies and justice, health, climate, and the environment.

All aspects of this political and economic cooperation stem from the rule of law. Every action the EU takes is authorized by treaties that are democratically and voluntarily agreed on by the member nations. This is evident for member states in the institutions the Council of the EU and the European Council. Citizens themselves have their representation at the European Parliament.

The EU is able to boast of some significant accomplishments. It has ensured over fifty years of peace, prosperity, and stability on the continent. The organization has increased living standards throughout Europe, though not uniformly. Countries in the north and center have seen greater economic benefits and improvements than those on the periphery.

The EU also successfully launched the world's second most important reserve currency the Euro. These achievements received official recognition in the year 2012. That year the EU received the Nobel Peace Prize for its work in moving forward the democracy, reconciliation, peace, and human rights throughout the continent.

Benefits that EU citizens receive in the group have to do with freedom of movement. Removing the border controls between EU countries ensured individuals were able to travel without restrictions around the vast majority of Europe. They are allowed to work and live in the other EU countries as well.

This benefit extends to not only people, but also to goods, services, and money which are allowed to move freely back and forth as well. This has been a main economic advantage that the EU provided for decades. The EU also is working to come up with common cooperation in knowledge, energy, and capital markets to provide the optimal benefits from these to the various EU citizens.

The United States provided a diplomatic Mission to the EU since 1961. Both the EU and U.S. maintain close strategic ties and work together extensively. These issues extend from global problems like nuclear non proliferation to counter terrorism efforts. The EU has major investment and trade relations with the United States as well.

Exchange Rate Mechanism (ERM)

Exchange Rate Mechanisms are systems that were established to maintain a certain range of exchange for currencies as measured against other currencies. These ERMs can be run in three different ways. On one extreme they can float freely. This permits the systems to trade without the central banks and governments intervening.

The fixed Exchange rate mechanisms will do whatever it takes to maintain rates pegged at a specific value. In between these two extremes are the managed ERMs. The best known example of one of these is the European Exchange Rate Mechanism known as ERM II. It is in use today for those countries who wish to become a part of the EU monetary union.

The European Economic Community formally introduced the European ERM system to the world on March 13, 1979. It was a part of the EMS European Monetary System. The goal of this new system centered on attaining monetary stability throughout Europe by reducing the variable exchange rates. This was set up to prepare the way for the Economic and Monetary Union. It also paved the way for the Euro single currency introduction that formally occurred on January 1, 1999.

The Europeans changed their system once the Euro became adopted. They introduced ERM II as a way to link together those EU countries who were not a part of the eurozone with the euro. They did this to boost extra eurozone currencies' stability. A second goal was to create a means of evaluating the countries who wished to join the eurozone. In 2016 only a single currency uses the ERM II. This is the Danish krone.

The European ERM ceased to exist in 1999. This was the point after the eurozone country European Currency Units exchange rates became frozen and the Euro began trading against them. ERM II then replaced the initial ERM. At first the Greek drachma remained in the ERM II alongside the Danish currency. This changed when Greece adopted the Euro in 2001. Currencies within the newer system may float in a fairly tight range of plus or minus 15% of their central exchange rate versus the euro. Denmark does better than this. Its Danmarks Nationalbank maintains a 2.25% range versus the central rate of DKK 7.46038.

In order for other countries that wish to join the Euro to participate, they are required to be a part of the ERM II system for minimally two years before they can become members of the eurozone. This means that at some point, a number of currencies for member states that joined the EU will have to be in the system. This includes the Swedish krona, Polish zloty, Hungarian forint, Czech Republic koruna, the Romanian leu, Bulgarian lev, and Croatian kuna. Each of these is supposed to join the system according to their individual treaties of accession.

In the case of Sweden, the situation is more complicated. The country held a referendum on becoming a part of the mechanism to which the citizens voted no. The European Central Bank still expects that Sweden will join the system and eventually adopt the euro. This is because they did not negotiate for an opt out of the currency as did the U.K. and Denmark. The Maastricht Treaty requires that EU member states all eventually join the exchange rate mechanism.

Britain participated in the mechanism from 1990 until September of 1992. On September 16, 1992 the British famously crashed out of the system on what became known as Black Wednesday because of manipulation of the pound by currency speculators led by Hedge Fund Billionaire George Soros.

Export Quotas

Export quotas represent a specific limit which a nation or block of nations establishes on the quantity of goods which may be legally exported in a given amount of time. They are also referred to as export controls. The main reason why a nation would set such a quota on its exports centers on optimizing the domestically available supply. This aids in controlling prices in the country and helps to ensure they remain lower. This practice is undoubtedly good for consumers, but it is not really beneficial for the national producers. In some cases it can have dramatic consequences on other countries, international buyers and producers, and multinational corporations.

Another way to define such export quotas is that they are restrictions on general or specific exports. Countries might choose to set exporting controls on nuclear materials or arms for the overall good of the country's security. During a time of famine in the land, the state could impose controls on wheat, corn, or rice in order to stave off shortages of food.

These export quotas limit the numbers of exports for particular goods and technology. They do this by establishing a maximum possible value denomination or literal quantity of goods permitted in that particular export. There are various kinds of such quotas. These include bilateral quotas, global quotas, seasonal time frame quotas, quotas set according to the purchases of national goods, quotas which are linked up to the performance of exports, politically motivated quotas, and quotas or controls of important and secretive technologies and products.

India and China are two examples of nations which have historically (and in the case of China still very much do) impose export quotas. India has many times implemented maximum exports on textiles (including acrylic yarn, knitted fabrics, and cotton fabrics) and clothing (including sweaters, T-shirts, and gloves) which might be exported away to the European Union, Canada, and the United States.

China similarly employs such export quotas concerning its oil and rare earth metals production. For example, the country elected to reduce its 2017 first round of licenses for exports by 40 percent on the national four oil majors,

Reuters reported. Traders were expecting the overseas oil allowances to be as high or higher than this past year's record- high levels. The Ministry of Commerce along with the General Administration of Customs sets these export quotas. They determined that the four major state oil producers would only be permitted to sell 12.4 million tons (or about 91 million barrels) of jet fuel, oil, and gasoline abroad. This was reduced from 20.5 million tons for the identical export licensing first round of 2016.

In the appropriately named rare earth metals, China is jealous and aggressive with its export quotas. This is all the more dangerous because China mines over 95 percent of all rare earth metals in the globe. These critical metals are necessary to make electric cars, smart phones, numerous components of computers, and a variety of military armaments which are highly technology intensive. China also controls and produces over 99 percent of the rarest of the rare earth metals, known as heavy rare earths. These may only be deployed in tiny amounts for electronics and clean energy uses, yet they are still necessary for the production of these goods and technologies nonetheless.

There are consequences to these export quotas, in particular on the rare earth elements markets which have no alternative suppliers to turn to for their many important needs. Manufacturers of high-tech goods find themselves in dire straights when they can not obtain affordable supplies, or even supplies at any price, no matter how high. Beijing has tremendous power over the world technology manufacturers and producing nations thanks to these export quotas. They are able to simply stop the global supply of the rare earth metals whenever it suits their national agendas, goals, or international policies.

Federal Debt

The federal debt is also known as the national debt. This represents the entire dollar value of the money which the U.S. federal government has borrowed from its various creditors over the years. Creditors to the government are made up of all governments, businesses, individuals, and other national and international entities which own the debt instruments of the U.S. government.

This national debt has resulted from numerous government deficit budgets where they spent more than they earned in revenues. It is important to realize that this federal debt never includes any of the money owed by municipal or state governments, companies, or individuals. Instead it is the total of all federal government outstanding obligations. This figure contains not just the money the federal government originally borrowed. It is also made up by the interest amounts that it has to pay back with the borrowed funds.

Governments fall into debt when they are not able to bring in sufficient revenues to pay for their expenses on a variety of government programs. This includes military spending and domestic programs such as retirement benefits, Medicare, welfare, and constructing bridges and roads. Revenues are derived from a number of sources. These are made up of personal income and corporate taxes as well as government fees on things like passports, cigarettes and alcohol, and national park admissions fees.

For 2016, the national debt had risen to an enormous amount of greater than $19 trillion. As a percentage of GDP this is over 105%. It has rapidly increased from the years 2006 to 2016, as in 2006 the debt came in at less than half as much at $8.4 trillion. This represented only 66% of the national GDP at the time. Because of this dramatic and ongoing increase, the debate is always heated regarding what should be done with the national debt. Many individuals and observers like the Congressional Budget Office feel that the debt needs to be paid down. Others argue that the debt proves to be a needed catalyst to keep up economic growth.

The debt has come from successive increases in the federal government's annual budget deficit. These annual deficits represent the amount of additional money the government spends over what they take in for receipts. All of these deficits combined together plus interest paid equal the national debt.

When investors see the debt grow higher and anticipate that there will be greater levels of inflation, they become concerned about the value of their debt holdings. Some economists have conjectured that the government only intends to inflate away the value of the debt over time. This is why debt holders can ask for higher interest rates when they make future loans to governments they suspect of inflating away their debts.

Federal surpluses can be used to pay down the federal debt. This has happened on rare occasions. Since World War II, the federal government has only managed to run less than 10 such surpluses. President Harry Truman was the first to turn the government finances around after President Franklin Roosevelt's years of deficits. President Truman had surpluses in 1947, 1948, and 1951.

President Dwight Eisenhower also managed to run smaller surpluses in 1957 and 1958. There was not another government surplus for more than forty years until 1998 when President Bill Clinton signed a deal with Congress that achieved an $87.9 billion surplus. This surplus grew to $290 billion by 2000.

The last surplus came under President George W. Bush who had a $154 billion carryover surplus in 2001. On these rare occasions, the Federal government was able to pay down the federal debt temporarily. These surpluses were followed by half a trillion to trillion dollar deficits per year for most of the next decade.

Fiat Dollars

Fiat dollars refer to dollars that do not possess any sort of intrinsic value. They are not backed up by gold or any other tangible asset, only by the full faith and trust in the United States government. Since the United States abandoned the venerable and stable gold standard back in 1971, the U.S. currency has been one of only fiat dollars.

Fiat actually refers to the Latin for "let it be done." Dollars that are fiat dollars are valued based on the decree of the government. They are not redeemable for anything else.

Until 1971, the dollar proved to be convertible into a certain set quantity of gold. This had been the case along with all other major currencies around the world for nearly two hundred years. Gold backed dollars and other currency proved to be extremely stable and constantly valued for huge spans of time stretching from forty to sixty years before some turbulence like the Civil War would impact their value for a few years. This resulted in part from governments only being able to print as many dollars and other currency as they had gold.

Since the U.S. currency became one of fiat dollars, its stability has vanished, along with its former constant value. One ounce of gold only represented $38.90 valued U.S. dollars at the end of 1970. Today the same ounce of gold equates to $1,350. Another way of putting this is that one 1970 gold backed dollar is equal to nearly $35 fiat dollars in 2010. You might also say that the Fiat dollar has declined by more than ninety-seven percent in the time span of almost forty years since it began its life as a Fiat dollar.

This says several important things about Fiat dollars. They are at the mercy of the international markets, since they are not backed up by any tangible value. They are also able to be printed or electronically multiplied in infinite quantities, since they are not restricted by a given fixed amount of gold. It also means that they are unstable in their values and can collapse fairly easily and quickly, since their real worth is only one of perceived value as determined by the confidence of buyers and sellers.

Fiat dollars are not the only currency that has been decoupled from real valued backing like gold. Euros, Japanese Yen, British Pounds, and practically all major currencies of the world are similarly only based on the faith and trust of their respective governments. The only currency among the major developed economies that might be considered to be non fiat is the Swiss Franc.

The Swiss constitution requires that the government holds a full quarter of the number of Swiss Francs in existence in gold in their vaults. This would give them a twenty-five percent gold backing to their currency. The truth is that since the Swiss value their gold reserves at $250 per ounce, and gold is trading consistently well over $1,200 per ounce to even $1,350 per ounce, at over five times the Swiss value of their gold, this means that they actually have their currency covered by in excess of one hundred percent of actual valued gold holdings, since five times their twenty-five percent gold reserve amounts to one hundred and twenty-five percent.

Fiscal Policy

Fiscal policy is a government policy for managing the economy. In these actions, a government changes its tax rates and spending amounts. They do this to influence the national economy in a certain way. Fiscal policy's sister strategy is called monetary policy. In this complementary series of government actions the central bank adjusts the country's money supply. They do this to pursue the national economic goals.

Governments adjust their fiscal policy by altering the government spending and tax levels. They do this to impact the amount of economic activity in the country. It is an attempt to change the aggregate demand to boost consumer and business spending. Aggregate demand proves to be the complete amount of spending in the economy. This is the total combination of consumer spending, business spending, and government spending.

There are a number of reasons that a government uses fiscal policy. They are to affect growth and inflation rates. Fiscal policy can effectively boost and encourage economic growth when the economy is suffering in a recession. It can also be used keep inflation under control at a targeted level. This is accomplished by cutting government spending levels. Ultimately the purpose of this type of policy is to stabilize the nation's economic growth. Governments hope to avoid the common boom and bust cycles in the economy this way.

Many times governments will use this fiscal policy alongside monetary policy. Much of the time governments prefer to utilize monetary policy in their efforts to stabilize the economy. Monetary policy is easier to change. It also makes less of a dramatic and potentially disruptive impact on an economy.

Expansionary fiscal policy is the type a government employs when the economy slows down. This is also known as loose fiscal policy. To engage in it the government must increase the aggregate demand. They will do this by one of three methods. They may increase the government spending to create more demand and jobs. They can cut taxes to put more money in consumer's and business' hands. This will increase consumer spending as they effectively receive a greater amount of disposable income. In some cases governments may choose to both boost spending and reduce taxes.

There are side effects of this expansionary policy. The government budget shortfall, or deficit, will worsen. As a result, the government must increase the amount of money it will borrow to finance the spending.

Deflationary fiscal policy is the opposite of expansionary policy. In deflationary policy the government becomes concerned about how fast the economy is growing. They attempt to slow it down. This is also known as tight fiscal policy. For a government to pursue this policy they must reduce the amount of aggregate demand. They will do this in one of three ways. They might reduce the government spending. Governments could also raise taxes. A higher level of taxes forces consumers to reduce their spending. The government might also both cut its spending and raise taxes in conjunction.

While this slows economic growth, it does have a positive side effect. The government budget deficit improves as a result of cutting government spending and raising taxes. The government can choose to reduce borrowing and pay down national debt.

Fiscal policy arose from the economic theory of John Maynard Keynes the British economist. He argued that government is able to affect change on macroeconomic levels of productivity. They could do this by raising or lowering public spending amounts and tax levels. According to Keynes, they are able to reduce inflation, keep the currency value healthy, and boost employment with this tool. These ideas are also called Keynesian economics in honor of his work.

Fiscal Year

The fiscal year refers to an accounting period which governments or companies choose to use for their own accounting and in developing financial statements. Fiscal years are not necessarily the same as the calendar years. The U.S. government employs a different starting and finishing point for its own fiscal year.

The IRS Internal Revenue Service permits companies to choose whether they will use calendar years or fiscal years in their tax computations. When individuals or companies discuss budgets, they often invoke fiscal years. They prove to be a useful reference point when contrasting corporate or government financial results over the medium to long term.

The IRS has its own definition of fiscal year. To them these are comprised of 12 contiguous months that conclude on the final day in any month besides December. This means that where tax reports are concerned, a fiscal year could run February 1st to January 31st. American taxpayers also have the opportunity to utilize either 52 or 53 weeks long fiscal years instead of a 12 month one. In the case of the weeks' version, the years will rotate back and forth between 52 and 53 weeks in length.

Because the IRS automatically uses a calendar year system, those who employ fiscal years will need to adjust their own deadlines for turning in specific forms and getting in different payments. The biggest difference concerns the tax filing deadline. For the majority of American households and businesses, this will be no later than April 15th after the year in question for which they file. Those taxpayers working with the fiscal year system instead must file no later than the 15th day in the fourth month that comes after the conclusion of their fiscal period. This means that a business choosing to have fiscal years that span from May 1st to April 30th will need to turn in all tax returns no later than August 15th.

The U.S. tax code makes it relatively easy for companies to use fiscal years in their income tax reporting efforts. All that they are required to do is to turn in on time their tax return which covers that particular fiscal period. The companies also have the right to opt back to using calendar years whenever it suits them. To make the change from fiscal back to calendar years, they need to obtain individual permission by asking the IRS. Otherwise, they will have to measure up to the criteria that they outline in their Form 1128 called the Application to Adopt, Change, or Retain a Tax Year.

These fiscal years have a particular way of being addressed. Individuals who are discussing them reference them either by the end date or alternatively the end year. This means that one would refer to the American federal government fiscal year that starts on October 1st and ends on September 30th by saying the government fiscal year which ends on September 30th, 2016. If instead they were referencing spending by the government that happened in November of 2015, they would have to call this expenditure one that occurred in the 2016 fiscal year.

Five Year Plans

Five year plans are economic and social roadmaps that China began issuing in 1953. These were based upon the old Soviet central planning procedures. The Soviet Union collapsed in the early 1990s. Its plans are now a historical footnote. China continues to implement these plans every five years like a clock. They consistently show the world what China is attempting to focus on and accomplish. China has a history of meeting many if not most of its five year plan goals.

The government drafts and implements its plans on many levels. These include the district, local, provincial, and central government sectors. Industry regulators are also a part of the process. Most of these government divisions have their own five year plans as well. The NDRC National Development and Reform Commission draft the central government's plan. In these are detailed economic goals that include GDP growth rates.

Social development focuses on improvements in other important areas like education and healthcare. They come up with these specific targets after consulting with a variety of ministries and experts in industry and academia. Chinese regulators on all levels utilize these targets as they work through the implementing the period of the plan.

China spends years preparing these plans. They started talking about the goals of the 13th five year plan to run from 2016 to 2020 back in April of 2013. These plans set directions for the government priorities and policies. China met the majority of both economic and social goals they set out in the 12th FYP that concluded at the end of 2015.

These attained goals included average growth rates of seven percent, GDP services share at four percentage points higher, and seven percent annual increase to rural and urban incomes. Areas they struggled in were reducing carbon targets, raising non fossil fuels energy production, and increasing energy efficiency.

China relaxed its 35 year old one child policy as the biggest change in its current 13th FYP. This showed how the government is concerned about maintaining economic growth in the future as its population ages. For main economic targets, they set a GDP growth rate of average 6.5% per year. They also want to raise disposable income per capita by 6.5% each year. The leadership felt that this would make them into a "moderately prosperous society."

The plan also continues on its path of reforms. Markets will have more influence and the state owned industries will be retooled. They will shift the economy to services from heavy industry. Services will represent a greater contributor towards GDP. The goal is for them to contribute 56% of the total GDP by 2020. China has also committed to lessen the state interventions into everything from account interest rates to gas prices.

They aim to increase the capacity of nuclear power to 58 gigawatts and the high speed rail network to 30,000 kilometers or 18,600 miles. The country is to build minimally 50 new airports for civilians. The government wants to develop a new 50 million urban area jobs. In support of this they want to see their urban residency rise to 60% of the whole population by the year 2020.

For other social changes China intends to significantly address the pollution problems of the past. They hope to limit energy consumption to less than five billion tons of coal equivalent. They also want to reduce their total energy consumption by 15 percent and cut carbon dioxide emissions by 18%. All of this working together is supposed to improve their sometimes horribly polluted air. The goal for city air quality is to see it rated at a minimally good rating for 80% of the time.

Flash Crash

The Flash Crash has also been called the 2010 Flash Crash and the Crash of 2:45. It occurred on May 6 in 2010. This stock market collapse occurred in the United States and caused a trillion dollars of equity to be temporarily wiped out. It began officially at 2:32 EST. The crash happened over only the next 36 minutes.

During this crash, major stock indices including the Dow Jones Industrial Average, the S&P 500, and the NASDAQ composite fell apart and then rebounded with unparalleled speed and volatility. At one moment, the DJIA set its largest point drop within a single day to that time. It fell 998.5 points representing over 9% of its value.

Most of this drop happened in only minutes. The index then went on to recover a substantial portion of the drop a little later. Up to this point, this represented the second biggest point swing in a single day at 1010 points.

Trading volume exploded briefly as volatility increased. The prices of stock indices, individual stocks, futures on the indices, options, and ETF exchange traded funds were all over the board. In 2014, the CFTC Commodities Futures Trading Commission released a report that called this just over thirty minute crash among the most chaotic points in all of the history of global financial markets.

The government responded by putting a number of new regulations into play after the 2010 Flash Crash. Despite this fact, they were insufficient to stop another such rapid crash on August 24, 2015. During this second episode, bids on literally dozens of stocks and ETFs plunged to as little as a single penny per share as ETFs decoupled from their underlying value, per the Wall Street Journal article of December 6, 2015. As a result of this second incident, regulators placed ETFs under additional scrutiny. This also led to the analysts at Morningstar stating that legislation from the Depression era was governing the digital age technology of ETFs.

It took the Department of Justice almost five years to charge an individual with criminal misconduct that contributed massively to the original flash crash. They charged the trader Navinder Singh Sarao with 22 counts of market manipulation and fraud. Apparently he had utilized spoofing algorithms to trick the exchanges.

Immediately before the crash unfolded, Sarao had put in orders for thousands of the stock index futures contracts known as E-mini S&P 500 contracts. These orders constituted $200 million in bets that the markets would then decline. Before the orders were cancelled by his algorithm, it modified or replaced them 19,000 times. Thanks to this individual action, the government and regulators banned front running, layering, and the spoofing of orders.

In the investigation that the CFTC conducted, they came to the conclusion that Sarao bore substantial responsibility for the imbalances of the orders in derivatives markets. These impacted the stock markets and made the crash so much more severe. The small time trader Sarao was operating from his parent's house in the suburban part of west London when he carried out these actions. He had started manipulating the markets back in 2009 when he purchased and modified trading software that would permit him to quickly and automatically place and cancel his orders.

A later CFTC report in May 2014 determined that the high frequency traders who were assigned much of the blame for the flash crash did not cause it themselves. They did contribute to the severity of it as their orders were taken before those of other participants in the market.

Floating Exchange Rate

A floating exchange rate is one where the price of the currency in question is set by the free forex market. This market sets the values of currencies using available supply and relevant demand as measured against other currency pairs. This is the opposite of a fixed exchange rate, where a national government mainly or entirely sets the rate for the country's currency. Most of the major economy currencies in the world have been free floating since the Bretton Woods exchange system irreparably broke down in 1971.

With a free floating exchange rate system in place, there will be countless short term movements in a currency value that result from investor and trader speculation and disasters or even rumors which are man made or naturally occurring. The longer term movements in these floating currencies occur because of the differentials in between interest rates and economic strength as relative to nations' peers. There can also be wild short term moves that happen because of central bank direct intervention in the currency markets, even while the system is still a free floating exchange rate environment.

The soon to be victors of World War II met in Bretton Woods Resort in New Hampshire in July of 1944 to hold the famed Bretton Woods Conference. The 44 nations at this key conference created the World Bank and International Monetary Fund. They also laid out specific guidelines to set up an exchange rate system that was fixed.

The scenario they established laid out a $35 per ounce gold price that all countries pegged up to alongside the dollar. The range of adjustment was limited to only plus or minus one percent at the time. This conference enshrined the U.S. dollar as the world's reserve currency. Central banks were able to engage in interventions by selling or buying dollars in order to stabilize or tweak exchange rates.

The system worked well until 1967 when fractures began to appear. That year, there was a gold run as well as an attack on the value of the British pound. This resulted in a shocking 14.3% sterling devaluation. Four years later, as numerous countries around the world watched the U.S. print limitless new paper dollars they began cashing in their dollars for gold in record numbers.

Faced with an impending shortage of American gold reserves in 1971, then-President Richard Nixon felt like he had no choice but to remove the United States from the gold standard. Only two years later, the Bretton Woods currency system had totally collapsed. Those currencies which had participated in the system morphed over to a floating exchange rate system instead.

Central banks are able to purchase and sell their own currency in a free floating exchange rate system. They do this to influence the rate of exchange for one of several reasons. They might want to calm down a volatile currency market. They could also wish to cut the currency exchange rate dramatically in order to stimulate exports to other countries.

The world's most important central banks often work in concert to affect the desired results. This includes the G-7 countries of the United States, the United Kingdom, Japan, Italy, Germany, France, and Canada. By working together, they are able to magnify their individual impacts on the currency markets.

These interventions do not always prove to be successful and are usually only short term in duration. Sometimes central banks choose to indirectly interfere in the markets by lowering or raising their interest rates instead to change the quantity of investor funds moving into their nation.

Foreign Exchange

Foreign exchange involves converting the currency of one nation into another nation's currency. Foreign exchange rates can be set in several different ways determined by the country's government. Free market economies allow their currency to float freely most of the time. The value of the money is determined by the markets according to supply and demand factors.

Other nations choose to peg the value of their money to a stronger and more stable currency like the U.S. dollar or the Euro. They might also choose to use a basket of currencies for such a peg. A third alternative is for a country's government to fix the value of their money at a set rate. The majority of nations choose to allow their foreign exchange rates to float freely versus the ones of other nations. This causes them to fluctuate up and down constantly throughout the day.

Sometimes nations which allow the value of their money to float freely will choose to intervene in foreign exchange markets to devalue their exchange rate. They might feel that their money's value has risen too fast and is hurting the competitiveness of their exports. As their exchange rate rises, the cost of their goods becomes more expensive to customers in foreign markets. In such a case, the country may announce that they are buying their own money at a lower rate or they may sell it off in Forex markets. Interventions like this tend to be less common except in volatile exchange environments.

Currency values are usually set by the forces of the market and are based on a number of national and international elements. These include trade and investment, flows of tourism, and geo political event risk. Trade and investment requires that the companies or nations purchase the host nation's money for the transaction. Investors may also want to purchase investments in another country. They would need that nation's money in order to make such investments.

When tourists come to visit a nation, they require the local money. They will exchange their own country's money for that of the one which they are visiting. Every one of these transactions constantly requires foreign exchange. This explains why the forex markets are the largest financial marketplaces in the world by far.

Banks handle this foreign exchange between each other on an international level. This creates a forex market that operates 24 hours per day and six days a week. The major centers of foreign exchange are disbursed around the world. These trades and transactions mostly occur in eight major forex centers. These are London, New York City, Tokyo, Singapore, Switzerland (Zurich and Geneva), Hong Kong, Sydney, and Paris. Each of the transactions comes under the regulation of the Bank of International Settlements.

Floating exchange rates are set by the supply and demand of all of these trades. More demand for a currency against a stable supply will increase the value of it against another. The rates are also impacted by numerous economic reports and geopolitical events. Some of the better known and followed ones are unemployment rates, interest rate levels and decisions, manufacturing data, gross domestic product changes, and inflation reports.

For countries that choose to go the route of pegged exchange, their governments must artificially set and maintain their exchange rates. These rates do not change up and down throughout the day. Instead the government will reset its value on reevaluation dates. Emerging market countries often find this a useful means of managing their foreign exchange rates in order to ensure that they are stable. They will be required to maintain large reserves of their pegged currency so that they can manage the inevitable supply and demand changes that affect their own foreign exchange.

Foreign Exchange Reserves

Foreign exchange reserves are comprised of any currency which is foreign to the central bank holding it. If the American Federal Reserve held British pounds, this would be an example of such reserves. These exchange reserves can include bank deposits, foreign banknotes, bonds, treasury bills, and various other kinds of government securities. The phrase also includes IMF SDR special drawing rights' units and gold reserves.

Such foreign exchange reserves can be utilized for a range of purposes. The main one is to provide the central government with necessary resilience and flexibility in any sort of currency crisis. If several currencies were to crash or become severely undervalued, these central bank vaults contain assets in other currencies which they can fall back on in order to outlast temporary market fluctuations and currency crises.

Practically every nation on earth, irrespective of their economy's relative size and strength, chooses to inventory substantial foreign exchange reserves. Over half of all such foreign reserves in the globe exist in the form of U.S. dollars. This is because dollars represent the most heavily traded global currency in the world. Other commonly found forms of foreign exchange currency reserves include the Euro zone's euro (EUR), the British pound sterling (GBP), the Japanese yen (JPY), the Swiss Franc (CHF), and ever increasingly the Chinese yuan (CNY). The euro is hands down the second largest form of such international exchange reserves. The yuan is the fastest growing component of foreign reserves today.

A number of economists and currency analysts concur that it makes the most sense to keep significant foreign exchange reserves in currencies which are not closely related to the ones of the nation in question. This helps to hedge the central bank from possible currency shocks and devaluations. It has become an increasingly Herculaneum task to do so since the majority of currencies are now closely correlated.

These days the People's Republic of China contains the most impressive array of international exchange reserves. This is due to their over 3.5 trillion dollars in foreign assets denominated in foreign currencies. The majority of these are based in the dollar and treasury securities proffered overseas by the U.S. Treasury.

Foreign exchange reserves serve the most common purpose of backing up the domestic currency of any country. This is necessary as currency by itself is inherently of no value. It is only an IOU from the government which issued it in the first place. The only assurance a receiver of this currency has that the currency value itself will be maintained is the good faith, trust in, and credit of the government and nation. This gives such foreign reserves great importance as a form of concretely backing up such assurance. Liquidity and security are critically important in defining what makes a reliable currency reserve investment.

Foreign exchange reserves are also utilized as an instrument in the tool kit of monetary policy these days. This is especially important for any country that is determined to use a fixed exchange rate. This helps a central bank to exercise control over its own currency value on the open market when they have other currencies to push into the markets against their own. Nations have opted to build up larger storehouses of foreign reserves since the untimely demise of the Bretton Woods system in 1971 over 45 years ago.

For example, China maintains simply enormous foreign exchange reserves so that it can control the exchange rates of its own currency the yuan. This helps it to foster beneficial international trading arrangements for its country and economy. They also keep such large dollar reserves because of the requirements of international trade which still mostly settles in U.S. dollars exclusively. Nations such as Saudi Arabia choose to keep huge foreign reserves because their entire economy depends on the one production and resource of oil to which their economy is almost entirely addicted. When oil prices plunge, their economy benefits at least temporarily from the flexibility provided by their heavy buildup of foreign exchange holdings.

FOREX Markets

FOREX markets are the world wide foreign exchange markets. They are called FX markets as well. FOREX markets are different from all of the other major financial markets in that they are over the counter and decentralized. They exist for the purpose of trading currencies.

Unlike with other markets, the FOREX markets are also open twenty-four hours a day during the week and on Sunday, since the different financial centers around the globe serve as trading bases for a variety of buyers and sellers. This foreign exchange market is the place where supply and demand mostly decides the different currencies' values for nations around the world.

The main point and reason for the FOREX markets are to help out investment and trade internationally through permitting businesses to easily change one currency to the other one that they require. In practice, individuals or businesses actually buy one amount of foreign currency through paying for it with a given amount of a different currency.

As an example, Canadian businesses may import British goods by paying for them in British Pounds, even though their income and base currency are Canadian dollars. The foreign exchange markets allow for investors to speculate on the rising and falling values of various currencies as well. It also makes the infamous carry trade possible, where investors are able to borrow currencies with low yields or interest rates and use them to purchase higher interest rate yielding currencies. Critics have said that the FOREX markets also hurt some countries' competitiveness against other countries.

This market is extremely popular and unique for a variety of reasons. It possesses the greatest trading volume on earth, managing in the three to four trillion dollar range every single trading day. This gives it enormous liquidity. It is also geographically centered all over the world, from Wellington in New Zealand to London in Great Britain to New York in the United States. Traders love that the market runs fully twenty-four hours per day except for on the weekends, when it reopens Sunday afternoon.

Finally, an enormous degree of leverage, that can be as much as two hundred to one, allows for even people with small accounts to make potentially enormous gains. Because of all of these factors and its world wide trading base, the FOREX markets have been called the ones where perfect competition is most evident. This is the case even though central banks sometimes intervene directly in these markets to increase or decrease the value of their currency relative to a trading partners' or trading competitors' currency value.

Free Enterprise System

Free enterprise systems are those which have limited government interference in the overall economy. Governments do not place many restrictions on the economic activity and commercial abilities of their citizens in this system. Ownership and business activities are not heavily regulated by the government. Other names for this system are capitalism or free market economies.

In such economic systems, individuals can spend their money however they would like. A number of companies compete for business in most industries. This creates the effects of higher quality products and better prices. Individuals can engage in any work or job that they like under this system.

The history of the free enterprise movement and system dates back to the 18th century. At this time people in countries around the world had to obtain governmental approval in order to start up a business. The philosophy of free market economies argued for limiting restrictions on business ownership.

The idea was that individuals should be permitted to trade with anyone they wished from any nation. Proponents of the system wanted to run their business as they saw fit. Adam Smith wrote about this system of capitalism and the invisible hand that guides free markets at this time in his timeless classic The Wealth of Nations.

The French came up with a similar concept Laissez-faire. This meant that government should keep its hands off individual business. Private party transactions were supposed to be left free from government tariffs, regulations, privileges, and subsidies.

In the early 20th century Communism developed as an opposing system to free enterprise. It argued for state owned control of industry and businesses. Workers were encouraged to labor for the good of the collective group instead of for their own benefit. Large sections of the world adapted this form of economic domination in Eastern Europe, Asia, and Russia particularly. In time this system became discredited. In the 1990s it collapsed in the former Soviet Union and Eastern Europe. It has all but disappeared except for in China.

A number of countries of the world have adapted many of the causes of free enterprise into their economies. This system of free enterprise became a major part of the U.S. and British economies' strength. There are free market representatives who continue to insist that the U.S. and other Western countries need less restriction on their economies.

Still other countries of the world participate in a third economic system. This is known as socialism. Socialist governments attempt to manage their capitalist economies. One of their goals is to protect workers' rights and benefits. They often place restrictions on free trade with other countries and erect barriers to competition. Larger industries are nurtured and are often part owned by the government. Smaller businesses are not as heavily regulated. They enjoy more of the benefits of free market economies. France is an example of this type of economy.

Free enterprise systems are characterized by a number of different traits. The spending of consumers determines what goods and services companies will supply. Markets permit individuals to obtain property, buildings, and real estate with few limitations.

Owners of businesses enjoy several advantages with this system as well. They are allowed to make their own prices and decide how much profit they will pursue. They can also choose their own material suppliers and with whom they will conduct their business. The government also will not limit them to the kinds of business which they are allowed to pursue.

G20

The G20 is the combined organization of developed and important developing nations. These countries make up 85% of the global economy and include two thirds of all the people on earth. As the powerful driving engine of the global economy, this group has been recognized as centrally important in tackling issues of world importance.

The G20 is comprised of central bank governors and finance ministers of the European Union (represented by the President of the European Central Bank and the European Council President) and the United States, the United Kingdom, Turkey, South Africa, Saudi Arabia, Russia, Mexico, South Korea, Japan, Italy, Indonesia, India, Germany, France, China, Canada, Brazil, Australia, and Argentina. The G20 is headed by a president. This individual position rotates every year among the constituent member states.

These central bank governors and finance ministers meet two times per year. They generally coordinate their meetings with those of the World Bank, International Monetary Fund, and the G20 summits. At the November 15-16 2015 meeting held in Turkey, around 4,000 delegates and 3,000 representatives of the world media participated or attended.

The G20 group actually formed back in 1999. The idea was to provide a more important voice and forum for developing countries in arranging the world economy. These meetings began as only informal sit downs of central bankers and finance ministers. The world's first G20 summit occurred in the midst of the 2008 global financial crisis from November 16-17. They met in Washington, D.C. Until this first summit, most important global economic issues and plans were tackled by the G8 or G7.

These represent only the economically important developed nations. At this first summit, the emerging market leaders wanted the United States to better regulate its financial markets. The U.S. at first refused. These developing leaders also wished to see the debt rating companies like Standard & Poor's and the hedge funds better regulated. They believed standards should be strengthened in derivatives trading and global accounting. G20 members blamed poor standards and regulations for the financial crisis that led to the worldwide Great Recession.

The 2015 summit meeting happened on November 15-16, 2015 in Antalya, Turkey. This particular meeting concentrated on an appropriate response to the Paris terrorist attack. Member nations consented to accepting refugees from the war on ISIS while promising to improve their border monitoring against potential terrorist threats.

The United States conceded to sharing more of its intelligence information with both France and the other member states. The U.S. refused to dispatch ground troops to Syria, but did promise to support the coalition of anti ISIS Iraqi and Syrian forces. The group agreed on additional steps to restrict the important sources of financing for the Islamic State.

The 2014 summit annual meeting occurred from November 15-16, 2014 in Brisbane, Australia. This meeting concentrated efforts on condemning the Russian invasion of the Ukraine. The membership also unanimously agreed to strive together to boost the growth of the global Gross Domestic Product to 2.1% by the year 2018. This would provide another $2 trillion to economies of the world.

Both the European Union and The United States twisted arms of other member states to act on worsening climate change. This was not in the official meeting agenda. Leaders agreed to help out the fight against Ebola virus in West Africa. President Obama also met on the sidelines with the leaders of Australia and Japan regarding a peaceful settlement to maritime conflicts over territories in the South China Sea.

The 2016 G20 meeting is scheduled to be held from September 4-5, 2016 in Hangzhou, China. It will be the eleventh such summit of the G20.

G8 Summit

The G8 Summit is a yearly meeting of the leaders of the powerful economies of the world. The annual G8 president for the year hosts the meetings. Technically there is no political or legal authority for the summit, and its outcomes are not internationally binding. Yet when the major eight world leaders concur on an issue, this promises enough authority to change the direction of global economic policies and growth. The G8 is made up of the United States, Great Britain, Canada, Italy, Germany, France, Japan, and Russia.

The founding six nations of the group held their first summit in Rambouillet, France back in 1975. In attendance were the U.S., France, Britain, Germany, Italy, and Japan. Canada joined the group the following year to round out the G7. In 1997, the other members consented for Russia to join, bringing it up to its format of eight countries. The group once again devolved to the G7 when Russia invaded the Crimea in the Ukraine and was suspended indefinitely.

The remaining members all agreed on disallowing Russia as a form of sanctions against its aggressive behavior against its neighbor in annexing Ukrainian territory. The G8 Summit regularly invites other critical global leaders to attend. This includes representatives for China, India, Mexico, the European Union, and Brazil. Other crucial international organizations are regularly invited, such as the heads of the United Nations, the World Bank, and the International Monetary Fund.

The G8 Summit proved its power and efficacy every year in over 30 years of annual meetings. In 2008 a noticeable shifting of power happened. The G8 discussed inflation in food prices and other critical world issues while entirely missing the impending 2008 global financial crisis and Great Recession.

This G8 Summit in 2008 occurred in July at the same time as Freddie Mac and Fannie Mae were failing and the LIBOR rates were sky rocketing. The Fed had just met in its first emergency meeting in more than 30 years to discuss saving Bear Stearns. This signified that the old financial world order had ended as the G20 met and took up the most important issue facing the world and its economies.

Their summit tackled the economic and financial crisis at its roots. They asked the United States to better regulate its financial markets. The U.S. refused, instead permitting credit default swaps and other derivatives to be unregulated and blow up the world economy. This crisis made it clear that the emerging market economies were a critical part of any global solution. They had mostly sidestepped the financial crisis and clearly saw the flaws in the developed market economies and financial markets which had caused it. From this point forward, the G20 had the reputation of being the most crucial meeting in the world of all the important global leaders.

The 2015 G8 Summit (G7 Summit) was held on June 8, 2015 in Emau Castle in Germany. The G7 came out with a plan to phase out fossil fuels around the globe entirely by the year 2100. It did not sufficiently address either a cohesive plan to take down ISIS or the ongoing Greek debt crisis. Instead it left this last matter to the IMF and EU for resolution.

The 2014 Summit was originally intended to be held in Sochi, Russia and hosted by Russian President Vladimir Putin. The G7 cancelled this meeting and opted for an emergency summit on June 7-8, 2014 in Brussels, Belgium. They pledged $5 billion in economic aid to Ukraine and strengthened the economic sanctions against aggressive Russia. They also agreed to provide greater support to the efforts of the WHO to lessen such dangerous infectious diseases as Ebola and Tuberculosis.

The 2016 G7 summit happened from May 26-28, 2016 in Ise-Shima, Japan. As has become a recent tradition, Russia was not invited.

Georgist Public Finance Theory

Georgist Public Finance Theory refers to an economic school of thought. Also known as geoism, this relates to the idea that economic value which comes from property including natural opportunities and natural resources ought to belong in kind to every individual in a society. They simultaneously believe the production value each individual produces should be owned by each contributing member according to what they produce.

The philosophy came from the works of Henry George. This Georgist paradigm provides solutions to ecological and social issues. It does this by depending on the concepts of public finance and land rights while striving to combine both social justice and optimal economic efficiency.

As such, this Georgist Public Finance Theory concerns itself with the fair distribution of economic rents created by pollution, monopolies, and the control over commons. This includes privileges and rights such as intellectual property and titles of ownership for natural resources. Those natural resources that have a limit on their available exploitable supply are able to produce economic rents. Georgists claim that placing a tax on economic rents is fair, efficient, and also equitable.

The principle policies of the Georgists maintain that taxes should be assessed based upon the value of the land. They feel that any revenues created by an LVT land value tax will eliminate or reduce those taxes on investment and labor which are both inefficient and unjust. Some of the followers of the Georgist Public Finance Theory argue for the redistribution of extra public revenues to be returned to the inhabitants via a dividend payment to the citizens or a basic income distribution.

Land value tax is called progressive by many economists dating back to Adam Smith and his *Wealth of Nations*. These taxes are mostly paid in by the landowning class of wealthy individuals. They can not pass them on to renters of the land, workers, or tenants. The idea behind land value taxes is that they should ameliorate inequalities in economics, increase wages, lessen the vulnerability which economies suffer from such as property bubbles and credit manias, and take away any motivations to abuse real estate.

The basis philosophically for Georgist Public Finance Theory hails back to a few of its early advocates like Baruch Spinoza, John Locke, and Thomas Paine. Yet the person who made the entire concept of gathering in public revenues from the privileges of natural resource ownership became popularized by the social reformer and economist Henry George via his first work *Progress and Poverty* which was published in 1879.

The ideas of Georgist Public Finance Theory became most influential and widespread in acceptance in the early 20th and late 19th centuries. There were whole communities, political parties, and even institutions which were founded on these ideas at the time. Early followers of George's philosophy on economics were many times called Single Taxers. This was based upon the idea of obtaining public revenues only from privileges on land. Today's Georgists have altered this foundational belief to include a wide range of government funds' sourcing.

There were a few communities founded under the Georgist Public Finance Theory principles back in the late 1800s and early 1900s in the United States. Three of them which still exist and function under these ideals are Fairhope, Alabama which arose under the governance of the Fairhope Single Tax Corporate in 1894; Arden, Delaware that Fran Stephens along with Will Price founded a few years later in 1900; and Altoona, Pennsylvania which still operates under only a single land tax to this day.

Internationally, the German sphere of influence in Jiaozhou Bay or Kiaochow within China fully implemented the Georgist Public Finance Theory policies. The only government revenue source that they relied on came from a six percent land value tax levied throughout the territory. The German Imperial administration hoped that this would eliminate the land speculation problems which had arisen in their southwest African colonies.

This objective was achieved successfully in their China sphere of influence as the hoped. These Georgist ideas became a part of the societal fabric in one form or another in such far flung nations and territories as Hong Kong, Australia, South Africa, Singapore, South Korea, and Taiwan. Such countries still assess one form of land value tax or another today.

Global Debt

Global debt is an issue that has become especially troublesome since the financial crisis of 2007-2009. Eight years following this crash and Great Recession, the planet is experience a debt problem that has never before been seen in the whole history of the world.

Total debt outside of the financial sector has increased by more than double in real dollars since the century began through 2016. By 2015, it had climbed to over $152 trillion. This figure that includes the debt of governments, households, and non financial firms continues to grow.

Global debt levels as of October 2016 reached a record setting 225% of the entire gross domestic product for the globe, per the IMF's Fiscal Monitor semi annual publication. Roughly two thirds of the total non-financial firm debt is owed by the private sector of businesses and consumers. The balance nearly a third of the total is considered to be government public debt. While other measures have this percentage higher, the IMF claims that government debt is up to 85 percent of GDP versus the 70 percent seen in 2015.

This enormous amount of global debt has made the job of worldwide policy makers much more challenging. Central banks have found that their efforts to stimulate economies are diminishing. It is up to government fiscal policy to increase growth to try to keep up with rising global debt. So far, few countries have seen much success in these efforts.

The surge in global debt borrowing hails back to the private debt boom that occurred before the financial crisis in 2008. Corporations and consumer households within the world's advanced economies began to retrench after the crisis. Despite this, debt deleveraging did not proceed evenly and in other cases debts continued to rise. Bad debts of banks especially proved problematic. Many of these have wound up on the balance sheets of governments instead.

The low interest rate environment that followed the financial crisis also encouraged a rising tide of corporate debt in the emerging nation markets. Private debt levels were already dangerously high in advanced countries.

Now they are also problematic in such important emerging economies as Brazil and China. Both of these are rightly thought of as systemically critical in the world's financial system.

The problem with deciding how dangerous global debt has become is there is no consensus on what percentage of debt versus GDP is critical. It is well known that financial crises are related to an overabundance of private debt in developing and developed economies. Beyond this, research has demonstrated that higher levels of debt come with lower rates of growth, even though a financial crisis may be side stepped. The IMF has been warning especially about the need for deleveraging to happen in both the euro zone area and China.

There are two more problems associated with rising debt levels. As debt increase outpaces economic output growth, more government debt equals a greater level of state involvement in the overall economy. It also guarantees a higher tax rate and number of taxes for the future.

Besides this, debt has to be rolled over regularly. The repetition of having to auction debt creates a scenario where governments face a vote of confidence on a routine basis. Should a government fail to inspire enthusiasm for its debt auction as has happened with a number of euro zone governments in past years, then the erring nation plunges head long into serious crisis.

Government Debt

Government debt refers to the total amount of government issued IOUs which have not been paid back at any given point. Governments issue such debt any time they chose to borrow money from the public or from overseas nations and companies.

As a government borrows this money, it provides government securities that give all of the important information on this investment debt. The face of the certificates states the interest rate which the government will pay on the original principal, the amount which they are borrowing, and the payment schedule for both principal pay back and interest payments. These outstanding securities are equal to the total debt amount which the government has not paid back. It is also the government debt.

Governments actually issue a variety of debt types. Economists classify such debt in different categories. The first would be by the form of governmental agency that issued such debt in the first place. Within the U.S., the principal governmental agencies which issue debt are state, federal, and local jurisdictions. Local debt is also further subdivided into sub-classes including city-, county-, or parish-issued government debt. All of these are considered a type of government bonds.

Yet another way to classify such government debt is according to the dates of maturity. This is why bond investors and U.S. Treasury officials with the Federal Reserve discuss thirty year and ten year bonds. These are the amounts of time between when the government originally issued the bond and the due date of the principal. With federal government debt, there are three easy to understand and remember types of maturities.

Treasury Bills are the first of these. They come with maturities amounting to a single year or under. This could be three month T-bills or year long T-bills. Treasury notes are the second designation. They have maturities that range from a single year to ten years long. Treasury bonds are the over ten year long maturity dates. With local or state level government debt, the terminology used is just bonds. This is true regardless of when they mature.

There are also bonds that carry infinite repayments. Analysts call these perpetuity bonds. With these bonds, the principal never becomes repaid. Interest payments will then be made forever. This would practically be until the government defaults, the country collapses financially, or the government buys back the bonds. Such bonds were at one time issued by the government of Great Britain. They called these consols.

A final means for classifying government debt bonds comes down to the revenue source which underlies the bonds' repayment. Those government debts that the entity plans to repay by utilizing revenues they garner from taxing their constituents they call general obligation bonds. Revenue bonds are those bonds that they pay back by employing particular user fees, sometimes from the project itself which the bonds will finance. This could be tolls on a new highway or a bridge. Only local and state government debt is classified this way.

The United States government debt has radically and exponentially increased over the past 15 to 20 years. Consider that in 2004 early in the year, the outstanding federal government debt amounted to around $7.1 trillion. In early 2017, that amount topped $20 trillion for the first time ever. Roughly half of this enormous debt amount the government owes to its pension funds - the Social Security Trust and Medicare Trust Funds.

Some economists like to say that the internal debt does not carry any public welfare or economic impacts, but they are incorrect with this assertion. Since the Social Security Fund will start to need its loaned out money paid back in 2020, it will require the government to issue either new debt to non-governmental buyers or to raise taxes dramatically to pay back the pension funds for the social security recipients' monthly benefits to continue.

This problem will only worsen over time through 2032 or 2033, when the funds will have exhausted all of their money the government owes them back. At this point, the federal government will either have to abandon the Social Security and Medicare programs entirely, dramatically reduce the benefits to where they are sustainable, hugely increase the age when retirees can draw on them, or vastly increase government revenues from somewhere.

Great Depression

The Great Depression represented the most serious economic contraction that affected the world in the twentieth century. It occurred the decade before the Second World War broke out, in the 1930's. The Great Depression began and ended in differing years in the various countries and economies of the world. In general it started around 1929 and held countries in its grip through the end of the 1930's and the early years of the 1940's.

The Great Depression turned out to be the deepest, hardest, longest, and most geographically encompassing depression that the world had seen. Nowadays, the Great Depression is still held up as the model for how badly the economy of the world can collapse. In the eighty years since the great depression began, economists have not named another economic contraction in the world or the United States as a depression.

The Great Depression began in the United States. It commenced with the stock market crash that began on September 4, 1929. The far steeper stock market decline of October 29, 1929 became known as Black Tuesday and eclipsed the worldwide newspaper headlines. This rapidly spread from the U.S. to nearly all countries around the globe.

Practically all nations of the world, whether rich or poor, felt the tragic and crushing impacts of the Great Depression. International trade plummeted by as much as one half to two thirds of its previous level. Along with this, profits, personal incomes, tax revenues, and prices plunged. In the United States, unemployment soared to twenty-five percent, but in other countries, this level reached even thirty-three percent.

Cities all over the globe suffered especially, particularly those that relied on heavy industry as their economic mainstay. In a great number of nations, construction came practically to a stop. Even farming suffered terribly with the prices of produce crashing by around sixty percent. The areas that depended on industries in the primary sector took the worst hit, including logging, mining, and cash cropping. Job losses in these industries turned out to be among the worst.

A few nations' economies began recovering in the middle of the 1930's. For most countries around the world, the terrible consequences of the Great Depression remained until the outbreak of the Second World War. The military output required by the conflict rapidly increased production and employment everywhere.

Numerous events and problems caused the Great Depression's original economic collapse of 1929. Structural weaknesses were present, only waiting for particular events to turn the crash into a worldwide depression. It is particularly interesting how the contraction ran from one country to the next like a wildfire in a forest. Regarding the structural weaknesses of the 1929 economic contraction, historians are quick to point out that enormous and widespread bank failures only became worse as the stock market crashed. Others hold up specific monetary policy like the Federal Reserve in the United States contracting America's money supply, and the British Empire choosing to go back to the pre-World War I parity of the Gold Standard with one pound equal to $4.86.

Great Recession

The Great Recession proved to be the worst American and world wide economic downturn since the 1930's era Great Depression. It began within the U.S. in December of 2007 and is said to have ended in June of 2009 officially. There is ongoing debate with some economists as to whether the full effects of the Great Recession have really ceased, or this is merely a lull in between bouts of a greater depression.

The Great Recession started in the U.S. but later spread to most industrialized countries around the globe. This world wide recession led to a severe drop in trade and a significant drop in economic activity. The financial crisis of 2007-2010 actually kicked off the Great Recession.

The financial crisis and resulting Great Recession ultimately stemmed from irresponsible lending policies practiced by banks on a widespread level and encouraged by the U.S. and British governments. Along with this, the increasingly common practice of securitizing real estate and mortgages led to the financial collapse. Mortgage backed securities from the United States were promoted and sold around the globe. They turned out to be far more speculative and risky than anyone had predicted or disclosed.

Besides this, a worldwide boom in credit encouraged a speculative asset bubble in stocks and real estate. As prices continued to rise, the risky lending only grew more prevalent. The crisis actually flared up as a result of severe losses on sub prime loans that started in 2007. These demonstrated that other loans were also at risk amid too high real estate prices. As the loan losses continued to rise, Lehman Brothers suddenly collapsed on September 15th of 2008.

An enormous panic ensued in the inter-banking loan markets. With stock and real estate prices sharply declining, historical and major commercial and investment banking institutions throughout both the U.S. and Europe showed how much they had over extended themselves with major leverage as their losses quickly mounted. The governments of their home countries had to step in with enormous amounts of public tax dollars in order to save many of them from imminent bankruptcy.

This resulting Great Recession has led to a substantial decline in international trade, dropping commodity prices, and high and mounting unemployment around the world. Although the National Bureau of Economic Research declared the Great Recession officially over at the end of 2009, other economic experts are not convinced. Nobel prize winning economist Paul Krugman has said that this Great Recession heralds the start of a second Great Depression. Others who are less pessimistic have claimed that true recovery in the United States will not emerge until the end of 2011.

A number of events have been blamed for causing the financial crisis and Great Recession. The environment that preceded the crisis included an unnatural rise in asset prices along with an accompanying boom in worldwide economic demand. These are believed to have resulted from the multi-year period of too easily available credit, insufficient regulation, and poor oversight from the regulatory bodies who all too often simply looked the other way when times were good.

Grexit

Grexit is the clever abbreviation for the idea of a Greek exit from the Eurozone. The feared event of Greece returning to its old currency until 2001 the Drachma never occurred thanks to a variety of bailouts in exchange for austerity measures. This did not stop it from threatening to collapse several European banks which held Greek debt and infecting the sovereign bonds of other similarly afflicted countries like Spain and Portugal.

The global financial crisis pushed over Greece's precarious financial position. In 2009 in only the first quarter, the country's GDP plunged by 4.7%. At the same time its deficit skyrocketed to more than 12% of the national GDP. Credit downgrades were not long in following. All three of the major agencies Moody's, Standard and Poor's, and Fitch began downgrading Greek debt until S&P finally cut it to junk level in 2010. The resulting yields on 10 year Greek bonds rose to over 44% at their worst point in March of 2012.

The socialist government began a series of cuts to attempt to stabilize its shrinking finances. In the initial austerity measures the socialist party passed in 2009 they cut the spending and government jobs wages by 10% and raised the age for retirement. During the next three years, they passed other austerity packages that severely cut back pay for government jobs, laid off public workers, increased taxes, cut minimum wages, cut pensions, slashed defense and health spending, and loosened the procedures for laying off employees.

Not all of these measures were evenly implemented. Interest groups with powerful allies were able to stall the ones that impacted them while those impacting the poor and middle classes moved forward. Unemployment soared from slightly more than 10% to around 28% by September of 2013. More than 40% of Greek children live in poverty. Nearly 50% of ages 15 to 24 year old Greeks are unemployed.

In order to qualify for international help from the IMF and EU, Greece was told to cut its expenditures still further. They were forced to begin a series of humiliating austerity measures and to enact painful structural reforms in order to receive the bailout money that was needed to stave off financial collapse.

Prime Minister Papandreou asked for a bailout from the IMF and EU in April of 2010. These groups responded to the calls for help by approving a €110 billion over three years ($147 billion when offered) bailout. This represented the largest bailout of a sovereign nation in history. In order to receive it, Greece had to go through yet another series of agonizing austerity measures.

Greece needed still more help and in February of 2012 received approval for a second package of bailout money. The EU nations, the European Central Bank, and the IMF known collectively as the Troika increased their money to Greece by another $172 billion bringing them to a total of €246 billion worth $319 billion in those days. Greece was required to lower its debt down from the 160% GDP at the time to 120% by 2020. Greek bond holding banks took a 53.5% haircut on their bonds' face value. This amounted to as much as 75% loss of the real value of the debt.

Regular Greeks felt betrayed by their own leadership and the leaders of fellow Eurozone countries such as Chancellor Angela Merkel of Germany. Their economy continued to slide in and out of recessions. Greece finally reached the point of a referendum on the policies and austerity that had brought the country to this low point.

More than 60% of Greeks who voted rejected austerity in the results. This led to fears that Greece would drop out of the Euro if the demands of Syriza party leader and Prime Minister Alexis Tsipras for a better bailout package were not met. This departure from the Eurozone never materialized, as Greece continued to receive periodic monetary help and support from the Troika every quarter. Greeks never saw most of this $320 billion in bailout money, as it instead generally passed through the country on its way to repay holders of Greek debt.

Gross Domestic Product (GDP)

GDP stands for the entire value in dollars of all goods and services that have actually been produced within the nation in a particular period of time, commonly a year. A simpler way of putting GDP is how large the economy proves to be.

The Gross Domestic Product turns out to be among the most closely watched and important measurements for how healthy the economy is. GDP is commonly given out as a comparison against a prior year or quarter. When the financial news reports that the Gross Domestic Product has increased by three percent year on year, it is referring to the economy having expanded by three percent during the last year.

Coming up with the actual measurement of Gross Domestic Product is complex. In simplest terms, it is figured up in one of two methods. The income approach works by totaling up the earnings of all individuals in the country over a year. The expenditure approach simply tallies up the money that everyone in the nation spends over the year. It stands to reason that through both means you should come to approximately a similar total.

With the income approach, economists take all of the employees' compensation in the nation. They add this to all of the profits that both non incorporated, as well as incorporated, companies have made throughout the country. Finally they add on all taxes paid minus subsidies given. This is known as the GDP(I) method of calculation. The expenditure based means proves to be the more typically utilized method. To figure up GDP this way, all government spending, net exports, consumption, and investment in the country have to be tallied up together.

You can not overstate the importance of GDP to an economy's growth and production. Almost every person within the nation is massively impacted by gross domestic product. If an economy is in good shape, then wages will rise and unemployment will prove to be low as businesses require greater quantities of labor in order to produce to keep up with the expanding economy. Major changes to Gross Domestic Product, revised to the downside or upside , have significant repercussions for the stock markets. The reasons for this are simple to grasp.

Economies that are contracting translate to smaller amounts of profits for corporations. This leads to lower prices for stocks. Investors also become nervous about decreasing growth in GDP, since it commonly means that the nation's economy is falling into recession or is already in a recession.

Conversely, economies that are expanding signify that corporations' profits in general will be higher. Investors bid stock prices up on this news as they become increasingly confident in the future economic prospects. Because of these effects of Gross Domestic Product on peoples' lives, it could be said to be the most significant economic measurement for all of the people in the country in general.

Hyperinflation

In the field of economics, hyperinflation proves to be inflation, or rising prices over time, that is extremely high and even beyond controlling. This state of the economy exists as the overall levels of pricing in a certain country are rising sharply and quickly at the same time as the actual values of these economic goods remain roughly the same price as measured in other more stable currencies. In other words, the nation's own currency is diminishing in value rapidly, commonly at rate that grows in pace.

The IASB, or International Accounting Standards Board, gives a precise definition of hyperinflation. They state that when the rate of inflation during three cumulative years nears one hundred percent total, or at least twenty-six percent each year compounded annually for three consecutive years, then hyperinflation has been reached. Other economists such as Cagan have declared hyperinflation to be when inflation is greater than fifty percent each month. Hyperinflation can witness the overall price levels go up by five to ten percent and higher even in single days for extended periods of time. This stands in sharp contrast to regular inflation which is commonly only reported over a quarterly or annual basis.

As greater and greater amounts of inflation are created in each printing of money instance, a truly vicious cycle takes effect. Such hyperinflation is clearly evident as the money supply grows at an uninterrupted rate. It is typically seen alongside the population's unwillingness to keep the hyper-inflationary currency for any longer than they have to in order to use it for any hard good that will prevent them from losing more actual purchasing power. Hyperinflation is typically a part of wars and their after effects, social or political upheavals, and currency meltdowns such as seen in Zimbabwe.

Hyperinflation is a phenomenon that is unique to fiat currencies that are not backed up by anything but a government's faith and trust. As the money supply is not limited by normal restraints like gold in a vault, it is instead run by a paper money standard. The supply of it is completely dependent on the discretion of the government.

Hyperinflation commonly leads to intense and long lasting economic depressions. This is not always the case though. In Brazil which suffered in the grips of hyperinflation for thirty years in the 1964 to 1994 period, the government managed to avoid economic collapse by valuing all non-monetary goods, services, and investments for the whole economy in an involved index. The government supplied this daily updated index that they measured with the daily Brazilian currency against the United States dollar.

In contrast to Brazil, Zimbabwe did not bother to set up such an index measured against the dollar. They did offer the day by day changes in the U.S. dollar as a comparison for everyone in the country to see. This voluntary comparison only served to worsen the problem and finally destroyed the real value of non monetary items that did not get updated as expressed against the Zimbabwe dollar. All monetary items in the country finally lost every bit of value during the hyper-inflationary meltdown.

Import

In simple terms, imports are goods that are utilized in one country that were produced in another country. The term import refers to the idea of bringing goods and services into a nation. It originally came from the concept of bringing these things into a port via ships. A person who is engaged in the practice of bringing these goods and services into the other country is called an importer. Importers live and are based in the country into which they bring these goods and services.

Export is the opposite of import. It refers to sending the goods made in one country abroad to the importing country. Exporters are based overseas from the importer and importing country.

Imports are then any items, such as commodities or goods, or alternatively services that are brought to a country from a different country in legitimate means. They are commonly used for trade purposes. Such goods are then put on sale to people in the importing country. Foreign manufacturers make such goods and services that are then offered to the domestic consumers of the importing country. Imports for the country receiving them are the exports of a country that sends them.

International trade is actually based on such imports and exports. Importing any goods commonly means dealing with customs agencies in both exporting and importing nations. Imports can be subjected to trade agreements, tariffs, or quotas much of the time.

Imports can refer to more than simply services or goods that have been brought into the country. They can also be the resulting measured economic worth of any goods and services that are being imported. Such imports' values are measured over periods of time, such as monthly, quarterly, or yearly. The abbreviation of I represents the value of such imports in macroeconomics.

From an economic strength point of view, imports are considered to be somewhat negative. Exports are nearly always regarded as positive, since they represent produced items that are being sold to others for currency consideration. When a nation's imports are greater than their exports, this leads to a trade imbalance, or trade deficit. Such trade imbalances must be paid for with something eventually. Much of the time it ends up being debt instruments that are exported back to the countries from which the imports come. Countries like the United States and Great Britain are guilty of having significantly greater values of imports than exports. They commonly run large trade deficits.

Import Quotas

Import quotas are numerical restrictions which a government of one country imposes on the imports of another competing nation. The main purpose of such quotas lies in decreasing imports while simultaneously boosting a country's own inherent domestic production. With the numbers of such imports restricted, the price of these imports will increase. This then fosters the production, purchase, and consumption of more domestically-produced goods and services by a nation's own consumers.

Import quotas prove to be among three of the most common foreign trade policies utilized to discourage imports while encouraging exports. Besides these are export subsidies and tariffs. National governments undertake to enforce these quotas as foreign trade policies. They are enacted with the intention of defending domestic production through limiting foreign competition.

Quotas in general are typically quantity limitations which a group slaps on activities, services, and goods. Employers typically run into hiring quotas for different national groups of people. Sales representatives also face such quotas in their sales activities and endeavors.

This is why import quotas as an extension of this idea are simply the foreign sector amount of imports which a domestic government will permit in a given industry or service sector. By increasing the numbers of domestically-produced goods in an economy while discouraging the numbers of competing imports, a nation's consumers are prompted to buy home-produced goods and services instead of foreign-based and -produced ones.

There are five principal reasons why import quotas are sometimes imposed on foreign imports of goods and services. The political pressure is such that domestic employment has to be protected and encouraged. Many domestic jobs proponents fear the competition of low foreign wages. By decreasing the number of imports from such countries, governments are able to lower the playing field for higher and better paid domestic employees.

Governments can also be concerned about unfair trade practices and infant industry worries. Unfair trade means that the foreign-created imports could be dumped at prices which are lower than possible production costs. Foreign exporters would do this temporarily in a market in order to reduce the ability of domestic producers to effectively compete and remain in business at the same time. China has been a major practitioner of dumping and unfair trade practices in industries such as steel around the world in the past. Infant industry refers to a comparatively new domestic industry which has not grown up sufficiently in order to benefit from the necessary economies of scale. Import quotas serve to safeguard this infantile industry while it develops and grows from cheaper and more efficient competition overseas.

A final motivating factor for import quotas revolves around the quite complex idea of national security. These quotas could be employed to discourage imports while encouraging domestic production of those goods which are called crucial for the nation's security and ultimate survival of its national economy. The military hardware production industry is one such example of a sector which many nations are eager to protect from less expensive foreign competition.

Economists are divided on the net effect and overall effectiveness of import quotas as they pertain to foreign trade and government policies. They do tend to help out the domestic economy for which they are the most advantageous. Domestic firms which are struggling against competition from stronger foreign competitors are most likely backers of such policies. The national companies see benefits from greater sales and profits, as well as additional income for the owners of the resources and factors of production. The problem with boosting domestic prices by restricting consumers' access to foreign imports is that such foreign trade policies will hurt the domestic consumers by increasing prices in stores and reducing both the ultimate quality and available choices offered.

Income Distribution

Income distribution proves to be the way that a country's entire gross domestic product is actually shared out among all members of the population. This has long been a main concern of the study of economics and related governmental economic policies. The classical economists of the discipline such as Adam Smith, David Ricardo, and Thomas Malthus were principally concerned about the factor of income distribution. This refers to the actual distribution of income as it pertains to the principal factors of production, such as capital, labor, and land.

More modern day economists have similarly turned their attentions to the topic in recent decades. They have been mostly preoccupied with the income distribution as it pertains to both households and individual consumers in economies. There are many public policy issues which involve such relationships as those of economic growth and income inequality. These have led to the creation of various measurements to analyze income distribution in a society and economy. Chief among these is the Lorenz Curve representation. It is correlated closely with such income inequality measurements as the highly respected and internationally utilized Gini coefficient.

There are many different related causes of and factors leading to income inequality in the world today. Some of the more important ones prove to be tax and other economic policies, fiscal policies, monetary policies by central banks such as the Federal Reserve and Bank of England, labor union policies, the labor market in given industries and regions, individual skills sets of specific workers, impacts of automation and technology, the negative effects of globalization, educational levels of workers in different regions and countries, race, gender, and culture.

Thanks to such useful concepts as the pervasive Gini coefficients, a few well respected organizations including especially the United States' Central Intelligence Agency and the international body the United Nations have been able to measure actual levels of income inequality on a country to country comparison basis.

The World Bank similarly employs the Gini coefficient index as it has consistently proven to be a dependable and accurate index measurement for comparing and contrasting income distribution on a nation by nation basis. This widespread index runs a measurement gamut of from 0 to 1. On this scale, 0 represents complete equality, while 1 depicts total inequality in the society or economy in question. As of the year 2016, the world's Gini index measures fittingly at 0.52.

Income inequality may be looked at through two different statistical approaches. These are intra country inequality that looks at the conditions within the nation itself. The other is inter country inequality that amounts to the various inequality levels between one country and the next one.

A May of 2011 report that the OECD researched and published demonstrated a disturbing trend regarding income inequality and income distribution among the OECD developed nations. The income gap between poor and rich in these developed nations, practically all of which represent the high income economies, "has reached its highest level for over 30 years, and governments must act quickly to tackle inequality."

The United States is a classic example of this troubling point. Income in America has become so unevenly distributed throughout the prior 30 years that the earners of the top quintile 20 percent now earn a greater share than the combined four quintiles or bottom 80 percent together do. This is the kind of dangerous and damaging statistic upon which violent class based revolutions are built.

Indemnity

Indemnity refers to financial compensation for loss or damages incurred by an individual or business. It comes from the original Latin word indemnis which translates to "without loss" and "undamaged" or "unhurt." The idea behind it springs from the premise of a contract between two groups, businesses, or individuals. One party will invariably promise to cover any possible damages or losses that they other party causes. When used in a legal setting, the word also pertains to the idea of gaining an exemption from being liable for damages. In the nation of Canada, the word means the salary which parliamentarians receive.

Insurance is a classic example of such indemnity. In these financial contracts, the insurer (who is the indemnitor) promises to provide compensation to the insured (who is the indemnitee) against any losses or damages. In exchange for this pledge, the insured will pay pre-arranged and agreed upon premiums to the insurer. Insurance contracts would not exist without such clauses.

These agreements will also feature a period of indemnity. This refers to the set time frame in which the guarantee is binding. There are also such contracts that provide letters of indemnity. These guarantee that the stipulations of the contract will be adhered to by both parties. If they are not, then indemnities have to be paid by the contract breaching party.

Clearly such indemnities are commonplace with contracts struck between businesses and individuals, as with insurance companies and their customers. On far grander scales, they are also prevalent in deals made between governments and companies, as well as in agreements made between governments of multiple nations.

There is also Indemnity Insurance. With such a policy, businesses and individuals are able to obtain protection in the event of any claims. Such a policy safeguards the policy holder from the necessity of having to pay out a large sum in indemnities. It does not matter if the policy holder is ultimately at fault or not. A great number of corporations require such insurance because of all the frivolous lawsuits in the United States.

There are countless examples of everyday insurance needs in this respect. Malpractice insurance and E&O errors and omissions insurance are two of the most common. Malpractice insurance is issued to protect medical providers. E&O insurance protects corporations and employees of the company in case customers make any claims against them. Other companies are so concerned about this problem of being held responsible that they pay for Deferred Compensation Indemnity Insurance. This forward-thinking policy actually safeguards money which the firm anticipates earning at some point and time in the future.

These specific insurance policies provide for the various costs associated with such a claim. This includes such expenses as settlements, fees, and the legal and court costs. The insurance amount may not cover the entire costs though. The particular limitations in dollars and types of fees will be specified by the policy itself and is often based upon past claims.

There are also indemnity clauses where property leases are concerned. Tenants who obtain a rental property will be responsible for any damages which arise from their own negligence, fines they incur, and associated legal fees. Each agreement will specify the particulars.

The concept surrounding indemnities dates back hundreds of years. The New York Times revealed in an 1825 article entitled, "French President Makes Unprecedented State Visit to Haiti" that the country was being required to pay to France a debt to cover French plantation owner losses because of the destruction of their plantation lands and the emancipation of their slaves.

Winning nations also exact war indemnities from losing countries after the end of many conflicts. Some of these war reparations required from years to decades to pay. The best remembered example of such long-lasting indemnities is the one which Germany had to pay for its part in starting and prosecuting the First World War. It took until 2010 for Germany to finally finish paying the war reparation debt, as the New York Times told in its piece from that same year, "Ending the War to End All Wars." This was almost a century after they began paying it.

Inequality

Inequality refers to a form of social ill that happens across countries as the national resources become unfairly and unevenly distributed. This happens as the normal allocation of resources occurs and creates classes of haves and have not's. Patterns of resource distribution typically occur according to social categories. Distribution of socially demanded goods occurs because of societal forces including religion, power, prestige, kinship, ethnicity, race, age, gender, and class.

There are also a range of social rights which fall under the topic of social inequality. These include access to labor markets and high quality jobs, health care, sources of income, equivalent education, freedom of speech, political participation, and fair political representation. Social inequality is closely connected to economic inequality. It stems from the uneven wealth and/or income distribution.

It is the social sciences of sociology and economics that study and create theories to understand and describe economic and social inequalities. These two disciplines work independently of one another to research unequal situations within society. They have also determined that both natural and social resources are also unfairly distributed in the vast majority of societies. This reinforces the concept of social status.

Regular means for allocating resources impact the distribution of a range of ideas and assets. These include privileges, rights, societal power, and access to publically distributed resources. Among the public resources which are impacted are justice, education, transportation, basic housing, financial and credit services, and banking opportunities. It stands out in glaring opposition to the idea of meritocracies which many nations of the world profess to encourage.

Meritocracy is the idea that economies and societies will only distribute their various resources based on the merit of every individual. Michael Young came up with this phrase with his "The Rise of Meritocracy" essay he penned in 1958. In this he showed how the idea among the elites that they succeed only because of their merits was somewhat fallacious but widespread.

Young described merit as the combination of intelligence plus effort. He feared that the British educational system which relied heavily on test scoring, quantification, and qualifications would lead to the rise of a middle class elite which was highly educated while the working class education would be inferior. This would lead to social injustice and finally a revolution in developed nations like the United Kingdom. His idea has been updated by the series 3%.

In fact, reality shows that resources are distributed along the lines of a hierarchical social arrangement. This is the way that resources are actually doled out, despite the fact that talent, intelligence, and other meritorious accomplishments are supposed to dictate resource distribution to a significant and meaningful point. The truth is that social injustice is closely connected to ethnic, racial, and gender inequality now as it always has been throughout history.

The Gini Coefficient proves to be the most heavily cited measurement for comparing and contrasting various forms of social injustice. This coefficient quantifies the income and wealth concentration in a given country using a scale of from 0 to 1. Zero equals completely evenly distributed income and wealth, while one means that a single person possesses all income and wealth in a particular country and society. The limitation to the Gini Coefficient is that despite the fact that two countries can possess the same exact coefficient, they may still showcase sharply different qualities of life and economic outputs.

Inflation

Inflation proves to be prices rising over time. It is specifically measured as the increase in a given basket of goods and services' prices. These goods and services are taken to represent the entire economy. Inflation is also the going up in cost of the average prices of goods and services as measured by the CPI, or consumer price index. The opposite of inflation is known as deflation. Deflation turns out to be the falling of an average level of prices. The point that separates the two from each other, both deflation and inflation, is price stability, or no change in the costs of goods and services.

Inflation has almost everything to do with the amount of money available. It is inextricably tied to the money supply. This gives rise to the popularly remarked observation that inflation is actually an excessive number of dollars chasing too small a quantity of goods. Comprehending the way that this works is easier when considering an example.

Pretend for a moment that the world possessed only two commodities: oranges that are gathered up from orange trees and paper money created by government. In seasons where rain is limited and the oranges are few as a result, the cost of oranges should go up. This is because the same number of printed dollars would be competing for a smaller number of oranges.

On the other hand, if a bumper crop of oranges are seen, then the cost of oranges should drop, since the sellers of oranges have no choice but to cut prices to sell off their large inventory of oranges. These two examples illustrate inflation in the former and deflation in the latter. The main difference between the real world and this example is that inflation measures changes in the price movement on average of many or all goods and services, and not simply one.

The quantity of money in an economy similarly impacts the amount of inflation present at any given time. Should the government in the example above choose to print enormous amounts of money, then there will be many dollars for a relatively constant number of oranges, as in the lack of rain scenario. So inflation is created by the number of dollars going up against the quantities of oranges that exist, or overall goods and services existing. Deflation, as the opposite of inflation, would be the numbers of dollars dropping compared to the quantity of oranges available.

Because of this, levels of inflation result from four different factors that often work together in combination. The demand for money could drop. The supply of money could expand. The available supply of various other goods might decline. Finally, the demand for other goods increases.

Even though these four factors do work in correlation, economists say that inflation is mostly a currency driven event. This means that in the vast majority of cases, it results from governments tampering with the money supply. Generally, they do this by over printing their own currency to have money to pay for spending, resulting in higher inflation.

Inflationary Bias

Inflationary Bias refers to the opposite of deflationary bias. Both of these are government monetary and/or fiscal policy prejudices. Governments are forced to take one of two positions with reference to their monetary policy and interventions in an economy. Inflationary bias turns out to be the one which the vast majority of central banks and sovereign nation policy makers pursue for several important reasons.

Such an Inflationary Bias results from discretionary policies of national governments. If they are utilized properly with regards to the labor market, these biases cause a higher than ideal inflation level without leading to any transitions in income increases. At the same time, this bias results from the goals of those nations which are saddled with public debt levels. They would pursue these policies with a goal of fostering inflation over the medium to longer term.

There are economic theories that persuasively argue governments have a natural affinity for and tendency towards Inflationary Bias policies. The Barro-Gordon model demonstrates that the government's ability to manipulate the economy will cause it to skew towards a bias that is inflationary by nature. According to such a model, countries will try to maintain the country's national unemployment rates at lower than the naturally occurring levels. This causes a wage and price inflation that is higher than their normally occurring level. In the end, this will lead to an aggregate inflationary level that proves to be greater than the normal level of inflation.

The economic theories that are more traditional also suggest that this Inflationary Bias will be present any time that fiscal and monetary policies become enacted at the discretion of the policy makers and central bankers instead of being rules based. Still other economists argue that this bias will even be present if the policy makers are not bent on reducing unemployment to lower than normal levels and even if the policies operate off of rules instead.

As there are so many perils from such Inflationary Biases, economists have suggested a variety of measures to stop it from occurring. Some of them have argued for appointing only conservatively ideological central bankers. According to these arguments, the countries ought to set out aimed for inflationary targets and goals. When these rates of inflation are surpassed by real economic data releases, there could be a punishment of some type given out to the central bankers.

In truth and point of fact, the majority of important countries now do state their optimal inflation rate targets in their policy setting meetings, press conferences, and notes from closed door meetings alike. For most Western nation policy makers and central banks like the United States Federal Reserve, Great Britain's Bank of England, the Euro Zone's European Central Bank, and the Japanese Central Bank, this level amounts to a desired two percent inflation target over the medium to long term time frame.

For those nations that opt to go with the opposite of an inflationary bias, the only other choice is the deflationary bias. The problem with deflationary biases is that they only work for countries, businesses, and consumers which are not saddled down with enormous debt levels. This is because a deflationary bias will cause debts to progressively cost more in real terms over time even as they reward savers and creditors. Governments are especially afraid of this policy bias as they are mostly running budgetary deficits year in and year out. Only a handful of countries run government budget surpluses in point of fact.

Interbank Market

The Interbank Market refers to the modern day financial system which involves banks trading cash and other instruments with other financial institutions and banks. This never involves banks trading money with non-financial businesses, consumers, or retail investors. It is possible for interbank trading to be pursued by banks for the benefit of their bigger customers, yet in general such trading between banks proves to be proprietary. This means that it happens between banks on the behalf of their own company accounts.

Interbank markets also involve FOREX foreign exchange services in a commercial capacity of buying and selling currency pair investments. There can be long-term trading as well as huge quantities of shorter term, speculative nature currency trading. The Bank of International Settlements stated in information which they compiled and analyzed in 2004 that around fifty percent of all transactions on the world FOREX markets are strictly interbank market trade.

It was after the failure of the Bretton Woods agreement and the catastrophic decision of then-American President Richard Nixon to abandon the gold standard back in 1971 that the present-day form of the interbank market arose and developed. Currency exchange rates for the majority of the big and economically important industrial countries became freely floating at this time. It was only on occasion that the various national governments chose to intervene in the interbank markets where their own currencies were concerned.

These markets do not have any central or single location or authority. Instead, the trading occurs all over the world in every time zone and during six days per week from Sunday afternoon through Friday afternoon. The only exceptions to this schedule are the few internationally and unanimously recognized holidays, such as New Year's Day.

The arrival of this new floating rate system of exchange happened to occur as the inexpensive computer systems and program revolution emerged. This happy coincidence permitted for quickly executed, globally-based exchange trading for the first time in history. At first, voice brokers utilized the phone and later fax machines to match up sellers and buyers in these earliest days of the interbank FOREX trading. These eventually became replaced by the new fast and far more cost-effective computer systems.

The computer systems which became connected by the Internet in time could scan huge volumes of traders and obtain the most optimal price in this way. Thanks to both Bloomberg and Reuters who created impressive trading systems which became ubiquitous around the world, banks gained the ability to trade literally billions of dollars in transactions at the same time. On the busiest days in the FOREX and interbank markets nowadays, daily trading volume exceeds more than $6 trillion.

The biggest market participants are the interbank market makers. Such financial institutions have to be both willing and able to extend pricing to other players in the market besides requesting prices for themselves and their own interest in trades. Interbank market deals have minimums which start at $5 million. The majority of transactions are vastly larger. Sometimes they exceed a full billion dollars in only a single transaction. The biggest players in the interbank markets by far are United States market makers JP Morgan Chase Bank and Citicorp, German and European market maker Deutsche Bank, and Asian market maker (London- based) HSBC.

The majority of such spot transactions agreed on the interbank markets will settle two business days following the trade execution. The biggest exception to this policy lies with the American dollar versus the Canadian dollar. It settles the following day. This settlement delay requires banks to maintain extensive credit lines (even when these are current spot trades) with their peer financial institutions so that they can trade continuously.

To lower the risks inherent with settlement, most banks engage in netting agreements. These agreements require that an offsetting transaction must be done within the identical currency pair which will settle on the exact same day as the opposing transaction. In such a way, the banks are able to drastically reduce the quantity of money which must change hands, as well as the default risks which could happen if one trading bank suddenly and unexpectedly encountered financial problems.

International Monetary Fund (IMF)

The International Monetary Fund represents an international organization with membership of 189 different countries. As such it counts nearly all countries of the world among its almost global membership. This IMF seeks to achieve financial stability, helps to encourage worldwide monetary cooperation, pushes for economic growth that is sustainable and for high unemployment, helps to facilitate international trade, and attempts to lessen poverty throughout the world.

Members of the United Nations created the International Monetary Fund back in 1945 as a result of the idea initially conceived of at the important Bretton Woods UN conference held in New Jersey in the United States in July of 1944. Originally 44 nations attended this conference and looked for ways to rebuild the global economy. They wanted to create a way of fostering economic cooperation. The group collectively hoped to not repeat the mistakes of the 1930s. A currency devaluing race to the bottom had led to the Great Depression in those years.

There were a number of original goals for the IMF. The organization was to encourage stability of exchange rates and monetary cooperation on an international scale. They were to promote and aid in the growth of a balanced international trade. IMF also had to help build up a system for balance of payments that was multilateral in scope. They also were designed to provide emergency resources to member states that suffered from problems with their balance of payments. Safeguards on the resources loaned out would b required.

With the early 1970's dissolution of the fixed exchange rates based on the gold standard set up at the Bretton Woods conference, their role changed some. They were no longer responsible for stable exchange rates and a balance of payments system based on pegged exchange rates. They became more of an organization that helps out member states in emergency economic need.

Today the IMF counts among its largest emergency borrowers Greece, Portugal, Ukraine, and Ireland. It also issues precautionary loans to members who may need to borrow based on particular conditions within their countries. The countries with the largest precautionary loan amounts agreed on include Poland, Mexico, Colombia, and Morocco. Between the two groups, the IMF has committed itself to $163 billion. Of this amount $137 billion has not yet been drawn.

The International Monetary Fund still works to safeguard the global monetary system. They watch over the system of international payments and free floating exchange rates so that nations and their populations can engage in transactions with each other. In 2012, the fund received an expanded mandate in part as a result of the chaos in the Great Recession. This bigger mandate includes all issues pertaining to the financial sectors and all macroeconomic issues that have to do with global stability.

The International Monetary Fund has its headquarters in Washington, D.C. Their governance is by an executive board. The board is made up of 24 directors. Each of these directors represents either a group of nations or a single nation. The IMF maintains a global staff of 2,600 individuals who hail from 147 different countries.

The majority of the IMF's money comes from its quota system. Every member is given a quota that they must contribute. This amount is based on the nation's economic size in the global economy. The member state's maximum contributions are limited to this quota. When countries join, they pay as much as one-quarter of their quota in a widely traded foreign currency like the pound, euro, dollar, or yen or as SDR Special Drawing Rights made up of a basket of these currencies. The other three-quarters they pay from their own currency.

John Maynard Keynes

John Maynard Keynes proved to be the English economist, professor, and journalist who also served in British government as a key economic advisor at the powerful British Treasury department. He has become best remembered for his at-the-time influential Keynesian economics. These theories had to do with the reasons for and solutions to long term unemployment.

Keynes was born to a middle class family of moderately successful prosperity on June 5th of 1883 in the famed university town of Cambridge, England. The man is best known for his economic theories that are still called after his name as "Keynesian economics." He wrote a critically important work entitled, The General Theory of Employment, Interest and Money from 1935-1936. This treatise argued that government-pushed policies of full employment could cure economic recessions. It has been called among the most influential books in all human history.

John Maynard Keynes had an academic for a father that helped to propel his lifelong passion for learning, teaching, research, and public service. John Neville Keynes his father served as economist and eventually academic administrator at the world-renowned King's College of Cambridge University. Even his mother could claim to be among the very first women graduates from Cambridge. Keynes attended the historic and prestigious university himself beginning in 1902. While studying there, Keynes came under the influence of economist Alfred Marshall. Marshall had such an impact on John that he switched from the classics and math studies to economics and politics.

In the 1920s, Keynes began to write pieces which were increasingly skeptical of the then-dominant laissez-faire style of economics that was very gently overseen by minor public policies. He stood against Britain returning back to the gold standard at a fixed rate in 1925 and demonstrated his concern about the long-term unemployment problems experienced by British textile workers, shipyard employees, and coal miners even before the Great Depression erupted.

Once Keynes wrote his internationally accepted greatest work The General

Theory of Employment, Interest and Money, he became the most influential economist of his time. In this magnum opus, he argued for an economic solution utilizing programs of government-sponsored or -provided jobs to solve the persistent and sky-high unemployment. Some critics have argued that his book was unclear enough that no one is actually sure what Keynes was really trying to say. His arguments seemed to be that reducing the rates of wages would not help governments to lower unemployment. Instead, it would take government spending increases to lower unemployment. This would lead to a budget deficit, which he claimed would be a necessary evil in order to solve these terrible economic and social problems of the time. World governments were eager to find reasons to boost their spending. This explains why they adopted all of his principal views with enthusiasm. The majority of his academic peers also ascribed to his ideas in the 1930s and 1940s.

Yet weaknesses in Keynes theories would emerge as reality challenged it repeatedly. He himself argued that his policies would only work optimally in a society that was totalitarian. From the later 1940s through the later 1980s his economic model remained a central tenet of economics and such textbooks. Yet economists finally began to move away from unemployment problem fixation and on to economic growth issues. As they learned more about the links between inflation and unemployment, his once-widely touted model lost its importance.

John Maynard Keynes is well-remembered for two major services to Great Britain and the world just before he died. He was a prominent figure at the post World War II and international order-establishing Bretton Woods Conference held in 1944 in the United States. Though he was not the main force behind the World Bank and International Monetary Fund agencies, he definitely played a role in the financial architecture of the world this conference established. The final major public role he carried out lay in his successful negotiation for Britain of a multiple billion dollar loan from its war ally the United States in 1945. Keynes died the next year.

Joseph Stieglitz

Joseph Eugene Stieglitz is an American-born professor of economics at Columbia University who is also regarded as the fourth most influential economist in the world. This is based on the number of citations individuals have used sourcing him in papers, government reports, and other areas of academic work.

He has received the world renowned Nobel Memorial Prize in Economics Sciences back in 2001 as well as the John Bates Clark Medal in 1979. He has served as former Senior Vice President and also Chief Economist at the Work Bank. Stieglitz also counts a stint at the Council of Economic Advisers for the United States president on his resume, where he served initially as a member and then finally in the prestigious role of chairman.

Controversial at times, Joseph Stieglitz has been an ardent support of Georgist public finance theory and critical in his viewpoints on the ineffectual management of globalization in the world today along with economists who espouse laissez-faire economic policies. He refers to these individuals by the tongue in cheek label of "free market fundamentalists." He is similarly critical of the World Bank and the International Monetary Fund, though he served even as Chief Economist and Senior VP at the former.

At the turn of the new millennium in 2000, Joseph Stieglitz established the Columbia University think tank known as the IPD Initiative for Policy Dialogue to ponder weighty issues of international development. He served on the faculty of ivy league school Columbia University from 2001 on. He has received the greatest academic rank which the university has to bestow back in 2003 as university professor. As the founding chairman of Columbia University's Committee on Global Thought, he similarly chairs the Brooks World Poverty Institute at the University of Manchester. Stieglitz has been a distinguished member of the Pontifical Academy of Social Sciences for years.

The then United Nations General Assembly President Miguel d' Escoto Brockmann appointed Stieglitz as chairman for the United Nations Commission on Reforms of the International Monetary and Financial

System in 2009 at the height of the global financial crisis. This financial collapse from which the world has still not completely recovered originated within the United States at the fall of Lehman Brothers. In this capacity, he provided oversight and participation on proposals and a report which made recommendations on reforming the international financial and monetary systems.

Joseph Stieglitz has also managed to amass fame with other nations' political leadership as well as in the United States and United Nations. He worked as the chair for the international Commission on the Measurement of Economic Performance and Social Progress which French President Nicholas Sarkozy established. They issued their official report entitled Mismeasuring Our Lives: Why the GDP Doesn't Add Up back in 2010. Presently, Joseph Stieglitz serves as the co-chairman for the successor organization called the High Level Expert Group on the Measurement of Economic Performance and Social Progress.

During the years 2011 to 2014, Joseph Stieglitz also worked as the International Economic Association IEA's President. He led the organization in its triennial world congress which occurred in a resort near the Dead Sea in Jordan back in June of 2014.

For academic recognition and international accolades, no living economist today compares with Joseph Stieglitz. He has been awarded over 40 honorary degrees, including from such internationally prestigious schools as Britain's legendary Oxford University and Cambridge University, and America's gold standard school Harvard University. He has received decorations from a range of governments including France, Korea, Ecuador, and Colombia. The French president appointed him to the Legion of Honor, Order Officer, as a member.

Time Magazine has named Joseph Stieglitz in 2011 as a member of their 100 Most Influential People in the World list. The man has written a range of books including the most recent *The Great Divide: Unequal Societies and What We Can Do About Them* from 2015, *Rewriting the Rules of the American Economy: An Agenda for Growth and Shared Prosperity* from 2015, and *Creating a Learning Society: A New Approach to Growth Development and Social Progress* in 2014.

Keating Five

The Keating Five refers to a corruption scandal of 1989. At the time, five important United States Senators were accused of corruption related to the Savings and Loan crisis in 1989. This political scandal came to represent all that Americans found (and still today find) wrong with their nationally elected congressional representatives. The five senators implicated as part of this Keating Five Scandal were California Democrat Alan Cranston, Arizona Democrat Dennis DeConcini, Ohio Democrat and former astronaut John Glenn, Arizona Republican John McCain, and Michigan Democrat Donald W. Riegle, Jr.

The five Senators endured serious accusations of having unethically involved themselves on the material behalf of banker Charles H. Keating, Jr. who was then Chairman of the Lincoln Savings and Loan Association in 1987. This bank became the subject of a more than routine regulatory investigation run by the Federal Home Loan Bank Board, the FHLBB. This government group later backed away from acting against the bank, apparently without sufficient reasoning.

Naturally the investigation revived two years later in 1989 as the Lincoln Savings and Loan institution spectacularly collapsed to the tune of a $3 billion loss to the federal government. An incredible 23,000 plus bondholders of the bank suffered wipeout losses along with countless investors who saw their entire life savings evaporate overnight. What caught the attention of journalists who investigated the mess were the major political donations Mr. Keating had directed to the campaigns of five senators. These questionably generous donations amounted to $1.3 million.

The Senate Ethics Committee began a long-running investigation into pressure which it was alleged the Keating 5 had brought to bear two years earlier on the FHLBB. Three of the five accused Senators, Cranston, DeConcini, and Riegle, were found guilty of unethically interfering with the government investigation of the bank that might have allowed them to wind down the bank before it imploded at a loss of billions of dollars. Of the three, only Senator Cranston received an official reprimand from the Senate. Both Senators John McCain and John Glenn were fully cleared of any charges of wrongdoing by the investigatory committee. Yet the two men still received a minor slap on the wrist in being told that they had "exercised poor judgment" in being at all involved.

Each of the Keating Five senators was allowed to serve out their remaining Senate terms. When it was time for reelection, both McCain and Glenn ran again. The two men each held onto their seats. McCain emerged apparently unscathed, as he was able to run for the President of the United States twice, emerging as the official 2008 campaign Republic Party nominee.

The Keating and Lincoln Savings scandal became a symbol of all that was inherently crooked about the financial system and ethics in American society. In the spring of 1992, a playing cards deck had been created, marketed, and sold under the name of the "Savings and Loan Scandal." On the card faces were Charles Keating, Jr. holding up his hand. For the faces of the puppets on each of his fingers were the portraits of the Keating Five Senators.

Polls were taken which demonstrated that the majority of American found the doings of these five Senators to be only typical of the actions of Congress in general. Even political historian Lewis Gould wrote about it that "the real problem for the Keating Three who were most involved was that they had been caught."

Key Performance Indicator (KPI)

Key Performance Indicators are measurements that aid companies and other organizations in assessing the progress they are making towards their key goals. It is important for any organization to start out by deciding on its mission and determining its goals. Once they have done this effectively, they can decide on the best means of measuring their incremental progress to reaching the goals.

A characteristic of Key Performance Indicators is that they are measurements that are quantifiable. They must also be relevant to the organization's particular benchmarks of success. These will be different for various organizations. A business and a community service organization will not have the same KPIs.

Businesses could have KPIs that relate to their total profits or amount of income that they derive from repeat customers. Customer service departments could use KPIs that measure the number of calls they answer in under a minute. Schools' Key Performance Indicators could center on the percentages of students who graduate. Community service organizations might look at a KPI that revolves around the number of individuals they are able to assist in a given year.

There is no one right or wrong Key Performance Indicator. KPIs only need to be measurable, relevant to the goals of the organization, and a core part of the group's success. As an outfit's goals evolve or are met, the KPI goals may shift as well.

Key Performance Indicators have to be definable and measurable to be useful. It is no good setting a KPI that is subjective or a matter of opinion. Their definitions also should be consistent year in and year out. This is the only way that the targets set for each KPI will be meaningful.

If a company sets a goal to be the best employer, then they might use their company Turnover Rate each year as a Key Performance Indicator. This will work so long as they are using the same turnover rate definition and measurement each year. Reducing turnover by a certain percent annually is an understandable goal that different departments can act on and address.

Another important attribute of these Key Performance Indicators is that they have to be relevant to the organization and its goals. A business whose goal is to become the most profitable company in the sector will need to use KPIs that address profits and relevant finances. They might choose profits before taxes. Schools that are not interested in turning profits would not utilize such KPIs.

For Key Performance Indicators to be helpful they also need to be a core part of an organization's success. KPIs are only practical so long as they relate to the elements that the organization needs to work on so that they can attain the goals. Another important facet of these KPIs is that there should not be too many of them.

The idea is for the members of the organization to be able to focus on the identical Key Performance Indicators. It is possible for the organization as a whole to have three to five KPIs while departments have several others that help to support the overall goals. So long as these goals can be neatly categorized under the company's larger ones, this is acceptable.

Key Performance Indicators make a good tool for performance management. When everyone in the organization is aware of the goals, then they can take appropriate steps to help reach them. KPIs can be posted on company websites, in employee break rooms, and in company conference rooms. All of the activities of the members of the organization should be focused towards meeting or even surpassing those KPI goals.

Keynesian Economics

Keynesian economics represents a system of economic ideas that the British economist John Maynard Keynes developed in the first half of the twentieth century. Keynes became best known for his easy to understand and straight forward arguments for the underlying causes of the Great Depression.

His theories of economics found their basis in the concept of the circular flows of money. As his ideas became more and more widely accepted, they led to a range of intervening economic policies towards the end of the Great Depression, particularly in the United States.

Keynes explained all flows of money in terms of their impact on other people and entities. He said that a single person's spending contributes to the next individual's paycheck. That person spending their pay would then supply the earnings of another. This virtuous circle goes on and on and assists in maintaining a healthy economy that is working properly.

As the Great Depression settled in, the natural inclination of people to save and hold their money increased. Keynes proposed that this cessation in the normally occurring circular money flow is what caused the economies of the world to grind to a screeching halt.

More than only explaining economic problems, Keynes offered solutions as well. He claimed that the best cure for this disease lay in priming the pump. With this expression, he intended for governments to intervene in order to boost their spending. They might do this by purchasing things on the open market or by growing the money supply itself.

At the time of the Great Depression, such an answer did not turn out to be well received at first. Even so, the actions of American President Franklin D. Roosevelt in spending enormously on defense for the Second World War are generally credited for beginning the United States' economic revival.

Because Keynesian economics strongly makes the case for the government to jump in and help out the economy, it represented a serious break from the prior system of laissez-fair capitalism economics that predated it. This laissez-fair, or hands off, approach had endeavored to keep government out of the markets. The system argued that markets left undisturbed would find their own balance in time.

Keynes' ideas represented a direct challenge to the many supporters of free market capitalism, such as the Austrian School of economics. Frederick von Hayek proved to be among its earliest founders who lived in England and represented a bitter public rival to Keynes. Their ideas on government influence in private citizen's lives battled back and forth for years in public policy debate.

Keynesian economics discourages an excessive amount of savings, which it calls an insufficient amount of consumption and spending for the economy. The theory furthermore argues in favor of a great amount of redistributing wealth as necessary. Keynes thought that giving the poorest members of society money would lead to them probably spending it, which would support economic growth.

Keynesian economics has been a major force in international economic policy since World War II. Though its influence is less in the past three decades, it has not died out. Its tenets are again gaining ground in the light of the failures that led to the financial collapse and the Great Recession.

Local Money

Local Money is money that is created, printed, issued, and traded by an individual community. Communities that are struggling to keep their economies going are in need of a way of boosting the local economic picture. In creating money that can only be utilized by individuals and businesses in their own local area, they attempt to address this problem.

In the United States, local money's history originated in the difficult era of the Great Depression. During this decade of the 1930's, banks were failing in numbers not seen before. This created a real shortage of currency and loans in local communities and towns. Individuals and businesses worked together to find a solution to the problem. They teamed up and created their own currencies that became known as Scrip. Utilizing this newly created local Scrip, trade and exchange continued to go on even with a shortage of banks and hard currency in the smaller towns throughout America.

Today's local money concept has made a comeback in the wake of the financial crisis and the Great Recession. Businesses began working with area banks to come up with their own local currency that could be purchased and issued to consumers in the area. In communities where local money has arisen again, a great number of businesses have signed on to the idea and consented to taking payment in the bills of this localized currency money. This is necessary in order for area consumers to feel compelled to obtain the local money in the first place.

The way that local money works in practice today is interesting. The currency is printed up and then offered by area banks in a participating community. The currency is then sold at a significant discount to its actual value. For example, $100 local money could be sold by area banks for only $95 United States dollars. The $100 local money can then by spent by the consumer at its full value in any business that takes the local money as a method of payment.

Already, over a dozen area communities throughout the U.S. have created their own local money currencies that are being honored on a fairly large scale. Not only is this helping out area businesses by keeping the locally earned paychecks in the communities, but since the currencies are sold at a five to ten percent discount to dollars, it allows struggling workers and families to stretch their incomes by using them. In communities that honor local money, they can be utilized to pay for groceries, gasoline, and even Yoga classes, as examples. Among the more successful and widely accepted local monies these days are the Ithaca Hours of Ithaca, New York; the BerkShares in Western Massachusetts; and the Detroit Cheers in Detroit, Illinois.

The BerkShares for Western Massachusetts are a model case study of successful local money. They can be purchased from twelve banks throughout the area. BerkShares are accepted at in excess of three hundred seventy different businesses in the region. As the largest local money network in the U.S, the BerkShares have so far circulated almost two and a half million dollars. Successes like these have encouraged other communities like South Bend, Indiana to begin creating their own local currency.

Ludwig von Mises

Ludwig von Mises turned out to be among the very last thinkers of the original epoch of the Austrian School of Economics. He obtained his law and economics doctorate late in the period of the Austrian School in 1906 at the University of Vienna. His writings and teaching had a tremendous impact on the young people of his day and age, especially Americans of that and future generations.

The Theory of Money and Credit proved to be among the best and most influential of Ludwig von Mises' works. This ground breaking work became published in 1912. It served as a principal banking and monetary textbook for fully the following two decades. In this influential work, von Mises took off on the Austrian marginal utility theory to expand the idea to money. He observed that no one demands money simply to possess money for its intrinsic nature. Instead, individuals are attracted to its utility in buying goods with it. This was revolutionary thought at the time.

In the book, Ludwig von Mises also postulated that the business cycles of economies occur because governments allow limitless expansion of credit by the banks. Mises then went on to put his ideas into place by founding his Austrian Institute for Business Cycle Research in 1926.

The students of Ludwig von Mises were many and some of them were important to later generations. Friedrich Hayek became the most influential of them. He eventually expanded and extrapolated further on Mises' ideas on business cycles.

Besides these important ideas, Ludwig von Mises made other important contributions to the fields of political and economic thought. He argued that socialism would fall because its economy collapsed first. He penned a 1920 article which postulated social governments would be unable to engage in the necessary economic calculations which were needful in order to establish complicated and efficient economies. Social economists of the time Abba Lerner and Oskar Lange vehemently disagreed with his arguments. Today the majority of economists side with von Mises and his arguments which were further expounded on by his star pupil Hayek.

Ludwig von Mises felt certain that self-evident axioms made economic truths in practice. These economic principals were not able to be tested empirically he believed. Finally he reached the point of writing his magnum opus great work entitled *Human Action*. In this and other publications, he spelled out his full world view of economics and human interaction. Unfortunately at the time, von Mises was unable to persuade the majority of economists living in his age who were outside of the Austrian School of Economics. He strongly championed laissez-faire economics, arguing that the government had no place to be involved in any portion of a national economy. There were points where he violated his own rules with some important exceptions. He believed that war justified forced military conscription, a sharply anti-free market idea.

Ludwig von Mises served as a professor without pay for the University of Vienna during the years 1913 through 1934. He worked officially for the Vienna Chamber of Commerce as economist at the same time. While in this role, he labored on behalf of the Austrian national government as their main economic advisor. When Nazism took root in his native Austria, von Mises immigrated to Geneva, Switzerland in 1934. There he became professor in the Graduate Institute of International Studies. He served in this capacity until he eventually immigrated on to New York City in the U.S. in 1940. He worked as a visiting profess there in New York University from 1945 through his eventual retirement in 1969.

Sadly for Ludwig von Mises, his economic policy ideas were out of political favor policy wise in the years of the Keynesian revolution which swept across the American elite and political landscape between the 1930s and the 1960s. He became increasingly bitter after Hitler wrecked the land of his birth and as the Keynesian ideas became a full blown revolution in Washington D.C., London, and Paris. He went full circle from believing himself to be a mainstream member of economics to a final dismal view of himself as an economic outcast. This is evident in his book *The Theory of Money and Credit*. In the early sections he wrote in 1912, he argues calmly and rationally, while in the final section penned in the 1940s, he is vehement and argumentative.

Despite this pitiful end to his great life and work, Von Mises had a profound legacy, especially in the United States. His powerful impact on the young people of his generation and that of his successor Hayek caused the

Austrian School of Economics to enjoy a powerful resurgence in the U.S. after his death.

Maastricht Treaty

The Maastricht Treaty is the main treaty of the European Union. It was originally known as the TEU Treaty on European Union. This agreement was signed in Maastricht, the Netherlands on February 7, 1992. Members of the European Community debated it in their individual countries and then signed it. The treaty came about as an effort to fully integrate Europe into a closer political and economic union.

The treaty established the European Union. It also set the groundwork for creating the euro, the single currency of the EU. The Maastricht Treaty was subsequently amended by several other agreements. These included the Amsterdam, Nice, and Lisbon treaties.

This treaty represented a significant milestone in the process of integrating Europe. It modified other previously signed agreements like the treaties of Paris and Rome, as well as the Single European Act. These earlier arrangements had economic goals for the community. The original stated objective had been to create a common market for trading and investment.

With the Maastricht Treaty, the Europeans signed on to a spelled out vision of political union for the first time. After the treaty came into effect, the European project no longer went under the name of European Economic Community or EEC. Instead, it became known as the EU or European Union. Article 2 in this treaty called for "the process of creating an ever closer union among the peoples of Europe."

This Maastricht Treaty had a structural base of three pillars. The central pillar referred to the community dimension. It set out arrangements that pertained to common community policies, citizenship in the EU, and economic and monetary union. These were laid out in the Euratom, the ECSC, and the EC treaties. This pillar led to the eventual creation of the European Central Bank and the euro.

The second pillar concerned the CFSP Common foreign and security policy. Under this idea, the countries of the European Union would create a foreign minister for the EU to represent their single voice and policy objectives overseas. They also began working to come up with a common defensive policy with the intention of eventually creating an EU military force. This pillar also pertains to immigration and border control issues. It has suffered a serious challenge since the European refugee crisis has brought more than a million mostly Syrian and Iraqi refugees across the external borders of the E.U.

The third pillar of the Maastricht Treaty is the idea that there would be police and judicial cooperation. This pertained to criminal issues and concerns. It established a European Court of Justice whose decisions supersede those of the national country high courts.

The Maastricht Treaty also laid the grounds for the creation of the European Commission and the European Parliament. These bodies govern many budgetary and even political affairs within the block.

The Maastricht Treaty set in motion the discontent that led to the Brexit vote and the United Kingdom's decision to leave the EU. The pillars on common security and judicial cooperation turned out to major sore points with the British people. On the one hand, they despised the loss of control over their immigration policy and borders.

On the other they did not like the fact that they had also lost judicial control. A number of high profile court cases decided in the highest British court were subsequently overturned by the European Court of Justice. This all helped to explain why the majority of the British voted against the ever further political union which article two of the treaty established.

Macroeconomics

Macroeconomics refers to the division within economics that concentrates its study on the workings of large national economies, or even regional economies, in their entirety. This field proves to be extremely general as a result.

It is mostly concerned with big picture measurements like the rates of unemployment, as well as with the developing of models whose purpose is to detail the various indicators' correlations. An opposite to macroeconomics might be said to be microeconomics that focuses on the activities of individuals and businesses instead of bigger pictures and scales. Macroeconomics and microeconomics are considered to be complimentary studies.

Because of the Great Depression that occurred in the 1930's, the study of macroeconomics evolved into a practical area of economics on which economists might concentrate their efforts. Up to that point, economists did not distinguish between the activities of individuals and businesses and an entire national economy. The most influential developers of macroeconomics proved to be those economists who made it their business to relate what had caused the Great Depression. The British economist John Maynard Keynes is among the chief of these economists who developed the study.

Until just a few decades ago, Keynes' ideas on macroeconomics overshadowed the entire field. Followers of Keynesian thought depended on the concept of aggregate demand, or total demand, to grapple with hard questions in macroeconomics, like the way to explain what stood behind particular unemployment levels. Today, Keynesian models are not the underlying philosophy of macroeconomics any longer, as neoclassical economics has successfully challenged it. Still, the presently used models bear great influence of the Keynesian precursors.

To date, no one economic philosophy has come up with a single model that is able to correctly and totally reproduce the ways that economies literally work. This causes different economists to have varying understandings of economics. Because of this, gaining an understanding of macroeconomics involves studying the ideas of each major economic school of thought.

As a result of the field of macroeconomics, governments have taken proactive approaches to managing economic cycles and changes. They do this through governmental policies that are utilized to create changes with the goals of either avoiding or lessening the impacts of economic shocks, such as depressions. This management of large national economies is affected in practical terms through two types of government policies. These are monetary and fiscal policies. Monetary policies involve the governmental control of the nation's money supply and the national interest rate levels. Their goals are both stable prices with low inflation and low unemployment levels.

Fiscal policies are amounts of spending that a government engages in, as well as taxes that they collect, to influence the economy. For example, the government can expand the economy by spending a good deal more money than it collects in tax revenues. It might similarly contract economic activity by spending less money than it actually brings in from taxes. Besides this, a government can stimulate the economy by cutting tax rates, or shrink the economic activity levels by raising tax rates.

Market Sentiment

Market sentiment refers to the all around attitude investors have with regards to a certain financial market or specific security. It is the tone and feeling in a market. This is displayed via the price movement and activity of various securities which trade in a given market. Some have called it the market crowd psychology or investor sentiment. Rising prices in a market are indicative of bullish market sentiment, while declining prices indicate the sentiment in a market is bearish.

What makes market sentiment so interesting is that it is sometimes not based on the underlying fundamentals of the security or market in question. At times it instead is based on emotion and greed rather than actual business valuations and fundamentals.

This market sentiment matters immensely to both technical analysts and to day traders. These individuals read technical indicators in order to measure shorter term price movements which the attitudes of investors can cause in a given security. They attempt to profit from these price fluctuations. Such sentiment also is important for contrarian investors. They prefer to place trades in the opposite direction of any prevailing sentiment. When all other investors are buying, a contrarian will use this sentiment to instead sell.

In general, market sentiment is referred to as either bullish or bearish. As the bulls have control, the stock prices are running up and away. As the bears are dominant, prices of stocks are declining or even plunging. Since the markets are subject to and driven from the emotion of the collective traders, the sentiment of the markets is often not correlated to the underlying fundamental values. This means that market sentiment is more about group emotions and feelings while the fundamental value is more about the actual business performance.

Traders realize profits when they find those stocks which are either undervalued or overvalued because of their market sentiment. Traders and investors alike utilize different indicators to attempt to ascertain what the sentiment of the markets actually is. This helps them to decide which stocks are the best ones for them to trade. There are a number of these helpful indicators. Among the more popular ones are the following: VIX CBOE

Volatility Index, Bullish Percentage, 52 Weeks High to Low Sentiment Ratio, 200 Days Moving Average, and 50 Days Moving Average.

The Fear Index, or VIX, runs off of the option prices. Such options prove to be like insurance contracts. A rise in the VIX means that traders see the need for more insurance within the markets. When traders instead feel like there should be more risk, this reveals a greater amount of price movement. Traders can simply compare the present VIX against the historical moving averages of it to decide if it is actually lower or higher.

Bullish Percentage quantifies the numbers of stocks that have bullish patterns. It relies on point and figure charts to do this. Typical markets will demonstrate a 50 percent bullish percentage. If the figure turns out to be at least 80 percent or greater than this, then the sentiment of the markets is highly bullish. Another way of saying this is that the market is actually overbought. Similarly if the figure is 20 percent or less than this amount, it signals the sentiment of the market is bearish. This makes it oversold. Traders can simply sell as the market is too overbought and buy as the markets are oversold.

High To Low Sentiment indicators will take the stocks which have made 52 week long highs and compare these against those stocks which have just made 52 week long lows. If stock prices trade around the lows universally, then the trading community is bearish in its sentiment on the markets. Conversely, if the stock prices trade near or at their highs, the same traders are instead showing their bullish market sentiments.

Market Trends

Market trends refer to the idea that financial markets tend to move in a given direction. Among the different types of these trends are secular, primary, and secondary kinds. Secular ones refer to longer time periods. Primary trends are those which happen over medium time frames. Secondary trends turn out to be those that occur over shorter time frames.

Traders try to figure out and predict such trends with the study of technical analysis. This study provides a means of characterizing such trends in the market as predictable patterns, especially when prices reach resistance and support levels, which vary with time. The dilemma with predicting trends is that they are only truly knowable after they have begun. This is because future prices can never be fully predicted with accuracy.

Secular markets actually cover those longer term trends which run from five to 25 years in duration. They are made up of a group of primary market trends. This means that a secular bull market would be comprised of bigger bull markets and smaller intervening bear markets. Conversely, secular bear markets are comprised of bigger bear markets and smaller intervening bull markets.

An example of a secular bull market was the period in U.S. markets from 1983 through 2000 (or sometimes considered to be through 2007). The intervening bear trends would be considered the Black Monday Crash in 1987 and the dot-com crash from 2000 to 2002.

Primary market trends are those which instead last only a year to several years. They generally enjoy significant and broad based support in the whole market while they are happening. In a primary bull market, the prices are generally rising. The bull market begins with a great deal of pessimism which is nearly universal. Somehow the despondency gives way to first hope, then belief before finally peaking out at irrational exuberance. At that point, the bull market has finished.

The average bull market has lasted around 8.5 years, according to the market data Morningstar compiled from 1926 through 2014. Annual gains in these types of markets averaged between 14.9 percent and 34.1 percent.

Important bull markets in the U.S. occurred from 1925-1929, from 1953-1957, and from 1993-1997. Two of the three ended badly in the Great Depression and the Dotcom crash, an ominous warning to investors.

In primary bear market trends, the markets are deteriorating over a given amount of time. Vanguard defines these as minimally twenty percent price declines in a given two month period. Bear markets followed the great Wall Street Crash of 1929, occurred from 1937 to 1942, and following the Arab Oil Embargo crisis from 1973 to 1982. More recent examples were from 2000 to 2002 and from 2007 to 2009 in the wake of the Great Recession and Global Financial Crisis.

Secondary trends are those which are short term in nature. These generally last for several weeks to several months. Market corrections are actually a kind of secondary market trend. Such corrections are defined as a shorter term decline in market indices by from around ten percent to around twenty percent. From April 2010 through June 2010, the S&P 500 dropped from 1,200 to around 1,000. Investors at the time believed this was the end of the bull market and the start of a bear market. In fact it was only a correction as the markets turned and continued going back up afterward.

There can also be bear market rallies within the secondary market trends. These are better known as dead cat bounces. They are comprised of a price run in the markets amounting to from ten percent to twenty percent before the bigger bear market trend continues again. Such a dead cat bounce actually happened in 1929 after the initial Black Friday crash. The markets then descended into the ash can through 1932 and more or less through 1942. Another such false bounce occurred in the latter years of the 1960s and early 1970s.

Middle Class

In the United States, the Middle Class is a broadly defined social group found throughout America. There are no exact definitions of what comprises the middle class. Depending on whose standard you use, the middle class in the U.S. is made up of from twenty-five to sixty-six percent of families.

The middle class in America have been responsible for many of the country's greatest accomplishments. Middle class people are known by characteristics of creativity, coming up with concepts, and consultative abilities. Most middle class people have either obtained a college degree or at least been through some years of college education.

Middle class values are central to the recognized American way of life. These values center around sticking to intrinsically held ethics and beliefs, independence, and innovation. Middle class people prove to be more politically motivated and active than do the other demographics throughout American society.

The income of the middle class ranges widely. It can be from around the national median income to over $100,000 per year. This means that the standard of living for middle class people can similarly vary greatly, dependent on the size of the household in question. This means that families with two incomes that have many members can earn more than a smaller family in the upper middle class that only has one income, even though the latter's standard of living would be considerably higher.

The middle class in the United States remains the most influential group in American society. They are responsible for the vast majority of teachers, writers, voters, editors, and journalists. The majority of trends within the United States begin with the middle class.

The middle class also pay the majority of the taxes within the U.S., making them an extremely critical group economically. The top twenty-five percent of earners, the overwhelming majority of whom are considered to be middle class, pay eighty-five percent of all taxes in the United States. Meanwhile, the bottom fifty percent pay only three percent, while the wealthiest one percent pay up to thirty-seven percent of the total share of taxes.

Even though the Middle Class are considered to be indispensable to American society and the economy, their ranks are dwindling with time. Data on income demonstrates that the American Middle Class have benefited from much slower growth in income than the top one percent of wealthy wage earners, according to data going back to 1980. This stands in contrast to the rise in income seen in the years after World War II, when the income of the middle class grew at the same pace as did the income of the rich. In the years since then, the rich have out gained the middle class considerably.

As an example, from 1979 to 2005, the after tax earnings of the top one percent grew inflation adjusted by 176% as opposed to only sixty-nine percent for the top twenty percent of wage earners as a whole and only twenty-nine percent for the top forty percent of workers. As a percentage of total gross yearly household income, the top one percent currently make over nineteen percent of all earnings, representing their greatest share of the wealth since the late 1920's.

Further proof that the critical middle class is shrinking is revealed by the June 2006 Brookings Institution survey. It demonstrated that the neighborhoods of middle income Americans as a percent of all metropolitan neighborhoods have decline dramatically over a thirty year period. From 1970 to 2000, this percentage decreased from fifty-eight percent to forty-one percent. According to this data, the middle class have already fallen well below the significant half of the country's population that it always represented in the past.

Milton Friedman

Milton Friedman proved to be one of the leading proponents of monetarism. He stood as opposition to the dominant thought of the day Keynesian economics. Today's supporters of the ideas of free markets owe Friedman and his followers the Chicago School economists a great debt of gratitude for their successful efforts.

Friedman opposed Keynes from the very beginning. Keynes had argued that shorter term solutions could fix economies. He believed that consumers would alter their spending habits if given a stimulus check from the government. This way the state would not have to relinquish future taxes to help the economy.

Friedman used empirical studies to attack this premise as he did with all Keynesian ideas. He demonstrated that individuals would only change yearly spending patterns if significant changes came to their lifetime income. A raise in a job would cause a more meaningful spending change than would a one time stimulus.

Friedman argued that economies could be better improved by reducing the involvement of the government. He proposed stopping policies that caused inflation and reducing taxes. Milton demonstrated that inflation tricked consumers into believing they earned more. In reality higher costs of living cancelled any gains they made in income.

The Keynesian multiplier represented another area that Friedman and the Chicago School economists constantly attacked. Keynes had assigned a higher spending multiplier to even government debt spending over private investment. Milton showed that such spending by the government only crowded out private investors who hold their money while the government is footing the bill.

Friedman published several influential economic books as part of his work in developing monetarism. Among these was *A Monetary History of the United States*. Here he demonstrated that misguided monetary policies led to the Great Depression. It had not been any free market form of capitalism that failed.

After he studied about a century of government monetary policy in response to recessions, depressions, booms, and crashes, he concluded that the Federal Reserve had created the Great Depression by massively reducing the money supply by more than one third from 1929 to 1933. These actions transformed a fairly common stock market crash into a long term depression.

Friedman's concentration on money's role within the economy only grew with time. Though he started out as a fan of the gold standard he changed his views to those of a hard monetarist. With this he argued that the amount of money circulated should grow apace with the economic growth of the country. This would still act as a check on governments printing limitless money.

It would also permit the national money supply to expand enough to continue the country's economic growth. He became a controversial figure for defending free market capitalism in the 1960's with his book *Capitalism and Freedom*. Some of the ideas in the book included a negative income tax for those who earned less and school vouchers. These received attention and eventually became main stream.

Finally in the 1970's the Keynesian system began to collapse thanks to the weight of stagflation. The powerful academics gave Milton Friedman and his hard money anti-inflation ideas another serious look then. His monetarism began to surpass the influence of the old Keynesian proposals at first in academic circles.

In the next decades Friedman and his fellow Chicago School of thought economists rose to the posts of economic advisors in not only the U.S government but others around the world. They argued for and promoted smaller government and hard money policies. In this way, they were pushing for a return to the ideas and policies of Adam Smith and his *Wealth of Nations* masterpiece.

Milton's work and ideas were honored by Nobel Prizes in economics. Both he and his Chicago School of thought won several of these awards for their efforts in taking apart the worse ideas of Keynesian economics. Friedman went to his death feeling that they had become accepted for their ideas which were not fully implemented. He and his monetarists argued governments loved Keynesian practices because they pardoned excess inherent in big government. They also allowed for the projects that were the most wasteful.

Monetary Policy

This is one of the two tools the government has to influence the overall economy. With monetary policy, a nation's central bank takes action to influence the economy. In the United States, the Federal Reserve Board is the central bank. They regulate the interest rates and money supply available in the country to stabilize the national currency and to control inflation. Monetary policy is the sister policy to fiscal policy.

Monetary policy is effective because the Federal Reserve or other central bank is able to change the real cost of money. This allows them to influence business and consumer spending behavior and the amount of money they use. With this policy, central banks are able to mange their nation's money supply. It allows them to oversee stable economic growth.

The money supply is made up of several components. These include cash, checks, credit, and money market funds. Credit is among the most important and biggest categories of money supply. It covers mortgages, loans, bonds, and other promises to repay.

There are two goals in which central banks utilize monetary policy. They are attempting to manage inflation levels and to lower unemployment rates. The United States Federal Reserve maintains particular target ranges in these two goals.

The Fed desires its core inflation rates to be around 2% and no higher than 2.5%. They are seeking to keep unemployment rates under 6.5%. The U.S. believes a healthy unemployment rate ranges from 4.7% to 5.8%. On top of this, the Federal Reserve is looking for steady rates of economic growth. By this they mean a yearly increase of from 2% to 3% in the Gross Domestic Product.

There are two types of monetary policies from which central banks can choose. They use expansionary monetary policy to increase economic growth. Central banks decrease interest rates, increase liquidity to the markets, and purchase securities from their member banks to affect this.

Central banks employ contractionary monetary policy to slow down economic growth. They may sell securities in open market operations, increase interest rates, and increase liquidity to banks and markets in order to create this impact. Central banks have several different tools they can utilize to pursue their monetary policy. They perform open market operations by purchasing short term government bonds or selling these. Buying bonds increases the money supply while selling them decreases it.

They can also raise or lower their main interest rates like Fed Funds rate in the U.S. or LIBOR in the U.K. This changes the price at which consumers and businesses can borrow money. Cheaper money means consumers purchase bigger, longer term goods using cheap credit. Businesses pursue expansion and hire more people with cheaper priced debt. Savers are encouraged to put their money into stocks and securities to earn higher returns than savings accounts pay when interest rate are low.

Central banks can also change the reserve requirements that banks must keep. Higher reserves reduce their ability to make loans and help to decrease inflation. Lower reserves allow them to make more loans but drive inflation higher.

Since the Great Recession in 2008, different central banks have engaged in more unconventional monetary policy in an effort to kick start declining economies. Quantitative Easing has been among these policies. It involves buying financial assets from banks with money the central banks print.

From 2008 to 2013 the U.S. Federal Reserve massively expanded its balance sheet by trillions of dollars by purchasing mortgage backed securities and Treasury notes. Encouraged by the relative success and so far limited consequences of these actions, the Bank of England, the Bank of Japan, and European Central Bank have also engaged in their own quantitative easing policies. Critics have warned that such quantitative easing will massively increase inflation at some point in the future.

Monopoly

Monopolies refer to markets where a single producer or supplier controls all or nearly all of the market. This means that they have the ability to set prices for the good or service they produce. For there to be a true monopoly, there can not be any near substitutes for the product in question. The term monopoly has also come to represent the company which dominates the market of the good or service. Monopolist is another better name for the supplier who controls the market.

When a monopoly exists, there is no competition in the price of the good or service. The monopolist is able to set the price. They will usually choose to make it as high as the market will bear.

Monopolies usually occur because there are particular factors that prevent other companies from competing effectively against the monopolist. These factors are called barriers to entry. There are a number of different barriers to entry which can cause a monopoly to arise.

Sometimes a company exclusively owns a critical resource that companies need to produce the product. This can help it to become a monopoly. Exclusive knowledge of a process to make something would also count as sole ownership of a critical resource. This is what makes pharmaceutical companies monopolies in various types of medicine which they develop and first release.

Government protected ideas can also create monopolies. This can exist in the form of copyrights and patents. In these protections, the government guarantees these companies a minimum period of time to produce the goods or services without any competition. This creates a temporary monopoly until the intellectual property protection expires.

Markets where a good or service is new typically see these types of monopolies. Governments justify copyrights and patents as the means to encourage invention and innovation. Without this temporary protection, many companies would not invest resources needed to create new inventions and products.

A related monopoly is a government franchise. Governments create these types of monopolies when they give the exclusive ability to operate in an industry to a single business. This could happen with a business that is owned by the government or a private company. Train operators and mail delivery companies like the postal service are good examples of this type of government franchise.

Natural monopolies sometimes arise on their own without government help or intervention. This is most often the case when the costs are lower for a single company to service the whole market. Numerous smaller companies competing against each other could actually raise costs and prices in these instances.

Some companies have limitless economies of scale. This means that they are so large and powerful in an industry that no new players could compete with their prices. This could be because the costs to enter the industry are so high that no one will bother. They also represent natural monopolies. There are a number of technology infrastructure companies in this position. Some of the more common industries where these types of natural monopolies occur include telephone operators, Internet service, and cable television providers.

It is not always clear if a company possess a monopoly in a given industry. Some people consider certain brands to be monopolies because of how popular they are. This is true even when they do not control all of the product market share.

The Coca Cola Company has a monopoly on producing the soft drink Coke. This is not the only soft drink on the market, but there is no exact substitute for it. Even though rivals Pepsi Cola and Dr Pepper Snapple Group control a large share of the soft drink market, neither of them produces Coke. This is why the debate for monopolies continues to rage on about what constitutes a close substitute. Anti-monopoly regulators constantly wrestle with the question.

National Bureau of Economic Research (NBER)

The NBER National Bureau of Economic Research is an organization whose purpose centers on creating and disbursing economic research. They are committed to encouraging better understanding of the way the economy functions for individuals, businesses, and policymakers. As part of this they write and distribute unbiased economic reports.

The NBER got its start in 1920 as a not for profit, private, non-political group. Their objectives from the start were undertaking research on economics and sharing it with business people, politicians, and academics. The researchers who are connected with NBER study a great range of different economic and business subjects.

Along with this they utilize numerous research methods in their studies. The group focuses on numerous different topics. Chief among them are creating quantitative economic behavior models, coming up with new ways to measure statistics, and studying the impacts that public policies cause.

The history of the NBER shows they covered many important ground breaking economic issues within American society. Their early efforts centered on longer term growth for the economy, the full business cycle, and the aggregate economy. In the formative years Wesley Mitchell wrote an important paper about the business cycle. Simon Kuznets pioneered the topic of national income accounting.

Milton Friedman researched and argued for money demand and what determined consumer spending. All of these proved to be in the earlier studies performed by the National Bureau of Economic Research. In 1984, Solomon Fabricant wrote a summary of their initial work and development entitled Toward a Firmer Basis of Economic Policy: The Founding of the National Bureau of Economic Research.

The NBER has greatly expanded and grown in influence over the years. Today it is considered to be the foremost group for not for profit research on economics in the United States. Among the economists who were affiliated with NBER are 25 Nobel Prize winners. There have also been 13 heads of the Presidential Council of Economic Advisers among their affiliated members.

NBER researchers today include over 1,400 business and economics professors who teach throughout universities and colleges around the U.S. and Canada. These researching scholars are considered to be the leaders within their own fields. The vast majority of those researchers who hold NBER affiliation have a title of RA Research Associates or FRF Faculty Research Fellows. These Research Associates are tenured by their home university or college. Their appointments to this senior status must be NBER Board of Directors approved. Faculty Research Fellows usually prove to be junior scholars in their fields.

The NBER does not receive direct tax dollar support. It operates based on a variety of research grants. These supporting grants come from private foundations, government agencies, corporate and individual contributions, and investment income.

The NBER is well organized and run by a board of directors that governs it. Its headquarters are based in Cambridge, Massachusetts. The group also maintains a branch office in New York City. The members of this board come from and represent both important national economics entities and foremost American researching universities. The board also hosts members who are important economists at academia, trade unions, and corporations. Being a board member of this national economics group is a prestigious honor.

In 2016 the Chief Executive Officer and President of the NBER is James Poterba. He is served by 45 personnel who staff the organization. These employees are besides the Faculty Research Fellows and Research Associates located around North America. The research group is governed by various important documents. These include their NBER by-laws, incorporation certificate, and the conflict of interest policy for directors and officers.

Negative Interest Rates

Negative interest rates are those that fall below 0%. In the past, negative interest proved to be only a theoretical discussion that economists played around with for the sake of argument. In 2010 Sweden's central bank put these rates into practice as a means of stemming the flow of outside money into the country. Denmark followed suit in 2012. Since then, minor to major central banks have moved into the mostly uncharted waters of these negative rates.

The reason that central banks would be interested in such negative interest rates is that they help the economy. Central banks cutting the rates into negative territory creates a similar effect as simply lowering interest rates. Lower rates help consumers to spend and businesses to invest more.

They also boost prices in the stock markets and other risk assets. They reduce the level of the nation's currency. This helps exports to be more competitive against other country's goods. Finally lower rates cause people to expect higher inflation rates in the future. This encourages consumers to spend their money now as opposed to later when it will be worth less.

The world has many decades of knowledge of what happens when central banks influence economies by reducing rates from 3% to 2% because of downturns in the economy. In theory this shifting to negative interest rates is similar with the difference of a starting point at or below zero.

Such NIRP negative interest rate policies are called unconventional monetary tools. The idea is to move benchmark interest rates into negative territory. Doing so means breaking the centuries' long barrier of 0%.

Deflation is what caused desperate central banks to pursue these negative interest rates and policies. In times where deflation pervades an economy, the businesses and consumers tend to hold their money rather than invest and spend it. Eventually this creates a reduction in total demand that in turn causes prices to fall even more. Output and production slow down and unemployment increases as a result.

Stagnation like this is typically avoided when central banks pursue a loose monetary policy. The problem arises when the deflation becomes so powerful that dropping interest rates to zero is no longer enough to encourage lending and borrowing.

The result of negative interest rates is profound. Central banks charge their commercial banks money (negative interest) in order to keep their deposits at the bank. Commercial banks then pass along these costs to their larger account holders as they are able. The financial institutions have not much stooped to official negative rates on their depositors. Instead they charge fees for keeping money in these current accounts. This amounts to negative rates under the guise of a different name.

Central banks hope that the commercial banks will loan out money instead of paying to hold it. Instead many banks have been paying the fees themselves, and this has impacted bank profits. Banks fear passing along fees to small deposit account holders who may withdraw their money instead.

As of 2016, the negative interest rate policy has been adopted by the European Central Bank, the Swiss National Bank, and the Bank of Japan besides the Scandinavian Central Banks. Early evidence suggests that the Euro zone did manage to reduce interbank loans with the negative interest rates. Companies have not so far much benefited from the negative interest rates. This is because the risk is perceived to be higher with corporations who borrow than with governments. One notable exception is with Nestle the Swiss food conglomerate that has issued negative interest rate corporate bonds.

Nielson

Nielson Holdings PLC represents the British-based, truly global data, information, and measurement firm which was originally started in the United States. Today it operates in more than 100 countries around the world and counts 44,000 staff among its worldwide employees. In 2015, they announced aggregate revenues of $6.2 billion. As a company with enormous operations in the U.S., it is listed on the NYSE New York Stock Exchange and the London Stock Exchange. The company is presently an S&P 500 component.

For 2016, the American Marketing Association named Nielson as its top firm out of the top 50 Market Research Firms active in the United States. Arthur C. Nielson, Sr. originally founded Nielson back in 1923. He remains famous for his invention of the idea to measure competitive sales which led to the concept of "market share." He receives credit for coining and making famous this phrase that is ubiquitous within the United States and developed world today.

Though the company existed separately in the United States and Europe (where it traded and was headquartered initially in the Netherlands), a merger of the two sister companies in August of 2015 led to the creation of the present day (sole surviving) version of the unified company Nielson Holdings PLC based in London. The cross border merger allowed by the European Cross-Border Merger Directive allowed for this combination to occur.

Today's Nielson Holdings remains headquartered in the United Kingdom in both England and Wales. Nielson has become the leading, multinational, independent data and measurement firm of consumer behavior, quick-selling consumer goods, and media. Its presence in over 100 countries means that its reach extends to over 90 percent of the world's population and total GDP. Nielson delivers an exhaustive understanding of what consumers are looking at in advertising and programming to its customers. It also reveals what they purchase in products, brand names, and categories on a local, domestic, regional, and global scale and how these choices meet and intersect. As such, the firm is active in both developed and emerging markets throughout the world.

It is interesting that the Nielson brand is usually thought of in connection with its famous Nielson TV ratings. Yet as a percentage of the company's revenues and business it only comprises about a quarter of the total. The company has labored for years to simplify the organization of its vast and far flung, diverse business enterprises. As a result of these intensive efforts, they have reorganized their business lines along two reporting divisions. These are "Buy," the consumer purchasing analytics and measurement division, and "Watch," the media audience analytics and measurement division.

The Buy division represents around 55 percent of this global behemoth's revenues. It mainly assists retailers, packaged goods makers, and Wall Street analysts with understanding the interests and purchases of consumers in broad categories and specific products and brands. The aim of this division is to gather and measure all of the purchases consumers make even while their purchasing behavior is fragmenting continuously over both market segments and channels.

This division's data actually determines the amount of Diet Pepsi vs. Diet Coke and Diet Dr. Pepper which stores sell, as well as the amount of Colgate versus Crest toothpaste retailers vend. They do this in practice by buying and analyzing enormous quantities of retail data showing what the stores are selling. They combine this with their own data from household panels of surveys which gather information on what consumers bring home. This division's most important clients include Nestle, The Coca-Cola Company, Unilever Group, Procter and Gamble Company, and Wal-Mart. The buy division extends over 106 countries now, though the U.S. remains the biggest market of this division.

The other group is the Watch division. This segment represents around 45 percent of worldwide revenues. It mostly measures what consumers listen to and watch over the majority of devices and channels. This includes television, computers, radio, cell phones, over the top, and other mobile devices. As such, they measure consumers' interest in both advertising and programming over all points of distribution. They call their proprietary data measuring machine the Nielson's Total Audience Measurement system. This division's most important clients include NBC Universal, CBS, The Walt Disney Company, and News Corporation. It measures media performances in 47 nations which collectively represent around 80 percent of worldwide advertising budgets.

Office of Financial Research (OFR)

OFR is an abbreviation and stands for the Office of Financial Research. This government organization that has its headquarter in the Treasury Building works to supply information in support of the Financial Stability Oversight Council.

The OFR strives to encourage financial stability throughout the United States. They do this by scanning throughout the American financial system in order to find, measure, and consider risks. They also engage in gathering critical research and then compile and homogenize the financial data so that it can be easily referenced, understood, and compared.

The Office of Financial Research says about itself that its job revolves around illuminating the darkest parts of the financial system. As they do this, they are looking to see where the risks to the system are heading. They then determine the level of threat such risks pose to the system and the economy. Finally, they deliver financial analysis, data, and insight on these threats along with an available policy tools' evaluation in order to effectively address and diffuse the threats.

Congress created this Office of Financial Research back in 2010 under the Dodd-Frank Wall Street Reform and Consumer Protection Act. They established this new organization in order to provide material support to the all important new super regulatory entity the Financial Stability Oversight Council.

The OFR was also to deliver useful information on the risks to the system to the member organizations of the Council as well as to any interested and concerned members of the public. The Director of the OFR is both appointed at the discretion of the President and must be confirmed by a majority vote of the Senate. In 2016, this Director was Richard Berner. The group was created to work around two offices of a Data Center and a Research and Analysis Center.

The mission of the Office of Financial Research is to encourage American financial system stability via providing high quality financial standards, data, and analysis of the information on behalf of the Financial Stability Oversight

Council, its various member organizations, and the general public. To this effect, they maintain the vision of a financial system that is efficient, effective, stable, and transparent.

Every year, the Office of Financial Research produces several publications. Two of these that have become annual productions are the Annual Report to Congress on Human Capital Planning and the Annual Report to Congress. The Dodd-Frank Act itself requires that the OFR produces, compiles, and presents this general annual report once a year before Congress.

Every general annual report must include a complete analysis of the various threats to the American financial system and overall stability, the progress in their endeavors to meet the mission of the OFR, and the critical discoveries regarding threats from their research and analyzing of the whole United States' financial system.

The 2015 Office of Financial Research Annual Report to Congress is the fourth such yearly report since the office became established under the requirements of the Dodd-Frank Act. This particular report reviewed and analyzed the possible threats to American financial stability, reported on their important discoveries of risk, detailed their progress in meeting the OFR overall mission, and laid out the agenda of The Office for 2016.

The 2015 report stated that the various threats to United States' financial stability increased slightly from the prior year's report. They still consider the risks to be in the moderate to medium range. They did not change their threat assessment after the Federal Reserve FOMC raised the short term interest rates. A major portion of the 2016 agenda for the OFR is to affect a new programmatic approach in their work. They are striving to concentrate their initial efforts on the core areas of eight programs.

OPEC

OPEC is the globally famous acronym for the Organization of the Petroleum Exporting Countries. This permanently standing and frequently meeting intergovernmental entity arose over fifty years ago at the Baghdad Conference held back from September 10th through the 14th of 1960. Founding meeting nations at the time were Saudi Arabia, Iraq, Iran, Kuwait, and Venezuela. These five original Founding Members later found company as nine other states joined them. These were Qatar in 1961, Libya in 1962, United Arab Emirates in 1967, Algeria in 1969, Nigeria in 1971, Ecuador in 1973, Gabon in 1975, and Angola in 2007.

Indonesia is the ninth member. They have experienced a tumultuous history recently with OPEC. The Southeast Asian nation originally joined in 1962 but suspended its membership in January of 2009. They reactivated it once again in January of 2015 then again decided to suspend membership in November of 2016.

The original headquarters of OPEC lay in Geneva, Switzerland, but only for the first five years of the organization's history. After this, the group moved the home base of operations to Vienna, Austria as of September 1, 1965. They have remained there to this day.

The objective of OPEC lies in unifying and coordinating the diverging petroleum production and sales policies of the member nations. Their goal in doing this is to ensure that petroleum prices realized by the producers are both stable and fair. They are also interested in delivering and guaranteeing an effective, uninterrupted, and economically affordable supply of petroleum and petroleum products to the wealthy consuming nations of the world. Finally, they seek a fair return on investments for those who support the industry with capital.

Their mission is nearly the same as the above defined statute. They look to make certain oil markets remain stable so that the producers are able to receive a dependable and steady income stream and consumers are able to rely on routine, economic, and efficient supplies of the crude commodity.

The formative years of OPEC in the 1960s were interesting times for the member producing states. Many of them were only achieving their independence from protectorate overlords Great Britain or France at the time. Decolonization meant that many new fully independent nations arose throughout the developing world. At the time, the world oil markets were controlled by the so called "Seven Sisters" multinational corporations. They existed almost independent from the former communist Soviet Union (the FSU) and the other communist nations of China, Vietnam, North Korea, Eastern Europe, and Cuba.

OPEC came together and refined its group vision, established their Secretariat, and created their objectives. In 1968, it adopted its "Declaratory Statement of Petroleum Policy in Member Countries." This laid out the irrevocable rights of all nations to permanently control their own natural resources for the best interest of their own national development. By the end of the decade, OPEC had expanded to ten member states.

It was actually in the 1970s that OPEC came into its own. In this decade, they gained international notoriety as they assumed full control over their own internal petroleum industries. This allowed them to gain a huge influence over the crude oil prices on global energy markets. Thanks to their Arab oil embargo of 1973 the were able to inflict dramatic pain for national governments as well as individual consumers and businesses throughout the United States, Great Britain, and most of the wealthy developed nations of the world. By 1975, 13 countries had become members of OPEC.

Throughout the 1990s and 2000s, OPEC's influence and great power over world oil and energy markets gradually declined as the organization fell from prominence. This happened because of ineffective coordination of policy as the years dragged on, and as other non-OPEC nations such as Norway, Great Britain, the newly revived Russia, Canada, Mexico, and the United States became major oil producers in their own rights.

PCE Index

The PCE Index stands for personal consumption expenditures. This economic index is used to quantify the changes in the prices of consumer services and goods. The expenditures which are included in the index are real expenditures that the U.S. government claims actual households in the U.S. spend.

The index measures data that covers non durable goods, durable goods, and services. It does share some important characteristics with the CPI Consumer Price Index, though it filters out wildly swinging commodities' prices. The Department of Commerce's Bureau of Economic Analysis includes the PCE in the personal income report which it issues.

Many officials and economists consider the PCE Index to be very predictable. This is one of the features they like about it. Other analysts favor the CPI over the PCE because they claim that it helps to discern if there is economic stability or not. CPI utilizes a fixed, set basket of goods in its calculations. The Department of Commerce likes that PCE smoothes out the inflation numbers to eliminate speculative trading based price changes in commodities.

The Federal Reserve also prefers the PCE Index to CPI. CPI may be the better known economic indicator. The Fed still chooses the PCE as its favored index as it considers the conditions in the economy. The PCE helps the American central bank to determine its plans of action which will influence employment and inflation.

The Fed has a reasoning for choosing the PCE Index. It likes the variety of expenditures which the PCE covers. CPI is more limited in utility to them precisely because its basket components are always fixed. In contrast, the PCE manages to consider a wide range of expenses that actual homes spend money on around the United States. The PCE data comes from business surveys, which are usually more reliable than those consumer based surveys that the CPI employs.

The formula of the PCE Index is also useful. It takes into account alterations in the consumers' behavior over the short term. The competing

CPI does not factor in such an adjustment. All of these characteristics when taken together lead to a better rounded and all inclusive measurement of inflation. The Fed relies on the slight nuances which the PCE divulges. To them, even tiny quantities of inflation represent an economy which is healthy and expanding.

While the PCE Index breaks down to two main categories of goods and services, it subdivides the primary category of goods into two further ones. These subdivisions within goods are called durables and non durables. Durable goods refers to those which a household will be able to utilize for over three years. They come with higher price points.

In the durable goods category are televisions, cars, furniture, and refrigerators. Non durable goods are those referred to as transitory. This means that they have a life expectancy which is shorter than three years. Such items cost less and are constantly consumed. Examples of non durables include clothes, food, gasoline, and makeup.

Philips Curve

Philips Curve is a concept in economics which A.W. Philips created. This curve demonstrates that the relationship between unemployment and inflation is predictable, inverse, and stable. Philips' theory explains that when economies enjoy growth, inflation appears alongside it. This may sound like a negative side effect, but it is not necessarily according to Philips.

The growth coupled with inflation is supposed to create a greater number of jobs and lead to lower unemployment. The idea was generally accepted until the 1970s. At that point, stagflation brought on high unemployment along with inflation. This real world empirical data has at least partially disproven the idea under these circumstances.

The theory that underlies Philips Curve claims that when unemployment changes in an economy, this causes a predictable impact on the inflation of prices. This relationship is said to be inversely related. On the curve, this means that the correlation between unemployment and inflation shows it as a concave (outward) and downward sloping curve. Unemployment is demonstrated on the X axis while inflation is depicted on the Y axis. It pictorially shows how inflation increasing lowers unemployment. The reverse is also shown as higher unemployment reduces inflation.

In the 1960s, economists believed that the result of fiscal stimulus would lead to a higher total demand in the economy. This would case the demand for labor to grow. The total number of workers who were unemployed would diminish, causing firms to increase their wages to be able to competitively vie for the tinier pool of talent. Higher wages would boost costs at corporations. Companies would then choose to pass through these costs to the individual consumers. This would translate to higher prices and finally more inflation as the Philips Curve demonstrates.

Because many governments believed in these ideas, they chose to implement a so called stop-go strategy. They would affect this by establishing a target inflation rate. To attain the desired rate of inflation, they would adapt their monetary and fiscal policies as needed to contract or expand the economy. It no longer worked for them in the 1970s as the once stable and predictable model between unemployment and inflation broke down as stagflation appeared. This caused economists and governments to question the relevance and value of the Philips Curve.

Stagflation happens as economies suffer from poor economic growth at the same time as they have high inflation and more unemployment. Such a case directly contradicts the Philips Curve theories. Until the 1970s, the United States had never suffered from stagflation where such increasing levels of unemployment did not come along with reducing inflation rates.

This is because demand typically falls when economies are stagnant. It makes sense that workers who are unemployed will purchase less. This causes companies to lower their prices to encourage consumer spending. Yet from the years 1973 to 1975, the American economy managed to provide six different contiguous quarters where the GDP declined as inflation tripled. Economists now show that the 1970 occurring minor recession which policymakers aggravated with price and wage controls caused the stagflation to occur.

It was then United States President Richard Nixon who implemented such controls. His imitation of a stop-go strategy caused companies to be confused as to how to react. Because of this, they kept prices elevated more than they would have otherwise. The government no longer employs stop-go strategies since this episode of stagflation. Central banks maintain strict and rigorously enforced inflation targets now so that stagflation is less likely for the future. In the majority of economic circumstances, the Philips Curve is otherwise a true representation of the real world relationship between unemployment and inflation.

Price Controls

Price Controls turn out to be government decreed standards for maximum or minimum prices which they set on specific goods. These are typically put into place in order to intervene directly in an economy so they can arrange for essential goods to be made affordable. Governments are interested in affecting these controls on staple goods. These include such critical things as foodstuffs and energy. Within these types of controls, price ceilings are those which decree maximum prices which can be charged, at the same time as price floors are such controls which determine minimum prices.

Governments have a lengthy sordid history with attempting to implement price controls. Their attempts have demonstrated that the effects of these measures work only effectively for short time frames. In the long run, such controls always cause great difficulties like rationing, shortages, poor quality product declines, and black market transactions which become popular as an alternative means of providing the goods which are price controlled via unofficial distribution systems.

As prices are alternatively set by free market forces of supply and demand, the prices naturally rise and fall in order to maintain the equilibrium between such demand and supply. There has never been a successful effort by governments over the long term to defeat the all powerful forces of supply and demand. Governments which impose their controls end of creating either too much demand when price ceilings are established or too much supply when price floors are enacted. As a method of government intervention, these controls have been proven to never work in practice, even when governments have established them with the very best of end goals.

Examples of failed and botched efforts at price controls abound in the United States. Rent controls are a classic example of these and how ineffective they usually are. New York City widely implemented such rent controls to try to enable a sufficient supply of housing which is affordable. The real world impact has actually been to lower the total supply of rental units. This has caused still higher costs for rental in the rental housing market.

The true net effect of such rent controls has been that they discouraged entrepreneurs in real estate from getting into the landlord business. It has led to a supply crisis which means that a significantly lower amount of rental housing is now available than would have been the case if they had simply left the free market forces to work out the fair prices. Another problem that has arisen from these rent controls is that landlords do not have the necessary motivation to improve the rental properties or even to properly maintain them to an acceptable standard for the tenants. This has caused a significant deterioration in the quality of the available rental housing stock as well.

The U.S. also implemented price controls in the wake of the Japanese bombing of Pearl Harbor, Hawaii, which led to the outbreak of World War II in America. The feds began to expand existing controls and to establish new ones to preserve the critical elements of the economy. President Franklin D. Roosevelt on January 6, 1942 detailed his new production goals which were necessary to support the war effort he claimed. Practically all of the national economic industries were placed ever increasingly under direct control of the government.

Economists are typically dead set against these types of controls, but everyone agreed this was a national state of emergency at the time. To do this more effectively, the Federal Government created the agencies like the Office of Price Administration (OPA) and the War Production Board (WPB) in 1942 to help boost overall production output and to control prices and wages as well.

The National War Labor Board arose as the result of President Roosevelt's executive order on January 12, 1942. This implemented price and wage controls along with the firing and hiring of employees. This agency approved increases to wages and adopted what became known as the Little Steel formula to make wartime changes because of the increasing cost of living.

A final recent example of such botched price controls centered on the Nixon administration implementation of controls on gasoline products. This finally caused massive supply shortages, rationing of fuel, and lengthy, tedious lines at gas stations.

Price Gouging

Price gouging involves businesses charging higher prices than those that are considered to be fair or normal. It is most often done when there are crises or natural disasters strike. This gouging could also result from temporary boosts in demand that are not matched by supply. If suppliers' expenses rises, this is not considered to be a form of gouging when they pass it along to customers.

Because price gouging is usually considered to be unethical, it is generally treated as strictly illegal in a great number of places. Interestingly though, this gouging originates from what many economists call an efficient market outcome.

As demand goes up for a given product, this signifies that consumers will and are able to pay more to purchase an additional quantity of the good at the fair market price. Increases in a good's demand generally lead to short term product shortages. Suppliers are tempted when they see extended lines of people forming (to purchase their product) to both raise their prices and to increase the amount of their product that is available. Suppliers who are retailers will attempt to bring in more product into their stores. Supply and demand return to balance at a higher price in many examples.

When demand increases, everyone can not have the amount that they want for the initial market price. This means that if the price does not go up, shortages will occur. It is because the supplier needs an incentive to provide a greater amount of the goods in question. As supply and demand return to balance, all people who are capable of paying the market price can obtain as much as they need.

The supply and demand balance proves to be efficient economically. The goods go to all individuals who want the product for a greater price than they cost to make. Companies can maximize their profits as well. With shortages, there is no set way that the goods become rationed. Though usually this is on a first come, first serve basis, it might be resolved through bribes to the owner of the store. Such a bribe would amount to raising the price anyway.

It is critical to realize that in times of excessive demand, everyone can not obtain their full demand for the product at the original price. Higher prices will generally increase the amount of good supplied so that those who wish most to have them can. This should not be confused with price gouging per se.

There are many critics of price gouging, including most governments. These critic argue that short term supply can not be adequately resolved by higher prices. Demand increase in cases like natural disasters do not allow for suppliers to provide more of the product. They only lead to increases in the price or shortages. This is because supplies in these cases are limited to the inventory a store has on hand.

The critics say that such short term shortages and accompanying price gauging only leads to suppliers realizing excessive profits at the consumer's expense. Though higher prices are often illegal in such cases, these prices serve a purpose. They distribute the goods more efficiently than prices which prove to be artificially low will since they lead to shortages.

As a classic example, when there is an increased demand, higher prices will reduce hoarding by the people who arrive first at the store. This means that there should be more of the demanded good remaining for others who arrive later and are willing to pay more than the original price.

Quantitative Easing

Quantitative easing is the policy where the government purchases bonds and financial instruments by printing money in order to stimulate the economy. Quantitative easing proves to be a monetary policy that the Federal Reserve and other central banks around the world utilize in order to grow the money supply. They do this by boosting the cash reserves in the banking system. This is accomplished via purchasing the government's issued bonds in order to raise their prices.

Since prices and interest rates of bonds move inversely, higher bond prices lead directly to lower long term interest rates. Quantitative easing is commonly employed only after other more traditional means of dominating the supply of money have not worked. These other methods involve lowering discount rates, bank interest rates, and even interbank interest rates to around zero.

Once these traditional means have failed to stimulate the economy, the Fed then steps into the market and directly buys financial instruments. The assets that they purchase include agency debt, government bonds, corporate bonds, and mortgage backed securities, which they purchase from banks and institutions. This entire process is called open market operations. By depositing electronically created money into the banks' accounts, the banks gain additional reserves that permit them to create still additional money from thin air. The Fed hopes that this multiplication of deposits accomplished through the fractional reserve banking system will allow greater amounts of loans to be made to businesses and individuals in order to stimulate the economy.

This quantitative easing policy is not without its risks. It could be too effective or not sufficiently effective, should banks decide to hoard their extra money to boost their capital reserves. This is particularly the case in an environment of rising defaults in the banks' mortgage and other types of loans' holdings.

Recent examples of quantitative easing abound. This subtle form of printing money became more and more common as the financial crisis of 2007 to 2010 grew worse. In these years, the United States engaged heavily in it, tripling the world wide dollar reserves by creating money both at home and abroad. Other Central Banks, such as those of Great Britain and the European Union, similarly engaged in the practice to help mitigate the effects of the crisis and resulting Great Recession. These countries and economic blocks had all already lowered their interest rates to zero or near zero amounts, and they found quantitative easing to be their best remaining option for restarting economic growth.

Quantitative Research

Quantitative Research refers to methods of performing research in social sciences (and natural sciences) such as economics, sociology, and education. It stands out in contrast to its opposite form of research called qualitative methodology. Many individuals have a certain image in mind when they contemplate quantitative methods. This usually involves concepts of numbers, percentages, and statistics. People also typically assume that this form of research is exceedingly complex and difficult. This is not necessarily the case.

A detailed definition of Quantitative Research is that it is explaining phenomena by gathering numerical data which will be analyzed utilizing mathematically based methods, especially statistics. This sounds more challenging than it is. The definition becomes easier to understand when dissected one section at a time. Explaining phenomena simply means that the issues or concepts must be explored and then finally expressed.

In economics, these phenomena to be explained could be through a variety of questions. How does supply and demand determine prices and how can GDP growth reduce unemployment rates are both sample questions this Quantitative Research could attempt to explore and answer.

It is through collecting numerical data that this disciplined approach proceeds. Numerical data is critical for pursuing an approach that will work with methods which are ultimately mathematically and statistically based. Without numerical representations of data, it is impossible to do this approach. This is what separates Quantitative Research so sharply from qualitative research. Statistics can only analyze information which is in numerical form.

This also means that the approach of Quantitative Research works best with topics which involve numbers in the data and in the question. For example, the discipline might query how many females obtain their bachelors', master's, and doctorate degrees in American universities as compared to their male counterparts. How much money do male minorities in different parts of the United States make on average as compared to their white male colleagues would be another good question. Such are the questions that economists might analyze using quantitative methods. The reason is because the data necessary for the answer is strictly available to researchers in a number based format.

It is a valid consideration as to whether this limitation to questions which involve numbers, statistics, and numerically based data reduces the utility of the quantitative research approach. The answer to this is that it depends on the sociological discipline with which users are working. Economics lends itself ideally to this type of numerically based data, research, and questions, since it is ultimately a science of numbers. Other disciplines might not be so fortunate. Education or politics for example often involve questions which might be better served by approaching them from an alternative qualitative approach.

The ultimate goal of this quantitative research is to come up with theories and hypotheses which are based upon mathematical models that relate to the phenomena and questions the researchers originally asked. These researchers are able to effectively analyze the information utilizing the study and practice of statistics. Researchers like this methodology because they believe (or at least hope) that the numbers will lead to a result which is free of innate human bias. They can then take these results and apply them to a larger group, called a population.

With qualitative research though, researchers are able to ask broader questions and gather a wider range of data from both participants and research sources. These researchers will seek out themes to describe the information utilizing patterns which are unique to the given group of participants.

Recession

A recession is literally defined as the declining of the nation's GDP, or Gross Domestic Product, by a smaller amount than ten percent. This drop in GDP has to occur over greater than a single consecutive quarter in a given year. Gross domestic product stands for the total of all goods and services that a country produces, or the actual total of all business, private, and government spending on the categories of investment, labor, services, and goods.

The terms recession and depression are typically confused and sometimes used interchangeably. They are quite different from each other. Recessions are typically less severe than are depressions. Recessions are generally corrected in significantly less time and with less economic pain for individuals. Depressions furthermore involve drops in GDP of greater than ten percent.

There is no universal consensus on what makes a recession within an economy. Most economists agree on a few different factors that are commonly involved in causing such recessions. Prices might decrease substantially, or alternatively they could go up substantially. The decrease in prices shows that people are spending smaller amounts of money, and this will cause the Gross Domestic Product to go down. Conversely, higher prices can diminish the amounts of public and private spending, similarly causing the Gross Domestic Product to decrease.

As much as governments, individuals, and businesses hate recessions, many economists feel that they are normal for economies to go through, particularly mild ones. They claim that such economic pull backs are a built in part of society and economics. Prices go up and down, and spending and the amount of consumption similarly decreases and increases over time as well. Still, natural decreases in spending are not sufficient to provoke a recession into occurring. Some other factor changes suddenly and leads to sharp spikes or drops in real prices.

For example, the early 2000's recession came about as a result of the dot com industry suddenly and precipitously decreasing in activity. One day, the demand that they had anticipated turned out to be far less than expected. This created enormous failures of companies and significant layoffs that led to production decreases and finally spending cuts. This dot com drop created a shock effect on the gross domestic product, leading to a significant fall in production and output as spending dropped.

The recession had ended by 2003, yet the consequences of it turned out to be dramatic and can still be felt. High paying jobs suddenly disappeared, only to be outsourced to foreign countries. These jobs will likely never return to the United States. Still, as the Gross Domestic Product began growing again, the recession was deemed to have ended. This does not change the fact that numerous individuals still feel the impact of it in their own personal lives.

Similarly, the Great Recession that you saw stem from the financial collapse of 2007-2010 came about as a sudden seizure in the banking industry and credit markets. It has led to the highest levels of real unemployment since the Great Depression, reaching nearly twenty percent when measured by the formula that had been used until President Bill Clinton changed it. Even though this recession has been called over, the unemployment levels have not declined meaningfully. This means that for several more years at least, a great amount of economic pain and hardship will continue to be felt by those countless millions who have lost their jobs in the recession.

Reserve Currency

Reserve currency proves to be that particular currency which central banks (and sometimes important international financial institutions) hold. They keep such currency so that they are able to have an influence on their own country's exchange rate or to pay down their debt obligations which are international in nature. A substantial number of global commodities remain priced according to the reserve currency. This includes such heavyweight items as gold and oil. Nations require this currency to acquire these commodity goods.

There is an advantage to keeping quantities of a reserve currency. It allows nations or international companies to reduce their risk of changing exchange rates. The purchaser that possesses the currency reserve will not be forced to exchange their own currency to be able to complete the purchase. Since the last years of World War II in 1944, the American dollar has enjoyed the status of being the principle reserve currency which other countries use globally. This has caused other nations to carefully watch the monetary policy the U.S. pursues to make certain their reserve values do not suffer too much from inflation and currency debasement.

The second reserve currency of the world is the euro used by countries of the euro zone. Countries also can use the SDR Special Drawing Rights created by the International Monetary Fund to settle some international obligations, making it a third currency reserve. Increasingly, nations like China and Russia are trying to shift other nations away from the U.S. dollar as their currency reserve. China is going about this by signing currency exchange swap agreements with as many countries' central banks as it can to settle in Chinese Yuan.

The U.S. originally gained its status as dominant reserve currency because it came out of World War II as the globe's main economic power. This had enormous impacts on the economy of the world. In the immediate aftermath of the war, the U.S. GDP comprised 50% of global output. This made it inevitable that its currency the dollar would emerge as the world's currency reserve as happened in 1944. After this event, a number of other nations decided to peg their exchange rates up to the dollar. The dollar had the backing of gold in those days, making it comparatively stable. This pegging move helped other nations to stabilize their own volatile currencies.

In those early decades, the world as a whole gained advantages from such a stable and strong dollar currency. The U.S. benefited significantly and prospered as it enjoyed the most favorable exchange rate for the dollar. America began to undermine this arrangement when it printed extra dollars. The currency reserve had gold backing it, but the U.S. was able to get around this by issuing dollars that its Treasury debt backed. In time the gold which backed the dollars became less valuable as the dollars multiplied to finance U.S. deficit spending. Other nations' dollar currency reserves' value began to decline along with the gold value of paper U.S. dollars.

This eventually had to come to an end. With the U.S. printing and flooding markets with huge quantities of paper dollars to pay for the Vietnam War and Great Society spending, other countries became wary. They started converting their dollar reserves for the gold backing them. This central bank run on the American gold became so severe that President Nixon had no choice but to de-link the dollar from gold and float dollars against other currencies.

This led to the present day system of floating exchange rates. Gold skyrocketed as the dollar commenced its multi decade decline in value which has seen gold prices reach as high as over $1,900 USD per ounce. The dollar still remains the dominant currency reserve mostly because other nations had built up such large amounts of it and U.S. dollar denominated Treasuries.

Roaring Twenties

The 1920s were the original national era of irrational exuberance. In this decade, huge numbers of Americans believed that they could earn enormous fortunes in the stock markets. They ignored the fact that the markets could be volatile. This allowed them to justify investing all of their life savings in stocks. Those who did not have savings were able to get in on the action as well.

They purchased stocks on margin or credit. This worked well until the markets dove on Black Thursday, Black Monday, and Black Tuesday on October 29 of 1929. At this point the country was grossly unprepared for the stock market crash of 1929. The ensuing economic devastation that the crashes caused proved to be a critical element in kick starting the Great Depression.

The conclusion of World War I changed the national mood in the U.S. Americans were jubilant, confident, and optimistic about the future. They saw new inventions appear like radio and the airplane and everything seemed to be possible. The stock market already had earned its reputation for risk by this time. In the 1920s it no longer seemed risky. The country's mood encouraged this as the stock market for once appeared to be an investment in a bright future that could not lose.

With more and more individuals piling into the stock market, prices naturally started going higher. This first became noticeable in 1925. The rest of the year and in 1926 stocks trended higher and lower. In 1927 they put in a strong upward trend and showing. The powerful bull market fed on itself and lured still more individuals to invest in the markets.

A full fledged boom had started by 1928. This resulting boom altered investors' perceptions of the stock market. No one saw this as a place for long term investment at this time. Instead in 1928 the stock market represented a venue in which ordinary Americans felt that they could actually become wealthy quickly.

At this point the enthusiasm for the stock market turned feverish. Everybody all over the country talked about stocks. These discussions over stocks occurred everywhere ranging from barber shops to parties. Newspapers told stories about regular Americans like teacher, maids, and chauffeurs who had made millions of dollars in the markets. This only increased the enthusiasm to invest more.

Not every person could afford to purchase stocks. They solved this problem by allowing regular people to buy stocks on margin. When they could not front enough money to purchase them, their broker would take a 10% to 20% deposit of the price and loan them the additional 80% to 90% to purchase the stocks. This worked well while stocks were rising but in practice was very risky.

When stock prices fell below the amount loaned, brokers would demand that borrowers find the cash to cover the loan immediately in a margin call. Speculators who hoped they could make huge amounts of money in the stock markets ignored this risk and purchased the stocks on margin whenever they could. They felt confident that the practically never ending increase in prices would only continue. They ignored the risks that they were taking.

In early 1929, the race was on across the U.S. to invest in the stock market. Even companies were putting their corporate money into stocks as profits seemed to be a sure thing. Most dangerously, banks began investing customer monies into stocks and did not tell them about it. As long as stocks continue to roar ahead, everything appeared perfect. As the great crash approached in October, these businesses, banks, and speculators had a devastating lesson coming and were caught completely off guard.

Secondary Market

The secondary market refers to that securities trading market in which investors are able to purchase and sell securities that they own. Most individuals would simply call this the stock market. It is also true that stocks are additionally sold on the primary market at their first time and point of issue. Secondary markets in the United States include the NASDAQ and NYSE New York Stock Exchange. In Europe they include London's FTSE, the Euro Next, and Germany's Deutsche Bourse.

There are more than simply stocks traded on the secondary market. Stocks do prove to be the most heavily traded securities on these exchanges. Other types of securities available on such markets include bonds and mutual funds. Individual and corporate investors along with investment banks both sell and buy all three types of securities on the secondary markets. Besides this, Freddie Mac and Fannie Mae the GSE government sponsored enterprises buy mortgages on such a secondary market.

These transactions that take place on this secondary market are simply a step away from the original transaction which created the relevant securities in the first place. Looking at an example of this process helps to clarify it. JP Morgan will underwrite mortgages for customers. This actually creates the mortgage which is a security. JP Morgan might then choose to sell the mortgage security on to Freddie Mac in a secondary transaction in this market.

There are important differences between the primary and secondary markets. In the cases where corporations issue their bonds or stocks initially and then sell them directly to various types of investors, this is a primary market transaction. IPOs initial public offerings remain among the best-known and most heavily advertised transactions of the primary market. In such an IPO, the transaction occurs directly between the investment bank IPO underwriter and the buying investor. All resulting proceeds that come from the stock shares would then be delivered to the issuing company directly. The bank would subtract any agreed upon administration costs before handing over the funds.

Later on in the life cycle of these new stock shares, the first investors might opt to sell their individual stakes in the corporation. They would do this on the secondary market. All such transactions occur between investor parties. This means that the resulting proceeds from sales accrue to the investor re-selling the stock. They do not go back to the firm which originally issued the security nor its underwriter investment banks.

In general, prices on the primary market will be pre-arranged in advance of the transaction. Those prices from the secondary market are arranged by the interaction of supply and demand forces. When most investors are convinced that a given stock will rise in value and decide to race out to purchase it, this causes the stock price to rise generally speaking. When investors decide a company is out of favor or it is unable to deliver strong enough earnings results, then the stock price drops as the demand for such a security evaporates.

There are many more secondary markets than just one. The numbers are constantly going up because new financial securities always appear on the markets. Where mortgage assets are concerned, there are a few different secondary markets that exist. This is in part due to the fact that clever investment banks created bundles of mortgages. They then engineered these bundles into securities like MBS and GNMA pools. Finally they resell these to investors on the secondary markets.

The secondary market can also be subdivided further down to two other types of markets. These are the auction market and the dealer market. The auction market is a physical place like a stock market exchange where they bid on and sell securities publicly. The dealer market on the other hand involves purchasing and selling securities via electronic networks which are run over phones, customized order routing machines, or fax machines.

Seven Sisters Oil Companies

Seven Sisters Oil Companies is a phrase that was made famous by Italian state oil Company ENI Chief and Italian businessmen Enrico Mattei back in the 1950s. Mattei used this phrase disparagingly, which he coined in order to refer to the seven Anglo-American oil companies that had formed the "Consortium for Iran" cartel. They became so powerful that they soon dominated the universe of the worldwide petroleum industry in the years from the mid 1940s through the early 1970s.

The group was made up of seven American and British firms Anglo Persian Oil Company (today's British Petroleum), Gulf Oil (most of which became part of British Petroleum and the other parts which joined Chevron), Standard Oil of California or SoCal (today's Chevron), Texaco (later a part of Chevron in a merger), London headquartered Royal Dutch Shell, Standard Oil Company of New Jersey (Esso which became Exxon), and Standard Oil Company of New York or Socony (Mobil, which merged with Exxon to become ExxonMobil).

Before the 1973 oil crisis, the different companies from the Seven Sisters controlled approximately 85 percent of the global oil reserves. Since then, this has shifted dramatically away from the Seven Sisters Oil Companies over to a combination of the OPEC oil cartel nations as well as several state controlled gas and oil companies in the emerging world economies. These include notably Gazprom of Russia, Saudi Aramco of Saudi Arabia, China National Petroleum Corporation, PDVSA/Citgo of Venezuela, National Iranian Oil Company, Petrobras of Brazil, and Petronas of Malaysia.

The Seven Sisters Oil Companies' common history stretches back to the Iranian 1951 nationalization of its foreign dominated oil industry. The Anglo-Iranian Oil Company, which became BP, at this time controlled the Iranian oil industry. Because Iran opted to nationalize its assets and seize the petroleum reserves, the international community placed an embargo on Iran. Once Iran agreed to return to the international oil markets, the State Department of the United States suggested that the oil majors create a major oil companies consortium. Interestingly enough, a few of them were the scions of billionaire oil man John D. Rockefeller and his original

American oil monopoly the Standard Oil Company. As a result of the State Department's appeal, the "Consortium for Iran" arose and saw seven oil majors brought on board the lucrative and influential project.

Anglo Persian Oil Company of the United Kingdom was the original player in Iran and a major player in the Seven Sisters Oil Companies consortium for Iran. The company changed names to the Anglo-Iranian Oil Company before finally becoming British Petroleum. After the company took over the Standard Oil Company of Indiana, which was better known as Amoco, and Gulf branded gas stations, British Petroleum shortened their name to BP back in 2000.

American Gulf Oil was the second company. SoCal acquired much of Gulf in 1984, and this larger firm changed its name to Chevron. Though some of its Gulf service stations in the Northeastern part of the U.S. still bear the Gulf name, the majority of these were bought out in the East coast by either BP or Cumberland Farms.

Royal Dutch Shell of Great Britain and the Netherlands was the third company. American Texaco was the fourth company. They were absorbed by Chevron in 2001. Chevron itself arose from the fifth company in the consortium Standard Oil of California, or the SoCal company of the United States. It changed its name to Chevron in 1984 after acquiring much of Gulf Oil.

The sixth company was American Standard Oil of New Jersey, or Esso. It later changed its name to Exxon before renaming itself Exxon Mobil in 1999 after it acquired the seventh consortium member Mobil. The American company Mobil itself was earlier known as Standard Oil Co. of New York, or Socony.

Interestingly enough, all of these oil companies were either American or British headquartered. ENI, the state oil company of Italy, wished to be a member of the Consortium for Iran, but was turned away by the other members of the Anglo-Saxon controlled Seven Sisters Oil Companies. These seven companies went on to dominate the oil production of the Middle East following the Second World War.

The phrase Seven Sisters Oil Companies became more popular still when

British author Anthony Sampson assumed the mantle of the term in his 1975 published book The Seven Sisters. In this work, he unveiled the shadowy world oil cartel that had attempted to crush its competition and to dominate control of the global oil and gas resources.

Because they were well-funded and -organized and operated effectively as an economic cartel, these Seven Sisters managed to exercise great power over the resources, markets, and politics of the Third World oil producers. Yet the power of these seven original oil behemoths became challenged by the rise of OPEC, which was established in 1960. The rise of the all-powerful state owned and run oil companies in many emerging national economies also dealt the Seven Sisters a body blow. Finally, there was a deteriorating global share of both gas and oil reserves held by their home countries of the United States and Great Britain over the years that weakened their home markets in the world oil production arena.

Today only four of the original seven sisters remain, thanks to merger and acquisition activities over the intervening decades. This became necessary for the oil majors to compete against OPEC and the state owned oil companies. The remaining entities are now BP, ExxonMobil, Chevron (Texaco), and Royal Dutch Shell. They are collectively a part of the seven or eight super-major oil companies of the globe also called Big Oil.

Sovereign Wealth Funds

Sovereign Wealth Funds are investment pools made up of foreign capital and currency reserves which the government of the country in question owns. The biggest such pools of investment belong to the few countries with a large trade surplus in their economies. This means that Norway, Singapore, the oil producing and exporting nations, and China are the principle sovereign wealth fund nations of the world. They bring in such foreign currencies as U.S. dollars in token of their substantial and valuable exports. Their respective governments then invest these currency reserves in order to obtain the maximum return they possibly can for the benefit of their nations as a whole.

The idea behind these Sovereign Wealth Funds is that the pools of money which the nation owns in foreign reserves can be invested wisely in yield-producing assets so that the economy of the country and its citizens as a group gain advantage. It is the excess central bank reserves in a net exporting nation which make these funds possible, as they accumulate from either trade surpluses or budgetary surpluses. Exports of valuable natural resources create such revenues which can be used for this kind of a fund.

The total wealth which these Sovereign Wealth Funds contain has increased by more than double since September of 2007. It grew rapidly from $3.265 trillion to fully $7 trillion by 2015. This means that the assets held by such funds have grown to be twice as much as the value for all of the global hedge funds combined. It makes these wealth funds substantial enough to move markets dramatically without ever trying to do so. During the financial crisis, they bought major stakes in troubled lenders Morgan Stanley, Citigroup, and Merrill Lynch. They were guilty of causing an asset bubble in real estate in both London and New York City. Their influence only grows apace as they evolve into increasingly sophisticated investors.

One sovereign wealth fund nation differs from the next in the kinds of permissible investments they are allowed to pursue and include. Some of the nations are worried about liquidity issues. This makes them restrict their investments to only those which are the most liquid types of public debt instruments, such as U.S. Treasuries, British Gilts, and German Bunds.

It was the rising and higher than average oil prices from 2007 to 2014 which actively encouraged the expansion of these enormous sovereign wealth funds. In that same time frame, almost 60 percent of all such assets came from the revenues of oil and gas production, sales, and distribution. Even though the 2008 Financial Crisis destroyed trillions of dollars in global asset wealth, it hardly slowed down the inexorable growth of the national wealth funds. They managed to attain the levels of $4 trillion by December of 2009 and $5 trillion by March of 2012.

There are a number of especially oil and natural gas producing nations which have developed and built up their SWF in order to provide diversification to their national income streams. The United Arab Emirates is one such model example. The overwhelming share of its national income and wealth is derived from oil exports. Because of this, the emirate dedicates part of its foreign currency reserves to a sovereign wealth fund which invests its resources in a range of diversified assets that can provide a hedge against oil-related price shocks. This fund has grown to be massive by any measure. By June of 2015, the UAE Abu Dhabi-controlled fund had increased to around $773 billion. This represented ten percent of all SWF assets at the time. In fact, these Middle Eastern oil exporting-based sovereign wealth funds comprise nearly a third of all wealth found in such national funds.

Despite the size of the UAE fund, it is not the largest on earth. The Norway Government Pension Fund proves to be the biggest in the world, with $873 billion by June of 2015. Its income is derived from the nationally owned North Sea Oil drilling operation. The plummet in oil prices and accompanying decline in the Norwegian Kroner may cause the fund to record a loss of $17 billion by the period which ended in first quarter of 2015. It is so very large that if the money from this national fund were equitably distributed to all Norwegian citizens, each of them would receive over a million Kroner in distributions.

Singapore also possesses two of the largest Sovereign Wealth Funds. Their two funds together contain $458 billion in total. They have amassed this enormous fortune because of the impressive investment and savings rates of the businesses and people in this world leading financial and trading center and city state. The Government of Singapore Investment Corporation, presently known as the GIC Private Limited fund, holds $344 billion as of 2015. Both funds are owned and operated by the government of the city state of Singapore.

China also possesses some of the largest such funds in the world. The China Investment Corporation is their largest at $747 billion. Hong Kong's Monetary Authority owns a $442.4 billion fund as of 2015. This is utilized to support and ensure stability for the public finances of Hong Kong in general and the Hang Seng stock exchange in particular.

Stagflation

Stagflation refers to the simultaneous problems of high unemployment, stagnated economic growth, and persistently high inflation. It is an unlikely scenario, as slowing economies typically reduce demand sufficiently in order to keep higher prices in check. When workers lose their jobs, they purchase less. Businesses are then usually forced to reduce their prices in order to convince remaining customers to buy. It is this typically slower growth in market economies that prevents inflation from running away.

Stagflation policies typically lead to hyperinflation. Central banks that expand the country's money supply as the national supply is restricted do so by printing up additional currency. Monetary policies then create additional credit. This increases demand from consumers. It is the simultaneous supply restrictions that keep companies from producing enough to keep up with the rising demand.

Such a scenario happened in Zimbabwe back in 2004. Their government printed up so much currency that it pushed well beyond stagflation and evolved into ruinous hyperinflation. A stagflation in the United States only transpired in the 1970s. At the time the U.S. government expanded its dollars significantly to try to create additional economic growth. While they did this, President Nixon's wage price controls severely limited business-produced supplies.

The name stagflation actually comes from the 1973 to 1975 era recession. In those six consecutive quarters, the U.S. GDP shrank in size. Inflation literally tripled in 1973 alone, jumping from a relatively tame 3.4% to 9.6%. In the time between February of 1974 and April of 1975, inflation stubbornly remained between 10% and 12%.

Experts today look back at the 1973 Arab-led oil embargo as the crisis that triggered first oil price inflation. At this time, OPEC nations drastically cut their oil exports to the United States, forcing prices to quadruple. The inflation from oil spread to many other parts of the economy dependent on oil and gasoline, such as shipping, rail, and trucking.

The mild recession of 1970 was the precursor to the problems. President

Richard Nixon in his bid to be re-elected introduced as series of four fiscal and monetary economic policies that helped to ensure he won. These unfortunately also created the conditions for stagflation a few years later.

Nixon's first mistake was the start of wage and price controls. U.S. businesses were unable to raise their final prices even as import costs were soaring. They could only respond by reducing costs via worker layoffs. That boosted unemployment and further slowed economic growth by lowering demand. Nixon secondly took the U.S. off the gold standard to stop an international run on American gold reserves. This only crushed the value of the dollar and created still higher import prices and yet more inflation.

In order to fight off the inflation, the Federal Reserve had no choice but to continue raising interest rates. These reached their peak of 20% by 1979. Because the Fed did this in an up and down motion, businesses became confused and chose to keep up higher prices.

Though stagflation has not yet reoccurred in the U.S., Americans became worried it might again in 2011. The Fed had begun employing aggressive expansive monetary policies to save the U.S. economy from the grips of the 2008 financial crisis and Great Recession. This caused many to fear that high inflation would return. The economy only grew at low levels form 1% to 2% at this time.

Economists observed stagflation was a viable risk if inflation rose while the economy continued to struggle. Instead, deflation became the serious concern of the day. Massive increases in global liquidity were used to try to fight off this opposite kind of problem.

Subsidies

Subsidies are types of financial support or aid which a government or organization extends out to an economic industry, institution, individual, or business. These are done for the purpose of fostering particular economic or even social policies. The government is the most common provider of this type of assistance, but such support can also come from Non Governmental Organizations.

Such grants can be derived from a number of different forms of aid. These include indirect help as with insurance, tax breaks, accelerated depreciation, lower interest loans, and rent rebates. They can also be direct assistance in the form of interest-free loans or outright grants of cash or other assets. The ultimate goal of such a subsidy is to alleviate a form of financial burden. They are often deemed to be to the overall advantage of the entire public and not a specific person, business, or interest group by the very nature of the group receiving the help.

Such a subsidy grant is often regarded by governments as privileges. This is because they help with a relevant burden which was somehow unfairly levied on the receiver. They could also encourage a certain behavior or ultimate result through delivering financial support, as with farming subsidies to encourage domestic agriculture.

In general, such a subsidy will typically benefit a segment of an industry within a national economy. These can be employed to help out markets which are suffering by reducing perceived burdens from which they struggle. They might also boost additional development within an industry or research line via offering financial support for the efforts and work. Many times, these areas of production or research do not receive the necessary assistance which they require from the workings of the mainstream economy. Sometimes they are even outright disadvantaged by the actions undertaken by rival economies and nations.

There are two principal forms of subsidy aid as mentioned previously. These are direct and indirect subsidies. The direct form encompasses payments specifically directed to a certain industry or a given group. Cash is usually the medium of exchange offered to the receiving parties.

With indirect forms of a subsidy, there is no preset monetary value at which the help is limited or specified when it is provided to the individual, businesses, or industry. This might involve special goods or services which are price reduced. It could also include another form of government support to the given industry. It helps the much needed items to be bought at under the present market cost. This level of savings can vary greatly depending on the amount of the given organizations' participation in the program.

Governments, in particular the American Federal and European Union governments, provide many different types of subsidies. These are not only limited to help for domestic industry or farmers. They can also involve welfare and social assistance as with payments, student loans, grants, housing loans, and a farm subsidy. When domestic farming struggles to endure within the intensely competitive international farming arena because of their lower prices of other countries' farms, the U.S. or EU government bodies may provide actual cash subsidies to the farmers in order for them to afford to sell their products at the lower market rates. The intended goal is that they will still reap financial rewards sufficient to justify continuing to farm with this outright monetary assistance.

More recently, the government has become involved with health care subsidy to private citizens on an individual and family level. The Affordable Care Act of the U.S. allows its citizens to receive subsidies dependent on their size and income of the relevant household. Such a subsidy is intended to reduce the enormous out of pocket expenses associated with high health care premiums and co-payments for households which earn under a minimum income threshold. The funds of the subsidies go directly to the insurance company in question. This reduces the amount of money which the insurance company requires from the individual or household.

Supply and Demand

Supply and Demand refers to a law that attempts to explain the interaction between the forces involving a resource or good's demand and available supply. It is this law that determines how much of a given product will be supplied and demanded at a certain price. When supply is low and demand is high, price tends to go up, while a higher supply and lower demand leads to falling prices.

This is considered to be a foundational economic law. It impacts the overwhelming majority of economic principles in some way. Supply and demand vie with one another as the market pricing attempts to reach equilibrium. There are many factors impacting both demand and supply, which means that there is no single way that they can affect the prices of the underlying commodity or goods in question. It is this equilibrium price, or market clearing price, that determines the set price for which producers will be able to sell off all of the units they can produce and at which the buyers will be able purchase as much as they want.

It always helps to look at a concrete example when considering a highly complicated topic like this one. If a business rolls out a new product, it may choose to start with a higher price. The problem will be that only a few consumers will purchase it at these higher prices. Because the business has large warehouses stocked with the new product, they will reduce the price to move their inventory. Demand will rise apace, yet now the business' supply diminishes. The company will then raise the price back part of the way to where it originally was now until it achieves the ideal price to balance out both consumer demands with its own available supplies of the product in question.

In the real world scenarios, there is rarely only one company producing a given good or resource though. This means that the supply will depend on a range of competing factors. Costs of production, capacity of production, and the quantity of direct competitors will all impact the amount of supply that the producers can prepare. There are other side factors which include weather, availability of sometimes scarce raw materials, and dependability of the various supply chains that also have an impact on available supplies ultimately.

Demand is a more straightforward concept. It often comes down to the straight up cost of a good and the quality which is produced. There will also be close substitutes which are available, price shifts, and advertising campaigns that all have an impact on the actual demand. When video game machine prices decrease, the games (on the system) demand may rise as a greater number of individuals purchase the game machine and demand related games to play.

This law of supply and demand applies to more than simply prices. It can also be utilized to effectively explain various forms of other economic activities. One of these is that when unemployment proves to be higher, the supply of available workers is elevated. Businesses will respond by reducing wages to match the supply of workers. At the same time, if unemployment is lower, the available supply of employees will also be lower. This leads to companies providing higher salaries in order to attract top employees to their firms. This also explains stock market prices. The laws of supply and demand will similarly aid in describing why a stock price rises or falls on any given trading day.

Tariff Programs

Tariff programs are tariff regimes that apply to imports. Tariffs prove to be taxes that governments put on goods that are imported. Every nation has its own tariff programs and amounts. There are five principle tariff types in any tariff program. These are revenue, specific, ad valorem, protective, and prohibitive.

Revenue types of tariffs are those that boost government revenues. A revenue tariff would be one set up by a country that does not grow oranges but imposes tariffs on the import of oranges. This way, that government makes money when any business chooses to import and sell oranges.

Ad valorem tariffs are those that a government places as a percent of the value of imports. An example of such a tariff is fifteen cents for each dollar value. This contrasts with specific tariffs that do not revolve around the imported goods' estimated value. Instead, they are levied as a result of the specific quantity of the goods in question. Specific tariffs can be figured up based on the volume of the goods that are imported, on their weight, or on any other form of measurement applicable to goods.

Tariffs that are prohibitive in nature turn out to be the ones that stop a business from importing a good at all. These tariffs might be used on goods that a government does not wish brought into the country. This might be for safety, health, or moral reasons.

Protective tariffs are set by a government in order to ensure that the sale price of goods that are imported do not destroy a local industry. These are employed to protect domestic markets from foreign competition. Higher tariffs will permit local companies that may not be so efficient to compete effectively against the foreign competitors within the local domestic markets. While protective tariffs have their time and place in building up the local firms and economy, they can have unintended consequences. They might cause an item to be so costly that companies have to charge more for their related products.

A good example of this pertains to the prices of gasoline. As they rise excessively through tariffs, companies involved in shipping, like trucking companies, have no choice but to charge retail businesses higher prices for getting their products to them. The retail businesses will then respond by increasing the prices of their goods to compensate for the greater costs of transportation. They have to do this to make the same level of profit that they did in the past. The final result will be that consumers bear the brunt of the tariff by having to pay higher prices for their products and goods.

All countries employ tariff programs for one reason or another. They may not apply them evenly to every import or industry, but they will utilize them somewhere. Sometimes countries choose not to put tariffs on goods being imported. This is known as free trade in these cases. Free trade is believed by many economists to permit higher levels of economic growth. Critics say that without tariff programs, economies will be forced to rely on global markets instead of their own local markets.

Total Public Debt

Total public debt refers to all of the national debt which the United States owes to its various creditors and other agencies within the government to whom it owes money. This amount grows in years where there are deficits as the government spends more funds than it receives in taxes.

The aggregate national debt shrinks in surplus years as the federal government receives a greater amount of money that it spends. Every year of the Obama administration has been a deficit year that increased the debt. As of the end of Fiscal 2016, the government's total public debt amounted to $19.7 trillion.

The total public debt includes all money owed to Americans and foreigners as well as other agencies within the government. As such, the gross national debt for the country is made up of two components. The first of these is marketable debt which the public and foreign countries hold. This includes instruments such as Treasury bills, bonds, and notes.

Investors regularly buy and sell this debt on the bond markets. Any investor who is not a part of the federal government is considered to be a part of this class of debt. This means T bills held by consumers, companies, banks and financial institutions, the Federal Reserve, and local, state, and foreign governments are all included in this category of debt. As of July 29, 2016 this portion of the debt amounted to $14 trillion.

The other category of the total public debt is the debt which other government accounts hold. This is also called intra-governmental debt. These debts are also comprised of Treasuries, only these can not be bought and sold. This category of debt is like IOUs kept in federal government administered accounts. The country owes it to beneficiaries of programs, as with the Social Security Trust Fund or the Medicare Trust Fund. These government accounts once had surpluses and invested them over time in Treasury securities. The amount which they are owed includes principal plus interest earnings. On July 29, 2016, this category of the total public debt equaled $5.4 trillion.

Together, the two categories which make up the total public debt equaled

$19.4 trillion on the July 29, 2016 date. This represented fully 106% of the prior twelve month national GDP for the United States. Foreigners held $6.2 trillion worth of the debt at this point equivalent to about 45% of the debt which the public held or 32% of the aggregate public debt. The largest foreign holders proved to be China and Japan. As of May 2016, China owned about $1.25 trillion while Japan held $1.15 trillion worth of U.S. government debt.

Usually, the government's debt goes up as and when the government spends monies on entitlements, interest on the debt, and budgetary programs. It similarly decreases as taxes and other monetary receipts accrue. Both categories change throughout the months of the fiscal year.

The government does not in practice issue Treasury debt itself on a day by day basis as it spends money. Instead, this is issued or redeemed according to the government's money management operations. The total amount of money which Treasury is authorized to borrow is restricted by the debt ceiling of the United States. Congress conveniently lifts this every time the ceiling is hit.

Trade Agreement

A Trade Agreement refers to a contract agreed upon and signed into force of law. These are made between two (or sometimes more) different countries regarding their trading relationship. It is entirely possible for such agreements to be either multilateral or merely bilateral. Multilateral trade agreements are those which exist with more than two nations.

In the majority of cases, international trade itself becomes regulated by a variety of one sided barriers. Among these different sorts of barriers are non-tariff barriers, tariffs, and restrictions on trade. A Trade Agreement is a way to lower such discouraging to trade barriers and restrictions. The generally held belief is that they will provide advantages which include more trade for all parties concerned.

It may come as a surprise to many that it is very complicated to successfully conclude a major Trade Agreement. The reasons for this are varied. There will always be coalitions of groups which do not want overseas competition to increase because of greater tariff-removed trade. Non-economic barriers to trade are also widespread in the world today. Some of them exist because of national security concerns. Still other government issues on trade concern the wish to protect a local culture and way of life from foreign "corruption," as was the case with Communist Eastern Europe and the former Soviet Union empire.

There are typically three principle elements which one Trade Agreement will often have in common with another. These are the reciprocity rules, treatment of non-tariff barriers, and a clause for most favored trading nation. Reciprocity rules must be a part of any kind of a trade agreement. All parties in the deal must each benefit from this type of arrangement or there will not be any incentive to enact it in the first place. For any such agreement to happen, all sides must assume that they receive minimally as much as they will lose from the deal. Simply put, if Britain drops tariffs on Australian beef, then they will rightly expect Australia to drop tariffs on British London high street fashions.

The second idea, a common treatment of non-tariff barriers is a clause that becomes necessary in such a Trade Agreement. The reason for this is one nation may slyly decide to put up other barriers to trade in place of the tariffs they agreed to reduce or eliminate. As an example, they might institute sales or excise taxes on certain goods, quotas, so-called health requirements, specific license requirements, voluntary restrictions on imports, and also outright prohibitions on certain goods. Rather than attempt to spell out and make illegal any kind of non-tariff regulation, the treaty parties must sign off on a clause that they will provide the same kind of treatment to their trading nation's businesses and goods as they would to those of their own country. Steel is one such industry example where this has occurred in the past.

Finally, there is the most favored trading nation clause. It mandates that one or more nations in the treaty must consent to not lowering barriers additionally on a non-participating country. It means that if Britain and Australia sign a reduced tariff agreement on beef, and then Britain agrees to a still lower tariff on beef with New Zealand, then Australia will automatically receive the same lower tariff on beef as New Zealand now enjoys.

Examples of several sweeping multilateral trade agreements do exist in the modern world. Two of the largest, best known, and most successful prove to be the European Free Trade Association from 1995 and the North American Free Trade Agreement (NAFTA) from 1993. Both of these deals became more possible because of the rules established by the World Trade Organization.

Trade Associations

Trade Associations refer to those groups which offer a means for businesses in a certain industry or segment to interact in a way that benefits all parties concerned. Such an organization will be funded by member company contributions. These associations typically work to promote the industry's image to the public.

It might also deliver a single voice in the form of a government legislative lobby. They interact with government officials on issues which will affect the industry itself. Besides such critical functions as these, associations have other roles. These could include a way for the organization to educate the consumers of the general public on the main products and concerns of its particular industry.

Much of the time such industry trade associations will be established as not for profit organizations. This allows companies which associate in the same segment to cooperate together on those issues which affect them all in common. It is also true that these organizations are particularly useful for safeguarding an industry's integrity. This is because they commonly establish behavior standards which all member companies have to honor in order to maintain a good standing record.

Those companies or groups which refuse to live up to the standards the group develops and enforces in common suffer from the consequences. The leaders of the trade association might eventually choose to expel the business from the trade association for continued misbehavior. This would cost the offending company a serious amount of credibility before not only the industry, but also buying customers of the general public.

It is these trade associations which typically maintain all necessary means to ensure the industry's undivided voice will be heard by the law makers in a given nation or jurisdiction. This is why many participating member corporations choose to operate through the trade association in order to encourage industry-friendly legislation which will best help their industry segment to succeed. Similarly, this association could choose to lobby against any legislation that they feel will harm their collective best interests and those of their industry as a whole.

It is true that a number of businesses will elect to back marketing plans and public relations campaigns on their own to increase the exposure of their products and name brand with the relevant consumers. The beauty of a trade association such as this is that it will similarly endeavor to create interest through making members of the public aware and educating them on the industry in general and also the various products it offers. They will not concentrate their efforts on the goods for sale by a given member company. Instead, they will back publicity and marketing or advertising campaigns which lead customers to buy and consume the given industry's goods they produce in general.

This starts with offering the public facts and figures which consumers can easily understand and appreciate. The idea behind such education efforts of the trade association is that it will make it easier for the marketing efforts of the individual companies within the industry to have maximum impact. Besides lobbying, educating, and marketing, these trade associations frequently act as conference sponsors for their member businesses to attend.

Such a conference's purpose and offerings typically center on boosting the industry's overall practical performance. They do this through delivering useful information that every conference participant is able to grasp and remember. Members then take home this information to the other members of their firm and share it with those who could not attend the conference. Practically every business or trade association will sponsor at least one or more of these forms of gatherings or conferences once every year.

Trade Balance

Trade balances are used to describe the difference between the value of goods and services that are exported versus those that are imported into a country. Countries might have positive trade balances, where they export a greater value than they import. They might also have negative trade balances, or trade deficits, when they import a larger value of goods and services than they export.

Positive trade balances create cash stockpiles and investment surpluses. Nations like Singapore, South Korea, Taiwan, and most of the Gulf Oil states like Saudi Arabia, Kuwait, and the United Arab Emirates continuously run positive trade balances. Negative trade balances create currency outflows or government debt that must be issued and sold domestically or exported as payment for the extra imports. Countries like the United States and Great Britain commonly run negative trade balances.

Positive trade balances are beneficial and constructive to a nation. They can be run forever in theory, so long as other countries continue to purchase their goods and services at high levels. Negative trade balances, or trade deficits, are harmful to a country over long periods of time. They can not be carried on forever, since eventually the negative trade balance running countries will reach a point that they have spent all of their money covering the imports or issued an amount of debt that finally becomes unsustainable and undesirable to investors any longer.

The United States' trade balance specifically refers to the differences between the value of American goods and service exports versus goods and services imported into the United States. This trade balance proves to be among the largest Balance of Payment components. America's Balance of Payments is constantly pressuring the U.S. dollar's value. These deficits minimally bring down the value of the currency for a country that continuously runs them.

Trade balances are reported in the United States and other advanced economies. The problem with such reports is they commonly come out some time after the data is current. This means that most of the information contained within such trade balance reports has already been anticipated and affected the markets. The Foreign Exchange markets do move based on these trade balance reports though, since trade balance data helps to form or support foreign currency trends. To this FOREX market, the Trade Balance report has proven historically to be among the most significant released from the United States.

Trade Barriers

Trade barriers are those restrictions to free international and bilateral trade which governments throw up in an effort to protect domestic industries and businesses. These government created restrictions often take a number of different forms. Among them are tariffs, import quotas, import licenses, subsidies, embargoes, voluntary export restraints, local product requirements, currency devaluations, and outright trade restrictions. Whatever forms the barriers to trade actually take, they generally work off of similar principles. The idea is that a heavy cost be imposed on trade which increases the cost of the traded (and especially imported) goods, services, and capital. When two or more countries continuously employ barriers to trade one against the other, a trade war often becomes the end result.

The majority of economists mostly concur with the idea that such economic barriers are harmful to both countries which impose them and those which experience their direct consequences. They lower all around economic efficiency and harm or distort national comparative advantages. Free trade is the concept of removing all such trade barriers besides those which are considered mission critical to national security. The truth is that even the biggest champions of free trade in the modern world, such as the United States and Great Britain, engage in subsidies of favorite industries like steel and agriculture as they deem it to be expedient for these critical domestic industries' long term survival.

While there are many different types of trade barriers which countries can erect, the most typically utilized ones are tariffs, subsidies, duties, quotas, and trade embargoes. While the concept of free trade is a popular catch phrase in the post-modern world, the reality on the ground is that no country fully practices such free trade. In fact, all countries are guilty of employing some types of trade barriers for their own exclusive benefit and those of their industries and companies.

Tariffs are probably the most common type of barrier to trade. This means that a company places taxes on certain goods which are imported into the nation via its ports, railroads, or airports. Though it is unusual, tariffs could also be placed on national exports. Tariffs throughout history have always been an important government revenue source. They were easy to enforce and collect since ships had to come in through the closely government monitored ports.

Subsidies are yet another typical kind of barrier to trade. They are generally set up to safeguard and encourage important domestic industries and companies. They can also be utilized to ensure that important critical goods and services are available at a price which residents can afford. It often makes the imports uncompetitive as a byproduct. Food crops are often heavily subsidized so that the population can comfortably afford a consistent food supply at prices they can manage. Steel is another product that often benefits from heavy subsidies. This is because many nations deem domestic steel supplies to be vital to their national economic interests. Steel supplies which are domestically available are essential in wartime when shipping lanes may be interdicted.

Probably the most extreme version of trade barriers is embargoes. These more or less outlaw the export or import of any goods or services with a particular nation. This is typically enacted to punish an offending country or to cause them to make radical internal political changes as a result of the pain of a weakening economy. Throughout much of human history, embargoes were war tactics and led to the outbreak of official war. Today these barriers to trade are not a cause of wars.

There are several important trade bodies globally today which work to reduce and eliminate barriers to trade of different countries. The broadest and most effective of these is the WTO World Trade Organization which enacts and enforces stringent rules on member states regarding the legality of tariffs and other trade barriers. This has driven some countries and economic blocks to employ other trade barriers than tariffs. The EU simply bans the importation of most any generically modified product. This outlaw bans the overwhelming majority of American food products in practice. The WTO has gotten wise to this tactic and begun to investigate these types of barriers too.

Trade Credit

Trade credit refers to special financing terms which are many times given to a business by a supplier. This situation arises when a business buys supplies or goods and the financial officer or owner of the vendor agrees to provide either all or half of the purchased order on credit. In the case of half on credit, the balance half would become payable on delivery of the merchandise to the business.

When businesses receive a half order trade credit, they have several possibilities for paying for the balance on delivery. If they have ample resources, they can simply pay with cash. Otherwise, they can borrow the money to pay for the other balance on the inventory. This is why such credit remains among the most critical means of lowering the amount of working capital smaller businesses especially require. It is even more common and necessary with retail operations.

Suppliers normally extend such trade credit to a purchasing business once they have been a regular client for anywhere from 30 days, to 60 days, to 90 days. This trade credit has the advantage of being interest free. An example of this concept helps to make it clearer. Perhaps a supplier ships the Great Sweater Company knitted hats. The bill might normally be due within thirty days. Since Great Sweater Company enjoys these special credit terms, they would have an additional 30 days to cover the cost of the knitted hats which the vendor supplied.

When companies first start a new business, it is difficult to obtain such credit from the suppliers and vendors. In fact they will initially require each order to be paid by either check or cash on delivery. This will be the case until the new business demonstrates that it can successfully pay its bill in a timely fashion. It is a common practice in the business world. For those startups that need to raise money to make the operations work in the early days, it is important for them to be able to negotiate some form of this credit with their suppliers. It becomes easier earlier if the business owner can provide a well-developed financial plan.

It is important for businesses to properly utilize this trade terms credit. When they become trapped in the mentality of it being a necessary means of permanently financing the operations, then the business is in trouble. Instead it should be viewed as a useful source of funding for covering shorter term and smaller needs. This credit is not really a longer term solution to the funding problem.

For businesses who do not avoid this trap, they often times become heavily committed to working with the supplier who generously extends such trade credit terms. The end result of this is that the business is not able to choose a more aggressively competitive supplier that provides better prices, more timely deliveries, and/or a higher quality product because they do not offer such generous credit terms for their buyers. There is a trade off for everything in business.

It is important to realize that trade credit is rarely free. Every supplier may have its own terms. Yet most of them will provide a significant cash discount for those businesses that pay their invoices in 10 days or less. The same as cash price may be for 30 days. By waiting for the 30 days to pay the invoice, it is costing the business the two percent discount. If a business chose to do this for 12 months a year, it would mean the merchandise was costing an additional 24 percent versus the price of paying the 10 days same as cash terms.

When a business pays after the 30 days credit expires, most vendors charge from one to two percent interest in penalties. By being late for a year, this could cost an additional from 12 to 24 percent. This is why effectively utilizing trade credit means that a business will need to plan intelligently ahead so it does not lose cash discounts consistently or pay late fee penalties needlessly. Little details like this separate successful businesses from ones which fail.

Trade Deficit

Trade deficits are unfavorable balances of trade. With a trade deficit, a greater valued amount of goods and services are being imported than are simultaneously being exported. This stands in contrast to trade surpluses that occur when a larger amount of goods and services are exported by a nation than are imported in return. Trade deficits are also called trade gaps.

These trade deficits and trade surpluses are a part of the balance of trade, or net exports, which proves to be the total difference between imports' and exports' tangible value within a country's economy during a particular time frame. The balance of trade results from the relationship of the country's exports and imports.

Economists have held varying opinions on how negative or non important that trade deficits might be. Some have said that issuing paper money not backed by anything other than faith and credit of a government in exchange for valuable produced goods is not a bad thing. Professor Milton Freedom, the founder of monetarism, is one of the main proponents of this particular point of view. He felt that what would likely happen is that high exports would raise the U.S. currency value, while high imports would lower the U.S. dollar value.

Friedeman said that the worst case scenario for running trade imbalances would be that easily and inexpensively printed U.S. dollars would leave the country in order to pay for the excess imports versus exports. Friedman claimed that this produced the same result as if the country that earned the dollars through exports simply set them on fire and did not send them back to America. His policies became influential in the late 1970's and early years of the 1980's.

Other influential investors and businessmen have made opposite arguments. Warren Buffet is perhaps the greatest investor in American history. He claims that the constant U.S. trade deficit proves to be the biggest financial threat facing the national economy. He says that it is worse than the enormous annual national budget deficit and consumer debt levels together.

Buffet has said that other countries in the world own three trillion dollars more of America than we own of their countries. This investment imbalance has only increased since Buffet made these arguments nearly five years ago. Buffet and his followers are so worried about the imbalanced trade deficit that they have suggested instituting import certificates as an answer to the American problem and to bring balanced trade back to the country.

Trade War

A trade war is a potential worst case result of protectionism. This serious sounding series of events unfolds when the first country erects tariffs on the second country as a response to the second country placing their own tariffs on the first country's imports.

Such trade wars can erupt if one nation believes the other nation's trading policies to be unreasonable or unfair. It can also occur as trade unions within a country place intense pressure on the national politicians to discourage consumers from purchasing imported goods from other nations. Trade wars can also happen because the various groups of citizens, unions, and politicians in both countries do not properly understand the many proven and demonstrated advantages of free trade.

It is relatively simple for a trade war that starts out in only a single sector to expand into other sectors as well. It is also all too easy for such trade wars that start out between one nation and another to explode into one with other countries that did not start out as a part of the economic conflict.

Distinguishing the differences between trade wars and other economic actions which cause a negative impact on the trading relations between two states has to do with the goals. These economic conflicts are focused on free trade. Sanctions are another form of economic embargo that also have political, military, or humanitarian focused goals.

Trade wars should not be confused with tariff wars. In a tariff war, two nations duel economically because the first country increases its taxation rates on the exports of the second country. The second country then chooses to retaliate by boosting their own tax rates on the first country's exports. The higher tax rates are intended to harm the other nation financially and economically. This generally does happen as such tariffs lessen the chances of consumers purchasing products from external sources when they increase the aggregate final cost on those goods or services.

There are various reasons why nations might decide to begin a tariff war. They might not like their trading counterpart's political choices. A country could feel that through exerting sufficient economic pressures on their trade partner, they can create a sea-change in the behavior of that government. Such a tariff war as this is often called a customs war.

There are a variety of economists who concur on the idea that some economic protectionist policies entail greater costs than do others. This is because certain actions have a higher likelihood of instigating a full blown trade war. Looking at a prescient example is helpful to understand the argument. If the United States raised its tariffs on China, then China would likely respond by increasing its own tariffs on the U.S. and American imports. Yet if China instead increased its subsidies to steel makers, then it would be difficult for the U.S. to proportionally respond against these economic actions. Political constraints would likely limit the U.S. politicians in their abilities to respond in kind. This is why such subsidies can be hard to effectively counteract, even for wealthy developed nations.

Poor nations tend to be more susceptible to trade wars than do rich ones. They often lack the financial capability of offering meaningful subsidies to their own domestic producers. They also struggle to erect effective economic protections in the face of foreign trade partners dumping less expensive goods on their own domestic markets. By placing such tariffs on these foreign goods, they run the risk of increasing the prices of necessary products to levels which their own impoverished citizens simply can not afford at all.

Trading Blocks

Trading Blocks are pacts between various countries typically having a common geographical area. They form them for protections against non-member nations' imports. These trading agreements are also a type of economic integration that has more and more impacted the global trade patterns and trends. A few different kinds of trading groups like these exist today.

Preferential Trade Areas are the first and probably most common form. These PTA's occur when countries of a common geographical area decide to eliminate or at least reduce the tariff barriers that exist on certain goods which they import from other nations in the PTA. This represents the first small but critical step in the development of full scale trading blocks.

The next logical progression in the trading agreements development is to form a Free Trade Area. If two or still more nations within the region concur on eliminating or at least reducing the barriers to all trade on every good imported from the other members, they establish this second step in the chain.

The third step forward is to establish a Customs Union. This means that all trade barriers and tariffs between the group members are canceled, and a unified external tariff policy against non members is placed. It allows the member states to negotiate trading deals with third parties as a single more powerful trading block. They can enter agreements this way with other trading blocks or even the World Trade Organization if they wish.

Full economic integration begins to occur if the members of the trading block continue down the path towards its eventual logical conclusion. This leads them to a common market, the first major leap into economic integration. Member nations are now trading freely in every area of economics and resources, not only physical goods. It entails all services, labor, capital, and goods barriers being eliminated.

They also work to reduce and finally eliminate any non-tariff barriers. The common markets are only truly successful when all micro economic policies and other rules are brought into harmony as well. These include anti-competition laws and anti-monopoly regulations. Some trading blocks at this stage also begin to implement key industry common policies, like the EU's Common Fisheries Policy and Common Agricultural Policy.

There are numerous advantages to members of a trading block once they are fully formulate and established in practice. Free trade within the block allows member states to specialize in areas of production in which they have the greatest comparative or absolute advantages. Trade increases between key members as they have improved access to one another's national markets. Trade creation is the inevitable result. It refers to the phenomenon that free trade creates as more expensive domestic producers are outcompeted by more economically efficient and less expensive imports from other trading blocks members.

Lower priced imports also mean a greater consumption effect and higher demand. Economies of scale allow the producers in these nations to benefit and apply the savings to lower pricing for their customers. More jobs are often created because of the higher and growing trade between the block members. Finally, companies within the block may have to be more efficient against their own block rivals, yet they do gain effective economic protection against less expensive imports out of non-block member based corporations. The EU shoe industry is a good example of this. They are economically protected by tariffs on cheaper shoe imports from Vietnam and China.

There are some significant disadvantages of these trading blocks too. Trading blocks usually distort global trade by reducing the benefits of global specialization and comparative advantages of the world as a whole. Those producers which are less efficient than global competitors will be shielded from the outside of block more efficient ones. Trade is diverted away from the most efficient producing companies which are only guilty of being based outside of the trading block area.

Trans Pacific Partnership (TPP)

The Trans Pacific Partnership TPP represents a trade agreement that has been put together by twelve countries with borders on the Pacific Rim. Participants signed the final version of the deal in Auckland, New Zealand on February 4, 2016. This signing culminated the end of seven long years of negotiating the treaty. In order to enter into effect, the treaty must be ratified by the member states' legislatures. This includes the U.S. Congress, where opposition to the treaty has been intense and bipartisan from many members of both parties.

There are 30 different chapters to the Trans Pacific Partnership. Their goal is to encourage job creation and retention, economic growth, innovation, higher living standards, competitiveness and productivity, poverty reduction, better government and transparency, and better protection of the environment and labor. This TPP is made up of agreements that reduce tariff and non tariff barriers to trade. It also creates a means of resolving disputes through investor state settlement.

Originally the Trans Pacific Partnership was born from the Trans Pacific Strategic Economic Partnership Agreement that Singapore, New Zealand, Chile, and Brunei signed back in 2005. Starting in 2008, other nations on the Pacific Rim began to discuss a wider arrangement. This included The United States, Vietnam, Peru, Mexico, Malaysia, Japan, Canada, and Australia. This increased the nations who were a part of the trade negotiations to 12 countries.

Previously in force trade agreements of the countries participating will be amended to not conflict with the TPP. Deals that offer better free trade will still be in effect. The Obama administration looks at the TPP as a pair of treaties. Its twin is the still under discussion TTIP Transatlantic Trade and Investment Partnership between the European Union and the United States. The two deals are generally similar.

The original goal of the talks was to conclude negotiations in the year 2012. The final deal stretched on for another three years because of conflicts over difficult issues like intellectual property, agriculture, investments, and services. The 12 nations at last came to an agreement on October 5, 2015.

The U.S. Obama administration has made implementing this TPP one of its principle goals for trade. On November 5, 2015, President Obama announced to Congress he would sign the deal and released a public version of the treaty for any interested American individuals and organizations to review. The U.S. President along with the other 11 leaders all signed the TPP February 4, 2016.

In order for the Trans Pacific Partnership to take effect, all of the signors have to ratify it within two years. In case it is not completely ratified by all parties in advance of the February 4, 2018 deadline, there is an alternative arrangement. It will become effective after minimally 6 signing countries with a combined GDP of greater than 85% of all the signing countries ratify it. This means that the U.S. must ratify if for it to ever take effect.

Other countries may be able to join the trade block in the future. Countries that have shown an interest in joining include South Korea, India, Bangladesh, Cambodia, Indonesia, Laos, Thailand, Colombia, the Philippines, and Taiwan. South Korea did not get involved with the original 2006 agreement. The U.S. invited it to join after South Korea and America concluded their own free trade agreements. South Korea is likely to be the first country to join in a next wave expansion of the group. First it will have to work through TPP treaty issues in agriculture and vehicle manufacturing.

Transatlantic Trade Investment Partnership (TTIP)

The Transatlantic Trade and Investment partnership represents a U.S. and European agreement for mutual trade and investment. In essence it is a free trade deal that the two economic superpowers are working to ratify. The two parties began the initiative in the June of 2013 G8 meeting. U.S. President Obama, European Commission President Barroso, and European Union Council President Van Rompuy introduced the idea and began working on the project.

The goal of the TTIP is to encourage both trade and investment. Governments on both sides believe that this will result in more economic growth and jobs for citizens of both sides of the Atlantic Ocean. Negotiations have been complex and mostly held in secret. The U.S. side is headed by the USTR, or Office of the United States Trade Representative. The Europeans are led by the European Commission. This EC handles negotiations for all 28 EU member countries.

TTIP turns out to be the largest and grandest vision for a trade agreement that has ever been attempted. This is because the United States and European Union economic blocks make up nearly fifty percent of the GDP of the entire world. The impacts on trade are expected to be substantial. Small to medium sized enterprises will gain several benefits in access to the new markets. They will have other countries to which they can export. They will also gain the ability to import input materials from other countries. It is anticipated they will have the ability to gain investments in their businesses at a cheaper, better price as well.

Consumers are supposed to benefit also. Lower prices are expected in both economic blocks because of the reduced tariffs and increased competition. This will improve the purchasing power of residents on both sides of the Atlantic and also help to create more jobs.

Twenty-four different chapters comprise the actual Transatlantic Trade and Investment Partnership. These have been divided into three principal topics. The topics are Market Access, Rules, and Regulatory Cooperation.

Market Access pertains to opening up markets. The goal is to allow for improved competition. Besides this, the architects of the agreement are trying to make it easier for products to flow back and forth across the Atlantic.

The rules section has to do with trade and investment. This area's goal is to increase the fairness and ease of importing, exporting, and investing for American businesses in Europe and European businesses in America. Rules cover a number of different important concepts. These include Energy and Raw Materials, Sustainable Development, Small and Medium Sized Enterprises, Customs and Trade Facilitation, Competition, Investment Protection, Geographical Indications, Intellectual Property, and the Government to Government Dispute Settlements.

The area of Regulatory Cooperation pertains to important regulation differences between the United States and the European Union. Both groups often have the same quality and safety levels that they insist on from specific goods. The problem is that each side employs its own procedures in considering the identical product. This imposes high costs on companies who produce the items. It can be prohibitively expensive for smaller to medium sized businesses.

There have been a number of objections raised by protestors to this free trade agreement, particularly in Europe. Many individuals on both sides of the Atlantic oppose the secrecy that surrounds the negotiations. The protesters have concerns that interest groups are creating special rules for larger companies.

The European labor markets are worried that their working conditions and benefits will suffer. Environmental groups are all concerned that environmental standards and safeties that are higher in Europe will be watered down as a result of the free trade initiative.

Treasury Inflation Protected Securities (TIPS)

Treasury Inflation Protected Securities (TIPS) are a unique and useful form of Treasury issued securities. What makes them special is their expressed and close linkage to inflation levels in their coupon payments. They are set up this way to safeguard investors from the interest destroying impacts of inflation.

TIPS prove to be lower risk investments because they enjoy the expressed and unlimited backing of the U.S. government. Besides this, their par value increases at the same pace as the official rate of inflation as depicted by the CPI Consumer Price Index. The interest rate itself stays fixed with these investments.

The interest earned by these Treasury Inflation Protected Securities pays out twice a year on the same fixed dates. TIPS may be bought directly off of the U.S. government by utilizing the Treasury Direct system. This allows for simple $100 increment purchases of the TIPS in a minimum of only $100 order size. They can be obtained from the site with 30 year, 10 year, and 5 year maturity date options.

Unfortunately for the Treasury Inflation Protected Securities holders, the inflation adjustments of the TIPS bonds fall under the IRS definition of taxable income. This is the case despite the fact that investors do not realize any of those inflation adjusted gains until the point where the bonds mature or they sell out their holdings. Because of this, some investors opt to obtain their TIPS exposure by utilizing a TIPS mutual fund or ETF. Otherwise, they could simply buy and hold them within tax deferred retirement accounts like IRAs. This would save them the tax headaches of having to pay the IRS now on money they will not obtain for possibly years or even decades.

On the other hand, buying TIPS directly means that investors sidestep the costs and fees applied by mutual funds and even ETFs. TIPS bought directly also feature complete exemption from the double or even triple taxation of local income and state income taxes which some investors must pay, depending on where they reside. Residents of Puerto Rico do not have to pay any federal income taxes on these inflation adjusted gains or interest payments because of the Commonwealth's completely unique status which it enjoys within the U.S.

If investors purchased $1,000 worth of TIPS and held them through year end and received one percent coupon rates while there was no CPI measured inflation within the United States, the investors could count on obtaining $10 payments for the entire year in interest payments. Assuming inflation increases by two percent, the principal of the bond would increase by two percent or in this specific instance by $20, to reach a total value of $1,020. The coupon rate would remain locked at one percent, yet it would apply to the entire new principal amount of $1,020 to help the holder receive interest payments of $10.20.

In the extremely unlikely event that deflation reared itself, the bonds would similarly decline in total face value. Should the CPI decline by three percent, the principle would drop by three percent, or $30, resulting in a new par face value of $970 on the formerly $1,000 Treasury bond. This would reduce that next year's interest coupon payments total to $9.70.

When the bonds mature, investors would then get the principal equity which equated either to the $1,000 original par face value, or an applicably higher adjusted principal based on the CPI adjustments higher. Interest payments throughout the life of the bond will be calculated from the principal amount as it rises or falls. This does not apply to the downside if the investors hold their TIPS until they reach maturity. Investors who do not wish to hold their TIPS until this interval can choose to receive a lower amount of principal than the par face value by selling their investment via the secondary bonds market if they so desire.

Universal Basic Income (UBI)

Universal basic income (UBI) is known by a variety of names in different countries and continents. Among the more popular are basic income, citizen's income, unconditional basic income, basic income guarantee, universal demo grant, and UBI. This represents a type of social security welfare program and safety net. In it, all residents or citizens of a nation periodically receive an amount of money which the government or another public institution gives them unconditionally. They receive this on top of and regardless of any other income they earn from work or investment returns. When the money is given out to any persons who live with less than the government-mandated poverty line, it is also known as partial basic income.

This universal basic income and its distribution systems could be financed by the revenues and turnover of publically owned enterprises. These are many times referred to as a citizen's dividend or a social dividend. Such a strategy is a component of a market socialism model, as opposed to market capitalism in which participants' incomes are based on their abilities, hard work, and opportunities. Taxation is another means of paying for such basic income schemes.

It was Thomas Paine's _Agrarian Justice_ published in 1795 where he wrote about capital grants to be provided at the age of majority that began the debates concerning universal basic income within the United States. Up through the year 1986, the phrase which referred to this basic income concept most commonly was "social dividend." After that year, the universal basic income wording gained universal appeal. There are many well-known proponents of the social and economic philosophy. Among them are Ailsa McKay, Philippe Van Parijs, Hillel Steiner, Andre Gorz, Guy Standing, and Peter Vallentyne.

In the United States, this Universal Basic Income has been discussed on a number of different occasions as a serious idea for public policy. The numbers which have been bandied about for Americans amount to approximately $1,000 per month, which would be sent via check to every American. Among the conservatives who espoused the concept and argued for it to be implemented were legendary Nobel prize-winning economist Milton Friedman and former Republican President Richard Nixon.

The base case for this Universal Basic Income has been most effectively argued and written extensively about by Andy Stern, who was once the Service Employees International Union president and who serves as a Columbia University professor since then. He published a book called *Raising the Floor* in which he argued dramatically and effectively for the UBI.

Stern argues that the concept of a basic guaranteed income has become more necessary for two reasons. On the one hand, the wars on poverty programs have not been so effective nationally. On the other, the rapid advance of technology has led to unparalleled job dislocation and disruption for millions of American workers. This program would deliver an effective floor, or social safety net, to every American.

Critics of the plan in the U.S. have asked how the Federal Government would possibly afford to pay for this proposed program. Stern referenced the 126 existing separate government programs which each already distribute money to American citizens. Some of these might be rolled into the Universal Basic Income program. Besides this, additional taxes would have to be introduced in order to make the proposal a reality. Economists have predicted that implementing such a UBI would require around $3 trillion each year in funding.

Despite the fact that this concept has many critics, it is also possibly the only significant ideology in the early twenty-first century which has supporters on both the right and the left sides of the political, economic, and social spectrum.

The Swiss were given a vote on the UBI issue for their own country in the late spring of 2016, and they soundly rejected it. Interestingly though, the same voters answered an exit poll claiming they expected to see this policy implemented in Switzerland within the next 25 years.

Velocity of Money

The velocity of money proves to be the speed at which money is changing hands. When the velocity of money is higher, then money is rapidly going from one hand to the next. This allows for a comparatively smaller amount of the money supply to cover a significant number of purchases. Conversely, if the velocity of money turns out to be lower, then the money is going from one hand to the next at a slower rate. This requires a greater supply of money to cover the same quantity of purchases.

The velocity of money is never the same. Such velocity will change along with the preferences of consumers. Besides this, it goes up and down as prices or money's real value fall or rise. Should the real value of money prove to be lower, then the levels of prices are higher. A greater quantity of bills would have to be utilized to pay for purchases. Assuming that money supply is constant, velocity of money has to go up to be able to pay for all purchases. The velocity of money also shifts as the Fed changes the money supply. These changes might cause price levels and money's value to stay the same.

The velocity of money turns out to be the single most critical factor in determining the impacts of any changes to the money supply. As an example, pretend that you buy a piece of pizza. The waiter takes the money that he is paid from this transaction and employs it to pay for dry cleaning. The dry cleaner owner next uses the money to wash his car. This goes on again and again until finally the bill is removed from circulation. Since bills can stay in circulation for literally decades, one bill will generally allow for a vast number of multiples of its face value to be transacted along the way.

The equation that demonstrates how velocity of money relates to the money supply, output, and the price level is expressed as M times V equals P times Y. In this equation, M represents the money supply and V stands for velocity, while P represents the price level and Y is the amount of output. Since P times Y yields the country's Gross Domestic Product, you could also say that V equals GDP over M, or velocity is Gross Domestic Product over money supply. In practice, the equation tells you that a certain Gross Domestic Product level that contains a tinier money supply will require a higher velocity of money so that all purchases can be funded. This means that velocity will go up in this scenario.

Velocity of money equations can also be altered to give percent changes in velocity of money equations. With velocity of money equations, you might employ them to measure the impact that any changes in the velocity, money supply, and price level have on one another. Only the output, represented by Y, would be fixed in such changes, since quantity of output does not change in short time frames.

Volatility

Volatility in investments has to do with the possibility of stocks or other investments undergoing a dramatic gain or loss in price and value in a certain amount of time. Investors consider the volatility of stocks and other investments when they decide to buy more shares of the asset, sell their current holdings, or to buy shares of a new offering. Whatever an investment's volatility proves to be, investors' goal should always be to make the highest return that they possibly can for the lowest chances of experiencing losses.

With stocks, a great concern is how stable the assets of a company are that underlie the stock itself. A sudden loss of confidence in a public company would also likely cause a sharp decline in the price. The stock price drop and accompanying volatility is actually created by the public's perception of something within the company, like changing leadership or a coming acquisition.

In fact the stock might come back in a relatively short time frame as the public decides that the company is stable after all. But such factors might be more troubling and enduring, causing the volatility of the stock to become too high. When such volatility persists, many investors will decide not to buy additional shares or even to sell off the ones that they hold.

The overall conditions of a market can also influence investment volatility. As the stock market all around shows higher signs of volatility, individual investments will likely suffer the same fate. This occurs as consumers become worried about the whole economy, or if political situations force investors to take more conservative trading positions. Should such impacts grow sufficiently significant, then even stable stocks can become lightly traded while investors sit on the sidelines to watch for the troubling issues to get resolved. In the meanwhile, the stocks and their underlying options might make dramatic rises and drops in price from higher volatility.

Volatility is a fact of life that investors have to be capable of handling. Still, some stocks and investments demonstrate higher degrees of volatility than do others. Investors can gain an insight into this amount of individual volatility that an investment might have thorough looking into its historical levels of price and accompanying volatility.

Using this data with projected trends in the economy and markets, investors can get a good picture of the amount of an individual investment's volatility to determine if they are comfortable with it before they invest in the offering.

Voodoo Economics (Reaganomics)

Voodoo Economics is also known as Reaganomics. The term was originally used by President George H.W. Bush (Bush the Elder) to refer disparagingly to the economic policies of his predecessor President Ronald Regan. Ironically President Bush served for eight years as the vice president under Ronald Regan after he made those remarks.

Before eventual President George H.W. Bush served as the VP of President Reagan, he considered his one-day running mate's economic policies the Voodoo Economics as unorthodox and ineffectual. This was because Ronald Reagan loved supply-side economics, wanted to cut back taxes on corporate and personal income, and planned to restrict taxes on capital gains.

The more popular term for the so-called Voodoo Economics changed into Reaganomics over time as these economic policies became wildly successful. The policies of the United States' fortieth president who served from 1981 to 1989 were considered experimental at the time. President Reagan suggested that the economy (which was under a terrible recession since the time of President Jimmy Carter) could be massively stimulated by unconventional methods. These would eventually include massive and across the board tax cuts, significantly lowered social spending, greatly increased spending on the military, and the financial deregulation of American markets. President Reagan introduced these measures to combat the lengthy era of economic and financial stagflation which had started back under President Gerald Ford in the year 1976.

While pre-Vice President George Bush the Elder intended for the term Voodoo Economics to be negative and harmful, the later adopted phrase Reaganomics served both critics and proponents of the policies of President Reagan. This set of policies came from the ideas of trickle down economics theory. Such an idea believed that by decreasing taxes, particularly those on companies, the government could stimulate the economy and increase economic growth. The concept held that as corporations found their expenses were reduced by federal policies, these savings would eventually find their way on down into the remainder of the national economy. This would then cause a boost in the growth rate.

As part of his plan, President Reagan unleashed a four part strategy to lower inflation and to increase the job and economic growth. He started by cutting back the federal government's spending on programs which were domestically based. Next he cut taxes for especially businesses, but also on individual investments and personal tax rates. Third, he decreased the burdensome regulations that handcuffed corporations and companies. Finally, he fostered a lower growth rate of money within the U.S. economy.

While President Reagan did manage to lower the domestic program spending, he over compensated for it with his boost to military spending. This caused a financial net deficit and grew the U.S. debt burden during both of his four year terms. He did effectively slash the highest individual income tax rate down from an eye watering 70 percent to 28 percent. Corporate tax top rates declined from 48 percent down to 34 percent.

Reagan moved on by cutting through all of the restrictive economic regulations which President Jimmy Carter had enacted. He also finally put an end to the dreaded and stifling price controls which still remained on natural gas and oil, cable television, and long distance phone service. During his second term, President Reagan encouraged a Federal monetary policy which helped to finally stabilize the American dollar versus major foreign currencies.

Towards the close of the second term of President Reagan, he had increased the Federal government's tax revenue base from $517 billion of his incoming year 1980 to $909 billion by his final year of 1988, effectively almost doubling it. He had cut inflation back to four percent, and he had pushed down the unemployment rate to under six percent. Economists and politicians may continue to spar regarding the ultimate impacts of the Reaganomics/ Voodoo Economics, yet no one argues that it did bring on what has become among the strongest and longest lasting eras of continuous prosperity in the history of the United States. From the years 1982 to 2000, the DJIA Down Jones Industrial Average increased in level by almost 14 times. The economy increased the job base by 40 million new ones during those heady years.

Welfare

Welfare is a social program that the government uses to attempt to provide for its citizens' well being. This could happen with social security, social welfare programs, or even government sponsored financial aid. Corporate welfare is generally described as the government directly supporting companies instead of permitting the free market to close down inefficient businesses. Governments that grow their welfare programs excessively find that they are called welfare states.

Any type of program that has the government giving services or money directly to citizens in need of help can be called welfare. This means that lots of government programs are forms of welfare, even when the citizens and critics do not realize it. Still others say that still more welfare programs are needed to adequately take care of people's needs.

Social welfare provisions are what the majority of people are describing when they talk about it. These programs offer minimum income standards to those who have lost their jobs, are old, or are disabled. The government feels an ethical obligation to help these individuals who could not live without help. By allowing them a chance to find work again, the government ultimately helps out the economy and nation as a whole.

As an example, those who have lost their jobs can get welfare assistance in the form of unemployment as they are seeking replacement work. This is offered as cash assistance and sometimes as food stamps. If you become disabled and can no longer work, then you are able to obtain the same type of help, even though you do not have to look for work to be eligible.

A great number of countries today feature national health care programs. These prove to be enormous welfare systems. In these systems, every group in the country is able to access medical care when they need help. The U.S. does not yet have a functioning universal health care system set up, though one has been passed by congress and President Obama for the future.

A free universal welfare system that runs throughout the U.S. is free schooling until the end of high school. The government pays for all associated costs, even food and transportation when it is required. Because most critics do not consider free public education to be welfare, there is little controversy surrounding it.

Welfare Economics

Welfare economics concentrates its studies on the best possible allocation for goods and resources in an economy. It looks at the ways that allocating such resources will impact the welfare of overall society. This pertains to the school of thought on the distribution of income and the ways that this will influence the overall good of society.

As such this becomes a subjective form of study. It assigns quantities to usefulness and welfare so that it can develop models to measure the improvements of individuals. This science came into its own as a clearly articulated economics theory branch in the years of the twentieth century.

Writers before the development of welfare economics thought of general welfare as only the sum total of satisfaction of all people living inside an economy. After this, later thinkers decided that it might not be realistic to measure even a single individual's level of satisfaction. They made the case that it was not possible to compare two different people's individual levels of well being. They skeptically considered the long held belief that poor people gain greater satisfaction than the rich do when they realize an income increase.

Today the branch of welfare economics considers both how resources are distributed and the way that this determines the aggregate level of contentedness within the society and economy. It does it on both an individual level and a total societal level. The theory seeks to determine an ideal distribution of resources for the maximum happiness of all its members to be achieved.

Welfare economics makes use of the techniques and point of view in microeconomics. It can also be combined to produce a macroeconomic conclusion. There are those economists who follow this branch of economics who argue that higher levels of all- around social good can be attained if the government will redistribute incomes fairly in the economy.

It also models theories of economic efficiency in predicting an ideal place where social happiness reaches the maximum level it can hit. Once this point is achieved, it means the economy functions so that additional changes will raise the happiness of one segment of society at the expense of another one.

There are a range of issues from welfare economics that help governments to develop their public policies. Among its chief goals is to create bare minimum standards for quality of living. This means the proponents of this economic school of thought are striving to see the governments make available basic and necessary services to the populace. They also want to have affordable housing options and enough jobs that pay livable wages for all members of society.

Capitalist concepts are in opposition to welfare economics. Straight capitalism rejects the notion of intensive intervention from the government in economic issues. Capitalism concentrates on individual ability, development, and choices in the pursuit of happiness through personal gain. Capitalism argues that the "invisible hand" will cause individuals who are pursuing their own personal enrichment to pursue actions that benefit the overall good.

Utility is an interesting concept from this branch of economics. It explains the value of a given good or service from the point of view of an individual. This value describes whether or not purchasers believe the value they receive for the particular service or good is equal to or higher than the cost to buy it. It also argues that individual units of currencies, like dollars or Euros, have the same values to individual people as they do to companies. It does not matter how vastly their relative incomes vary.

Other Financial Books by Thomas Herold

The Money Deception - What Banks & Governments Don't Want You to Know

High Credit Score Secrets - The Smart Raise And Repair Guide to Excellent Credit

Other Books in the Herold Financial IQ Series

99 Financial Terms Every Beginner, Entrepreneur & Business Should Know

Personal Finance Terms

Real Estate Terms

Bank & Banking Terms

Corporate Finance Terms

Investment Terms

Economics Terms

Retirement Terms

Stock Trading Terms

Accounting Terms

Debt & Bankruptcy Terms

Mortgage Terms

Small Business Terms

Wall Street Terms

Laws & Regulations

Financial Acronyms

www.ingramcontent.com/pod-product-compliance
Lightning Source LLC
Chambersburg PA
CBHW071543210326
41597CB00019B/3099